Gendered Bodies

Feminist Perspectives

◆◆◆

JUDITH LORBER
Brooklyn College and Graduate Center, City University of New York

LISA JEAN MOORE
Purchase College, State University of New York

SECOND EDITION

New York   Oxford
OXFORD UNIVERSITY PRESS
2011

Oxford University Press, Inc., publishes works that further Oxford University's
objective of excellence in research, scholarship, and education.

Oxford   New York
Auckland   Cape Town   Dar es Salaam   Hong Kong   Karachi
Kuala Lumpur   Madrid   Melbourne   Mexico City   Nairobi
New Delhi   Shanghai   Taipei   Toronto

With offices in
Argentina   Austria   Brazil   Chile   Czech Republic   France   Greece
Guatemala   Hungary   Italy   Japan   Poland   Portugal   Singapore
South Korea   Switzerland   Thailand   Turkey   Ukraine   Vietnam

Published by Oxford University Press, Inc.
198 Madison Avenue, New York, New York 10016
http://www.oup.com

Oxford is a registered trademark of Oxford University Press

Library of Congress Cataloging-in-Publication Data
Lorber, Judith.
  Gendered bodies : feminist perspectives / Judith Lorber, Lisa Jean Moore.—2nd ed.
    p. cm.
  ISBN 978-0-19-973245-6 (pbk.)
  1. Human body—Social aspects. 2. Gender identity. 3. Sex differences. 4. Feminist theory.
    I. Moore, Lisa Jean, 1967   II. Title.
  HM636.L67   2011
  306.4—dc22   2010023199

9 8 7 6 5 4 3 2 1

Printed in the United States of America
on acid-free paper

Gendered Bodies

◆◆◆

◆◆◆

For Judith's grandchildren, Conrad, Charlie, and Joseph

For Lisa's parents, Linda and Richard

◆◆◆

Contents

*New to the Second Edition

♦♦♦

New to the Second Edition

Thoroughly updated throughout, the second edition incorporates fourteen new selections, which include such topics as evolution and motherhood; breastfeeding; breast cancer; world champion runner Caster Semenya and sex verification; disability, gender, and embodiment; and Palestinian female suicide bombers. It also adds new references and a concluding chapter, "Social Bodies in an Interconnected World." In addition, there is a new chapter (Chapter 6) which covers Sports and Gender.

◆◆◆

About the Authors

JUDITH LORBER is Professor Emerita of Sociology and Women's Studies at Brooklyn College and The Graduate Center, City University of New York. She is the author of *Breaking the Bowls: Degendering and Feminist Change; Gender Inequality: Feminist Theories and Politics; Paradoxes of Gender;* and *Women Physicians: Careers, Status and Power.* She is coeditor of *Handbook of Gender and Women's Studies, Revisioning Gender,* and *The Social Construction of Gender.*

LISA JEAN MOORE is Coordinator of Gender Studies and Professor of Sociology and Women's Studies at Purchase College, State University of New York. She is the author of *Sperm Counts: Overcome by Man's Most Precious Fluid,* the coauthor of *Missing Bodies: The Politics of Visibility* and the coeditor of *The Body Reader: Essential Social and Cultural Readings.* With Judith Lorber, she is the author of the second edition of *Gender and the Social Construction of Illness.*

♦♦♦

Acknowledgements

Parts of this book were adapted from Judith Lorber and Lisa Jean Moore, *Gender and the Social Construction of Illness*, second edition, Walnut Creek, CA: AltaMira Press, 2002, and from Lisa Jean Moore, "Polishing the Pearl: Discoveries of the Clitoris," in *Introducing the New Sexuality Studies*, edited by Steven Seidman, Nancy Fischer, and Chet Meeks, London: Taylor and Francis, 2006.

We would like to thank the anonymous reviewers for their helpful suggestions for this edition, Paisley Currah for guidance and assistance, and Sherith Pankratz and Taylor Pilkington for editorial support, and Julio Espin for help with production.

Judith Lorber
Lisa Jean Moore
New York City

◆◆◆

Introduction

Key Terms and Issues

The human body has been an object of fascination from the beginning of the human species, judging from the little prehistoric statuettes we see in museums. Many of them depict hefty females, with large breasts, buttocks, and thighs. They are often called "venuses" and thought to be icons of female fertility. Made 45,000 years ago, by people whose culture we can only guess at, what we see in them is a reflection of our own culture, our views of female bodies. As we shall see throughout this book, much of what we think of as nature and natural is cultural and socially constructed. Since Western society is a gendered society, ordered by a binary that divides people into two categories (male/men, female/women), the social constructions we will be exploring are gendered. Although our focus is on gendered social constructions of bodies and their consequences, we show how racial constructions, economic and class issues, and the influence of sexual orientations intersect with gender to make the human body a social body.

White people are privileged in the United States, so members of other racial and ethnic groups are under the burden of having to look and act "White" to improve their chances for a good job, admission to an elite school, or entry into a popular social circle. Latinas with plumper figures may go on extreme diets, and some Asians use cosmetic surgery to make their eyes look bigger and skin whiteners to lighten their complexions. Lighter-skinned African American media stars and politicians experience greater social acceptance, which can lead to rifts within African-American communities. Similarly, because homosexuals are so devalued, gay men and women in the public eye may choose to look "straight" in their appearance, even when they are open about their sexuality. Working-class women and men, who can't afford expensive beauty and fitness services, can't compete in appearance with toned, slim, surgically altered middle- and upper-class people. Size, comportment, and appearance of bodies are all modified and modulated in order to meet social expectations through extreme regimes but more often in completely unconscious ways.

1

These are some of the ways that social norms and expectations shape bodies. Other ways are stigmatizing fat people, disrespecting old people, making people with disabilities invisible, and assuming that everyone is heterosexual. Although it is impossible to separate gender norms from those imposed by social class, racial, ethnic, religious, and sexual communities, in this book we will be foregrounding gender.

GENDERED SOCIETIES

We live in a deeply gendered society, where work, family, and other major areas of life are organized by dividing people into two categories, "men" and "women," assigning them to different jobs and positions, and socializing them to do the work of their assigned category. The categorization of infants into "boys" and "girls" may originally be based on genitalia, but the systematic allocation of people into gendered positions is done through social processes.

Inequalities emerge through the distribution of privileges and rewards based on this allocation of social positions by gender, so that men's work is more prestigious and better paid than work done by women. Child care and domestic work are women's unpaid work for the family. Cultural and knowledge production reflects and legitimates gender divisions. The division of people by gender also permeates social relationships in friendships and other informal groups. In sum, we see ourselves and the world around us through a binary gender lens.

The division of society and our immediate social worlds by gender is so taken for granted that we rarely probe the processes that produce it. They are virtually invisible. Yet it is our actions and beliefs that construct the gendered social order. It is maintained by those who benefit from it as well as those who are shortchanged by the resulting inequalities. Women and men, for the most part, go along with gendered norms for appropriate masculine and feminine behavior because their identities, self-esteem, and social standing are built on meeting social expectations. A girl or woman who looks or acts masculine and a boy or man who looks or acts feminine is criticized, stigmatized, and sometimes ostracized. Feminine boys may be beaten up or subject to even worse violence by gangs.

In Western societies, most people are persuaded to accept gender inequalities by a belief that they emerge from nature. This belief claims that our "natural sex differences" explain why men and women have different roles and positions in work organizations, politics, education systems, and the other main areas of society, and why men predominate in positions of power and authority. These "natural" explanations are reinforced by culture, the mass media, religions, and knowledge systems, which obscure the ways in which social processes produce gendered bodies and behavior.

Using feminist social construction theory, we argue that the differences between women and men are produced through social practices that encourage boys and girls to use their bodies and minds differently and with different relative social value. Boys and men are expected to be strong, assertive, and rational; girls and women are expected to be soft, compliant, and nurturing. Gendered work organizations divide jobs into "women's work" and "men's work" with stratified compensation. Movies, television, and marketing focus women's lives on marriage and motherhood, men's on a wider range of physical and mental activities.

The socially produced gendered attributes and activities are differently valued and have different life outcomes. Boys' and men's bodies and behavior have a higher value in Western society and are intended to bring economic independence and political power. Girls' and women's bodies are often exploited sexually and maternally, and their behavior is intended to bring economic dependence and domestic harmony. These effects, we argue, are not natural to women and men, but are socially produced through many of the processes described in this book.

The overall system in which body evaluations are embedded is *patriarchy*. Originally, patriarchy was a social organization marked by the supremacy of the father in the clan or family, the legal dependence of wives and children, and the reckoning of descent and inheritance in the male line. Now, it is a belief system that presupposes the dominance or hegemony of certain groups of men, the priority of high-status men's agendas and interests, and the acceptability of men's acquisition of a disproportionately large share of social and political power.

BELIEFS ABOUT BODIES

According to feminist theory, claims about bodies are part of the social arrangements and cultural beliefs that constitute the gendered social order. As a social institution, gender produces two categories of people, "men" and "women," with different characteristics, skills, personalities, and body types. These gendered attributes, which we call "manliness" or "masculinity" and "womanliness" or "femininity," are designed to fit people into adult social roles, such as "mother," "father," "nurse," or "construction worker."

Men's physical capabilities are, for the most part, considered superior to women's. Feminist theories have examined the contexts of this superiority in sports and physical labor. As bodies prone to illness and early death, as well as higher infant mortality rates and lower pain thresholds, men's bodies are actually more fragile than women's. Feminist analysis has tried to tease the physiological from the social, cultural, and environmental in illness and death rates.

As some feminists argue, domination requires that the subordinate group be marked as different from the superior group. Thus, claims that women and men are physically different become fodder for the development and perpetuation of a gender hierarchy or a dominance system favoring men over women. Through the disciplines of science and medicine, socially constructed gendered body differences are recast as natural, physical, universal, trans-historical, and permanent. The common belief is that men's and women's bodies are different because they were born that way. We argue that male and female bodies are indeed different, but they are for the most part made that way by social practices and expectations of how girls and boys, women and men should look and act.

GENDERED BODIES

People experience their bodies, and these experiences produce different senses of self. Women's experiences of menstruation, pregnancy, childbirth, menopause, and breast cancer have been examined through critical feminist perspectives on science, medicine, and psychology, as have men's experiences of sexuality, impotence, and prostate cancer. In more specific contexts—sex selection, gene manipulation, ritual genital cutting, cosmetic surgery, rape, physical violence, sports, disabledness, and transgendering—feminist perspectives have grappled with cultural values and theories of power and control to analyze the complexities of these body-based phenomena.

The theme that runs through all of these topics is *gendered bodies*. Human bodies are not allowed to develop in all their diversity of shapes, sizes, and physical capabilities. Human bodies are not "natural;" they are socially produced under specific cultural circumstances. They are shaped by socio-cultural ideals of what female and male bodies should look like and be capable of (and further shaped by national, racial ethnic, and social class ideals for each). Bodies are socially constructed for dominance and submission and are symbolic in different ways. Simple attributes, like height, become ways of signaling superiority and inferiority. Western cultural beliefs posit that men should be taller than women, and we make it so: If a woman in a heterosexual couple is taller than a man, she wears flat shoes and stands one step below him for photographs. Women thus diminish their own bodily stature in order to maintain a socio-cultural script. The media reinforce these conventions: Michelle Obama is as tall as Barack, yet they are often positioned so he seems to be taller.

Feminism has increased awareness of how bodies are gendered by making visible the cultural and social dynamics that produce difference and dominance out of male and female bodies. Feminists have called into question many accepted "truths" about gender and bodies and have challenged the evidence on which dubious claims of men's physical superiority are based. In addition, the practice of feminism has the political aim of improving the status and treatment of women and girls by valuing women's bodies as much as men's bodies.

KEY DEFINITIONS

Feminists have tried to develop a precise vocabulary for referring to the body. We use the following terms in this book:

Sex: Biological criteria for classification as female or male: chromosomes (XX for female, XY for male), hormones (estrogen for female, testosterone for male), genitalia (clitoris, vagina, and uterus for female; penis and scrotum for male), procreative organs (ovaries and uterus for female, testes for male), gametes (ova for females, sperm for males).

Secondary sex characteristics: At puberty, in most males, testosterone increases muscle size and mass, deepens the voice, and accelerates growth of facial and body hair. In most females, estrogen produces breasts and menstruation, widens the pelvis, and increases the amount of body fat in hips, thighs, and buttocks.

Sex category: Self-identification and self-display as a female or male; the assumption is that identity and self-presentation are congruent with the sex assigned at birth, but they may not be.

Gender: Legal status as a woman or man, usually based on sex assigned at birth, but may be legally changed. Gender status produces patterns of social expectations for bodies, behavior, emotions, family and work roles. Gendered expectations can change over time both on individual and social levels. There is an assumed congruence between sex and gender although the actual biological evidence of sex is often limited. Rather, we assume that when we know someone's gender (their embodied behavior and presentation), we also know their sex (their physiological and biological status).

Gender display: Presentation of self as a gendered person through the use of markers and symbols, such as clothing, hairstyles, jewelry. Managing interaction with others using behavior and physical activities considered appropriate for one's sex category.

Sexuality and sexual identity: Attraction to and desire for a sexual object choice of one or both of the presumed dichotomous sexes, male or female, or genders, girl/woman or boy/man. Common identity terms are homosexual or gay and lesbian (erotic desire for same sex or gender), heterosexual (erotic desire for other sex or gender in the binary), bisexual (erotic desire for both sexes or genders), queer sexuality (erotic desire for fluidity and variety), transamorous (erotic desire for transgender and transsexual people). Individuals may move through sexual identities throughout the life span or be fixed in one sexual identity throughout their life.

Intersexual: A person born with procreative or sexual anatomy that doesn't seem to fit the typical definitions of female or male—appearing genitally female but having mostly male-typical anatomy internally, or a girl (XX) born with a noticeably large clitoris or lacking a vaginal opening, or a boy (XY) born with a notably small penis or with a divided scrotum resembling female labia. A person born with mosaic genetics, so that some cells have XX chromosomes and some have XY. Intersex characteristics may not show up until puberty, or at attempts to conceive. Some intersexuals are not identified until an autopsy is done after death.

Transgender: Identification as someone who is challenging, questioning, or changing gender from that assigned at birth. May include individuals who identify as male-to-female (MTF), female-to-male (FTM), transitioning (between genders), gender queer (transgressive, challenging gender norms).

Heteronormativity: A social environment that assumes that a "normal" (i.e., sex congruent with gender) boy or girl will inevitably fall in love with or have sex with a person of the other sex or gender. Heterosexuality is taken for granted as the natural, default state, and homosexuality is seen as a deviant, abnormal state. In general, the social pressures for compulsory heterosexuality are invisible, but heterosexuality is written into the tax code, medical practices, educational policies, and family scripts.

Medicalization: Labeling and treating body differences and preoccupation with these differences as diseases or illnesses that can be treated by the medical system with medical solutions. Thus, preoccupation with fitness has been called "muscle dysphoria." Preoccupation with one's looks in general is now diagnosed as "body dysphoria." Acting in ways that don't conform to gender norms is labeled "gender dysphoria." Criteria for inclusion in these categories and consequent treatment regimens often change markedly over time.

Racialization: Marking the body in ways that indicate racial ethnic identity other than White and Anglo-Saxon. These aspects of the body are then altered to emulate what White Anglo-Saxon people ideally look like. Examples are "bad" (nappy, frizzy) hair straightened so it is "good hair," noses that are shortened and reshaped, and skin that is artificially whitened. Ironically, White Anglo-Saxon people will also alter their appearance if they don't look like the "ideal."

PLAN OF THE BOOK

The intent of this book is to cover a broad spectrum of topics relating to the body, as a way of foregrounding the body in feminist social science theory. Although we understand feminism to be a theoretical and political movement composed of eclectic perspectives, feminist theories and activism have always considered the body as imperative, and some postmodern scholarship is entirely about the body and its problematics. Radical feminism has focused on sexual and procreative aspects of the female body, and on the politics of menstruation and menopause. Feminist studies of men and masculinities have incorporated body studies through examining sports, violence, and advertising representations of men. There have been many liberal and poststructuralist feminist critiques of Western culture's emphasis on thinness, Caucasian beauty, and cosmetic surgery. Theoretically, feminism has analyzed the interplay among the physiological body, the sexual body, and the social body. In this book, the focus is on gendered aspects of how bodies are shaped, used, and abused, with an emphasis on how gendered body practices perpetuate and reinforce hierarchies of power.

The book presents eight chapters of text with feminist readings chosen to show some of the feminist work on the topics covered in the chapter and to present a range of examples of what is discussed more conceptually in the text. Each chapter has an alphabetic list of key concepts that are covered in the text, three readings, and recommended books and articles. At the end of the book, we offer class exercises and a list of recent and classic movies with somatic themes.

There are other aspects of gendered bodies than those presented in this book that could be covered. We have tried to choose topics that would be of most interest to college students. Although we present examples from other cultures, our focus is Western developed countries.

Chapter 1. Neither Nature Nor Nurture: Theories of the Gendered Body reviews feminist critiques of theories of the gendered body and brain: loop-back systems in producing sex/gender differences, hormonal influences on women's and men's behavior, prenatal and genetic "hard-wiring" of brain structure, primate ancestry, and evolutionary development. We also take another look at a nature vs. nurture accidental experiment. Our argument is that social processes intertwine with genes, prenatal hard wiring, and hormones to produce gendered bodies. "Nature" is never unmediated. When we see biological sex differences as immutable "facts," we neglect the ways our gendered culture frames how we see and understand our bodies.

Chapter 2. " Are You My Mother? My Father?" Gendering Procreation looks at the social framing of fertility, conception, pregnancy, childbirth, and breastfeeding. Particular issues covered are prenatal sex and genetic testing, new procreative technologies, surrogacy, infertility, maternal responsibility and powerlessness in pregnancy and childbirth, breastfeeding as a boon and a burden, and gender representations of sperm and eggs in children's facts-of-life books. Procreation is considered women's responsibility, but their autonomy is limited by a medical system dominated by men's values.

Chapter 3. Eve, Venus, and "Real Women": Constructing Women's Bodies explores the combination of conformity, agency, and resistance evident in the social construction of women's bodies. The chapter discusses elective cosmetic surgery, breasts and body image, body size, the politics of menstruation, women's sexual bodies, and ritual genital cutting. For each of these topics, we examine the extent to which women make independent decisions that reflect prevailing social expectations but which they feel are important to their self-identity.

Chapter 4. Adonis, Don Juan, and "Real Men": Constructing Men's Bodies describes the social construction of the ideal Western male body and sexuality, and also shows how, in different contexts, a variety of male bodies and sexualities are valorized. Particular issues covered are idealizations of male bodies; Black, gay, and urban variations; the importance of sexual performance to men's gender identity; prostate cancer and masculinity; rectal examinations; and the controversy over routine circumcision of male infants. Men's bodily manifestations of masculinity reflect the need for validation of manhood in order to maintain the privileges of a dominant status.

Chapter 5. Aligning Bodies, Identities, and Expressions: Trangender Bodies looks at the ways gender is troubled and reestablished by transgender people. By examining how members of the transgender community live their lives as MTFs and FTMs, we understand how gender is constructed and maintained by everyone. Topics covered are issues in reassigning gender, transitioning and workplace discrimination, pregnant men, and disentangling sex and gender.

Chapter 6. Sports: The Playing Grounds of Gender looks at how organized sports construct a version of masculinity that is aggressive, competitive, and often misogynistic, and how women's sports are feminized or neglected. Topics explored are sex verification and intersex in classifying athletes as male or female, learning gender through sports, the media production of professional athletes, Title IX and gender equality and inequality, and the "locker-room" mentality in Western culture.

Chapter 7. You Don't Need Arms and Legs to Sing: Gender and Disability examines the ways gender socially constructs the experiences and identities of disabled people. Just as gendering is a social process, so is the phenomenon of "disabling"—identifying and interacting with those with seeming physical limitations as "other"—but, ironically, as gendered "others." Topics covered are gendering and disabling as social processes, disability and gendered sexuality, and transcending the body.

Chapter 8. Violent Bodies: Violence and Violations explores the ways violence in war and terrorism are gendered. Women are particularly vulnerable to rape and forced prostitution in wars and conflicts, but they can also be torturers and suicide bombers. Racial ethnic and social class status, as well as gender, produce military bodies, imprisoned bodies, the tortured and torturers, and terrorists. Femicide, the final topic, is an outcome of the patriarchal system of body honor imposed on girls and women in some societies, and the prevalent domestic violence against women in practically all societies.

Conclusion: Social Bodies in an Interconnected World summarizes the ways that physical bodies become social by incorporation into a community. At the same time, bodies are controlled by governments through laws and regulations imposed on everyday interactions and life-cycle events from birth to death. As social, economic, and political bodies we are integrated into a social world, but give up the promise of total autonomy. However, we can use our bodies to protest and resist governmental and community oppression, and reassert our individuality and diversity.

CHAPTER 1

Neither Nature Nor Nurture
Theories of the Gendered Body

Key concepts
evolutionary adaptation, genes and gender, hormonal influences on behavior,
loop-back systems, prenatal brain organization

Human bodies vary in many ways, but we tend to group them into contrasting types—attractive, repulsive; old, young; fat, thin; tall, short; strong, weak; and so on. When we first meet people, it is practically automatic to characterize their body types—are they masculine or feminine? Upper class or lower class? White, African American, Latina or Asian? The physical typologies are intertwined with social behavior—we think that physically attractive people have appealing personalities, that tallness conveys authority, that body strength is manly.

Generally, people assume that the physical traits of bodies produce an individual's social characteristics. But physical traits—genes, hormones, and anatomy—are also affected by behavior and environment. We are born with a skeletal type and the potential for physical functioning, but where we live; how much we exercise; what we eat, drink, and breathe; the traumas and illnesses we suffer; and the treatment and medications we are given all modify muscles, bones, and body shape throughout the life cycle. Diet is an obvious example—ethnic culture, social class, and available foods affect individual eating patterns. In the United States, among working-class communities, fattening fast foods are as near as the next McDonald's; the result is often childhood and adult obesity, high blood pressure, and diabetes.

We talk about "nature" versus "nurture" in the production of gendered bodies, but there is an interplay among the components we sum up as "nature and nurture." What is "nature" for humans is female and male procreative systems and secondary sex characteristics, hormones and genes, the evolution of human bodies, the structure of the human brain. What is "nurture" is personal life experiences, the social milieu of similarly located people, the culture of the society at a specific point in time, and the physical environment and its resources and hazards. As physical bodies we are the result of all the "natural" and "nurtured" input working together and affecting each other, producing behavior that further changes bodies and brains in a *loop-back system.*

A constant question of contemporary feminism has been the extent of women's and men's body and brain differences, and their origins and universality. If differences between women and men are "natural," there is not much to be done about altering them. Much could be done to insure that the differences are not used to legitimate unequal legal rights or discriminatory practices. Significantly though, there is constant debate over how equal women and men can be, given what seems to be a substantially wide and unbridgeable gap between their "natures."

The argument tends to come down to *sex differences* (biological) versus *gender differences* (social) as sources of women's and men's behavior and social positions. These views explain the social order in different ways. What are the determinants of who has power and authority, who produces knowledge and culture, who works at what, who nurtures, whose values prevail, and so on? Those arguing that *sex differences* naturally produce the social order tend not to see a need for change. Or else they feel that since the social order is the manifestation of biology and nature, it cannot be changed. Those arguing that differences between women's and men's behavior and social positions are produced and maintained by humans in a social order that perpetuates power inequities and hierarchies feel that it can—and should—be changed.

Many of those arguing that differences between women and men are caused by genetics or evolution usually accept racial ethnic and social class differences as socially produced. But not so long ago, racial ethnic and social class differences were also seen as products of biological inheritance (then called "blood") or evolution (social Darwinism). Those who argue for the social origins of the differences between women's and men's behavior and positions in society note that both are modified by racial ethnic, social class, and other group differences.

For the most part, explanations of the origins of the differences between women and men tend to focus on one cause. Because so many of these biological explanations have become extremely popular, we will discuss each in turn in this chapter. Our contention is that social and cultural effects are equally important, but are usually downplayed, and so we devote the rest of the book to how bodies get *socially constructed* as gendered.

GENES AND GENDER

Now that the human genome has been mapped, and the effects of more and more genes have been isolated, the belief that "it's all in the genes" is a prevalent idea about physical and mental differences between women and men. Feminists have critiqued this belief for its underlying assumptions about the universality and immutability of masculine and feminine behavior, and particularly for its legitimation of men's dominance of women. Any introductory cultural anthropology text has descriptions of assertive women and passive men, of men weaving and women building houses, of women heads of families, and of kinship structures where children belong to the mother's tribe, not the father's. The dominant status of men has varied throughout history and varies today. Some societies are much more egalitarian when it comes to gender than others, yet their women and men presumably have the same kinds of genes, hormones, brains, and evolutionary history.

In addition to the variation in women's and men's behavior cross-culturally and through time, the changes brought about through feminist activism in the last 35 years have modified what has seemed like genetically ingrained behavior. In January 2005, Lawrence Summers, then president of Harvard University, caused a furor when he said that the lack of women in science and engineering might be due as much to genetic differences as to social differences—discrimination and the difficulty of balancing demanding careers with family responsibilities. However, many more women today receive higher degrees in the science professions than they did thirty years ago. In 1970–71, women got 0.6 to 16.5 percent of the Ph.D.s in the physical, biological, health, and computer sciences. In 2001–02, they got 15.5 to 63.3 percent of the Ph.D.s in those same sciences (Cox and Alm 2005). Thirty years is too short a span for genetic changes, but it was a period of feminist protest against gender discrimination in higher education and the professions.

To say "it's all in the genes" ignores how genes work. Genes are proteins that turn body processes on or off. They are not one-time recipes for the production of bodies, minds, or behavior. Genes interact with the body's changes and with the physical and social environment in which the body lives. Genes may be triggers, but what sets them off are complex factors, and they don't work once but continue to interact with the body and environment. Furthermore, gendered behavior is complex; there couldn't be one gene for creating a gendered body or a gendered mind.

We need to think in terms of interactive developmental processes. Interactive models and biosocial perspectives did not emerge until the 1980s. They were, in part, a reflection of the work done in the sociology of the body, which argued for a continuous, life-long, loop-back interchange of bodily, behavioral, environmental, and social structural factors. In the following excerpt from *Sexing the Body*, Anne Fausto-Sterling, a feminist biologist, lays out the processes by which genes produce the proteins that affect cell development in a social and cultural environment.

"R" Genes Us?

◆◆◆

Anne Fausto-Sterling
Brown University

We live in a genocentric world.[1] The "genes 'r' us" habit is so deeply imbued in our thought processes that it seems impossible to think otherwise. We think of our genes as a blueprint for development, linear information that need only be read out of the book of life. We go to movies in which the major premise is that a DNA sequence isolated from a fossilized mosquito is all we need to create Tyrannosaurus rex. (The nicety, clearly found in *Jurassic Park,* that the DNA needed an egg to become a T. rex is lost in the shuffle).[2] And we hear almost daily on the news that the project to sequence human DNA molecules has led us from the genes for breast cancer and diabetes to Parkinson's and more. Present-day students of human genetics can do the rest, "discovering" genes for alcoholism, shyness, and—yes—homosexuality.[3]

Even when scientists are themselves cautious about imbuing all power to the gene, popular renditions of new scientific findings dispense with linguistic subtlety. When Dean Hamer and his colleagues published evidence that some male homosexuals possessed the same region of DNA located on the X chromosome, for instance, they used fairly cautious language. Phrases such as "the role of genetics in male homosexual orientation," "genetically influenced," or "a locus related to sexual orientation" abound in the paper.[4] Such caution did not, however, extend to other pages in the same issue of *Science,* the journal in which the Hamer group's report appeared. In the Research News section of the same issue, the headline ran: "Evidence for Homosexuality Gene: A genetic analysis...has uncovered a region on the X chromosome that appears to contain a gene or genes for homosexuality."[5] Two years later, coverage in a more popular venue, *The Providence Journal,* had, on the same page, headlines referring to "gay gene" research and "schizophrenia gene search."[6]

In shorthand, we sometimes say that genes make proteins; but it is precisely such shorthand that gets us into trouble. Naked DNA cannot make a protein. It needs many other molecules—special RNAs to carry the amino acid to the ribosome and secure it, like a vise, so that other proteins can link it to its next neighbor. Proteins also help transport the DNA's message out of the nucleus and into the cytoplasm, help the DNA unwind so that other molecules can interpret its message in the first place and cut and splice the RNA template. In short, DNA or genes don't make gene products. Complex cells do. Put pure DNA in a test tube and it will sit there, inert, pretty much forever. Put DNA in a cell and it may do any number of things, depending in large part on the present and recent past histories of the cell in question.[7] In other words, a gene's actions, or lack thereof, depend on the microcosm in which it finds itself.[8]

Genes, then, function as part of a complex cell with its own important history. Cells, in turn, operate as large, intimately connected groups that form coherent organs within a complex, functionally integrated body. It is at this level, when we look at cells and organs within the body, that we can begin to glimpse how events outside the body become incorporated into our very flesh.

Just after the turn of the twentieth century in the Bengal Province of India, the Reverend J. A. Singh "rescued" two children (whom he named Amala and Kamala), girls succored since infancy by a pack of wolves.[9] The two girls could run faster on all four limbs than other humans could on two. They were profoundly nocturnal, craved raw meat and carrion, and could communicate so well with growling dogs at feeding time that the dogs allowed the girls to eat from the same bowls. Clearly these children's bodies—from their skeletal structure to their nervous systems—had been profoundly changed by growing up with nonhuman animals.

Observations of wild children dramatize what has become increasingly clear to neuroscientists, especially in the past twenty years: brains and nervous systems are plastic. Overall anatomy—as well as the less visible physical connections among nerve cells, target organs, and the brain—change not only just after birth but even into the adult years....

How might social experience affect the neurophysiology of gender? The comparative neurobiologists G. Ehret and colleagues offer an example in their study of paternal behavior in male mice. Males that never have contact with young pups will not retrieve them in the spirit of good fathering (when they inch too far from the nest), but even a few hours or a day spent in the company of baby rats will evoke ongoing paternal pup retrieval. Ehret and colleagues found that early exposure to pups correlated with increased estrogen receptor binding in a number of areas of the brain and decreased binding in one area.[10] In other words, parenting experience may have changed the hormonal physiology of the father's brain as well as the mouse's ability to care for his pups....

How might all this apply to the development of sexual difference and human sexual expression? Answers developed to date have been impossibly vague, in part because we have been thinking too much about individual components and not enough about developmental systems.

During our lives, the brain changes as part of a dynamic developmental system that includes everything from nerve cells to interpersonal interactions. In principle, we can apply similar concepts to gonads and genitals. The gonads and genitals developed during fetal development continue to grow and change shape during childhood, affected by such things as nutrition, health status, and random accidents. At puberty anatomic sex expands to include not only genital differentiation but also secondary sex characteristics, which in turn depend not only on nutrition and general health but also on levels of physical activity. For example, women who train for long-distance events lose body fat, and below a certain fat-to-protein ratio, the menstrual cycle shuts down. Thus, gonadal structure and function respond to exercise and nutrition levels, and of course they also change during the life cycle.

Not only does sexual physiology change with age—so, too, does sexual anatomy. I don't mean that a penis drops off or an ovary dissolves, but that one's physique, one's anatomical function, and how one experiences one's sexual body change over time. We take for granted that the bodies of a newborn, a twenty-year-old, and an eighty-year-old differ. Yet we persist in a static vision of anatomical sex. The changes that occur throughout the life cycle all happen as part of a biocultural system in which cells and culture mutually construct each other. For example, competitive athletics leads both athletes, and a larger public who emulate them, to reshape bodies through a process that is at once natural and artificial. Natural, because changing patterns of diet and exercise change our physiology and anatomy. Artificial, because cultural practices help us decide what look to aim for and how best to achieve it. Furthermore, disease, accident, or surgery—from the transformations undergone by surgical transsexuals, to the array of procedures (applied to secondary sexual characteristics) that include breast reduction or enlargement and penile enlargement—can modify our anatomic sex. We think of anatomy as constant, but it isn't; neither, then, are those aspects of human sexuality that derive from our body's structure, function, and inward and outward image.

Reproduction also changes throughout the life cycle. As we grow, we move from a period of reproductive immaturity into one during which procreation is possible. We may or may not actually have children (or actually be fertile, for that matter), and when and how we choose to do so will profoundly affect the experience. Motherhood at twenty and at forty, in a heterosexual couple, as a single parent, or in a lesbian partnership is not a singular, biological experience. It will differ emotionally and physiologically according to one's age, social circumstance, general health, and financial resources. The body and the circumstances in which it reproduces are not separable entities. Here again something that we often think of as static changes across the life cycle and can be understood only in terms of a biocultural system.[11]

In their book *Rethinking Innateness*, the psychologist Jeffrey Elman and his colleagues ask why animals with complex social lives go through long periods of postnatal immaturity, which would seem to present big dangers: "vulnerability, dependence, consumption of parental and social resources." "Of all primates," they note, "humans take the longest to mature."[12] Their answer: long periods of development allow more time for the environment (historical, cultural, and physical) to shape the developing organism. Indeed, development within a social system is the sine qua non of human sexual complexity. Form and behavior emerge only via a dynamic system of development.

Notes

1. Hubbard and Wald 1993; Lewontin et al. 1984; Lewontin 1992.
2. Crichton 1990.
3. Hubbard and Wald 1993.
4. Hamer et al. 1993, pp. 321, 326. Rice et al. (1999) have been unable to repeat the finding that places it among a large number of genetic claims about complex behavior that continue to be in dispute.
5. Pool 1993, p. 291.
6. Anonymous 1995a; Anonymous 1995b.
7. Cohen and Stewart 1994; Ingber 1998.
8. See Stent 1981.
9. The ethical question of whether these children were "captured" or "rescued" is discussed in Noske 1989. See also Singh 1942; Gesell and Singh 1941.
10. Specifically, there was binding in the bed nucleus of the stria terminalis, the hippocampus, subiculum, lateral septal nuclei, entorhinal and piriform cortex, and medial preoptic area and arcuate nucleus of the hypothalamus. There was a decreased presence of

estrogen receptor binding cells in the periventricular gray area of the midbrain (Ehret et al. 1993).

11. For analyses of embodiment during pregnancy and of the effects of new technologies of fetal visualization on the embodiment of pregnancy, see Young 1990, chapter 9, and Rapp 1997.

12. Elman et al. 1996, pp. 354, 365.

References

Anonymous. 1995a. "Gay gene" research links homosexuality in males with heredity. *Providence Journal,* October 31, (Providence, RI), A8.

———. 1995b. Schizophrenia gene search getting closer, say studies. *Providence Journal* (Providence, RI), A8.

Cohen, J., and I. Stewart. 1994. Our genes aren't us. *Discover* (April): 78–84.

Criehton, M. 1990. *Jurassic Park.* New York: Knopf.

Ehret, G., A., Jurgens, et al. 1993. Oestrogen receptor occurrence in the male mouse brain—modulation by paternal experience. *Neuroreport* 4(11): 1247–50.

Elman, J. L., E. A. Bates, et al. 1996. *Rethinking innateness: A connectionist perspective on development.* Cambridge: MIT Press.

Gesell, A., and J. A. Singh. 1941. *Wolf child and human child: Being a narrative interpretation of the life history of Kamala, the wolf girl; based on the diary account of a child who was reared by a wolf and who then lived for nine years in the orphanage of Midnapore, in the province of Bengal, India.* New York: Harper and Bros.

Hamer, D., S. Hu, et al. 1993. Linkage between DNA markers on the X chromosome and male sexual orientation. *Science* 261: 321–25.

Hubbard, R., and E. Wald. 1993. *Exploding the gene myth: How genetic information is produced and manipulated by scientists, physicians, employers, insurance companies, educators and law enforcers.* Boston: Beacon Press.

Ingber, D. E. 1998. The architecture of life. *Scientific American* (January): 48–57.

Lewontin, R. C. 1992. *Biology as ideology.* New York: HarperCollins.

Lewontin, R. C., S. Rose, et al. 1984. *Not in our genes.* New York: Pantheon.

Noske, B. 1989. *Humans and other animals: Beyond the boundaries of anthropology.* London: Pluto Press.

Pool, R. 1993. Evidence for homosexuality gene. *Science* 261 (July 16): 291–92.

Rapp, R. 1997. Real-time fetus: The role of the sonogram in the age of monitored reproduction. In *Cyborgs and Citadels,* ed. G. L. Downey and J. Dumit. Santa Fe: School of American Research Press, 31–48.

Rice, G., C. Anderson, et al. 1999. Male homosexuality: Absence of linkage to microsatellite markers at Xq28. *Science* 284 (April 23): 665–67.

Singh, J. A. L. 1942. *Wolf-Children and feral man.* New York: Harper.

Stent, G. S. 1981. Strength and weakness of the genetic approach to the development of the nervous system. *Annual Review of Neuroscience* 4: 163–94.

Young, I. M. 1990. *Throwing like a girl and other essays in feminist philosophy and social theory.* Bloomington: Indiana University Press.

TESTOSTERONE, ESTROGEN, AND
GENDERED BEHAVIOR

A popular theory of sex/gender differences focuses on hormones—testosterone and estrogen. Increased levels of testosterone and estrogen shape male and female bodies at puberty. Testosterone increases muscle and bone size and mass, resulting in growth spurts in males. It thickens the vocal cords to deepen the voice, and accelerates the growth of hair on the face and body. In females, estrogen produces breasts, pubic and underarm hair, ovulation, and menstruation. The pelvis widens, and the body gets rounder from the deposits of body fat in hips, thighs, and buttocks. These physical signs of maleness and femaleness are accompanied by sexual desires and wet dreams, and by mood changes. The body changes and sexual urges are certainly distracting, but the changes in intellectual focus and academic accomplishment, particularly among adolescent girls and working-class boys, are much more the result of peer pressure and norms of femininity and masculinity.

Testosterone and estrogen are found in both women and men, and both are important for human development, but testosterone is the theorized source of aggression and machismo in men, and estrogen supposedly produces empathy and nurturance in women. There are certainly behavioral and emotional effects of hormones, but the pathway is not linear. There is a loop-back effect: hormones affect behavior and behavior raises hormone levels. A familiar example is that aggression raises testosterone levels in men, and these raised levels in turn produce more aggressiveness.

Stress, for men, sets off a "fight-or-flight" response. A recent study of responses to stress found that adult women don't have a "fight-or-flight" response, but rather a "tend-and-befriend" reaction. In situations provoking fear or anxiety, men tend to stand and defend themselves physically, or run away to protect themselves. Women often seek out support from other people, or they protectively look after their children. Since 1932, most of the subjects of the research on stress responses were men, so this alternative behavior was virtually unknown. Recent studies have revealed that the biological source of stress responses in men is testosterone; in women it is oxytocin, the same hormone that induces labor in childbirth and milk let-down in breast-feeding. There is also a social side to these differences in stress-response behavior. Women usually have children to protect, and so their responses may be psychologically or socially induced, and the high oxytocin levels may be an effect of maternal protectiveness rather than a cause of it—or there may be, more plausibly, a loop-back effect.

In animal studies, oxytocin affects males as well as females (Neuman 2008). The female/male overlap of hormones in humans and, more significant, the interplay of hormones with social interaction are often neglected in accounts of how hormones affect gendered behavior. Scientists and the media particularly like to highlight the effects of testosterone on men's risk-taking, downplaying the effects of the thrills of daring on testosterone levels. The recent economic boom and bust produced a flurry of these reports.

A study that was the basis of much of the media inflation of testosterone and the market meltdown suggested that elevated male hormones plus market volatility could lead to irrational choices, which would increase market volatility and further elevate the hormones (Coates and Herbert 2008). While the study linked hormones and the social environment, it missed crucial elements. It didn't include the masculine culture of corporations, which encourages aggressive, risky behavior. It treated men as a homogenous group; there was no indication of racial ethnic variation, and it didn't have a comparison group of women traders. When the economy imploded, the media said that because women respond to stress with raised levels of oxytocin, the "tend and befriend" hormone, they would be less prone to risk-taking and more prudent in their decisions. Nicholas Kristof, columnist for the *New York Times,* wrote:

> Banks around the world desperately want bailouts of billions of dollars, but they also have another need they're unaware of: women, women and women.

> At the recent World Economic Forum in Davos, Switzerland, some of the most interesting discussions revolved around whether we would be in the same mess today if Lehman Brothers had been Lehman Sisters. The consensus (and this is among the dead white men who parade annually at Davos) is that the optimal bank would have been Lehman Brothers and Sisters (2009).

FEMALE AND MALE BRAINS

Another popular argument for the biological source of gendered behavior is brain organization. *Organization theory,* which goes back to 1959, argues that the male brain is organized or "hard-wired" for masculinity by prenatal androgens produced by the fetal testicles. The female brain is organized for subsequent feminine behavior by maternal and fetal estrogen input. Brain organization theory was widely adopted by psychologists and neuroendocrinologists and became textbook knowledge by the 1960s. It is still a widely used explanatory model for female and male behavior, even though it was found in the 1970s that "male" hormones had to be converted to "female" hormones before "masculinizing" the brain. Information about the hormonal "mixed bag" hit the newspapers as new knowledge in the 1990s, concurrent with now-accepted ideas of the overlap of masculinity and femininity.

Organization theory was popular with animal researchers because it provided a method for showing the effects of pre-natal hormones on mature sexual behavior. Pregnant rats were administered large doses of testosterone or estrogen, which resulted in altered sexual behavior in the offspring. Female rats whose mothers had received testosterone mounted male rats, and male rats whose mothers had received estrogen presented themselves sexually to females; both are the opposite of non-altered behavior. These results were extrapolated to human sexuality as a theory of the origin of homosexuality, and by extension to stereotypical and non-stereotypical gendered behavior, including skills and career choice. The theory of "brain sex" suppressed evidence of male-female behavioral overlaps in humans and in animals, and did not allow for social factors in the gendering of human behavior. In fact, there was a great deal of effort to separate out the biological from the social causes of masculinity and femininity in the search for "bedrock" origins.

The problem here is that despite our constant contrasts and comparisons of boys and girls and men and women, human beings show a continuum of physiological and behavioral patterns that are not clearly and neatly divided into "female" and "male." The seemingly natural binary division of brain structure and behavior is a division imposed by researchers looking for differences between women and men. Similarities and overlaps are made invisible because researchers start with the assumption that there are two—and only two—clear-cut categories of different sorts of people, so they dismiss the in-between areas as aberrations. When researchers start with the variety of patterns they see and classify them into finer categories, and then run those categories against multiple social categories (combinations of racial ethnic groups, social classes, sexual orientations, and genders), they come up with many more than two contrasting sets of people. If people cannot be sorted into clear and separable sex groups, how can you validate sex differences in the structure of the brain and the sex-typed behavior they are supposed to produce?

Another problem with brain organization theory is that brain pathways do not get established once and forever prenatally or during infancy. Fausto-Sterling cites research that shows that brain structures respond to behavior by laying down new neural pathways which in turn affect behavior in a loop-back developmental pattern (2000, 195–232). Despite this evidence of changes in individual brains and behavior, theories of evolutionary psychology claim that there is a deeply embedded core of human behavior that was laid down in our primate ancestry and further ingrained by the food-gathering behavior of prehistoric humans.

ARE WE HAIRLESS PRIMATES?

A popular theory of the source of human behavior is that since we share 99 percent of our genes with our primate ancestors, we must act the way they do. Male primate behavior is usually invoked as an explanation for men's propensity for warfare (territorial defense) and sexual aggression (the alpha male has first pick of the females). But the behavior of gorillas, chimpanzees, baboons, and bonobos is very different. Bonobos, for instance, spend much of their time having sex and grooming each other, as a way of ensuring peaceful cooperation. The sex is social, not procreative, and often female-female and male-male. It is used to facilitate sharing and gifting, for reconciliation after disputes, to integrate a new member into the group, and to form coalitions (Roughgarden 2004, 153–165).

Another false idea about primates is that while they learn local skills, like how to crack nuts with stones, from each other (mostly from their mothers), their social behavior is genetically established and unchanging. An accidental experiment in changing male primate behavior occurred in a group of 62 baboons. Natalie Angier, *New York Times* science writer, describes what happened in the following article.

No Time for Bullies: Baboons Retool Their Culture

◆◆◆

Natalie Angier

...Among a troop of savanna baboons in Kenya, a terrible outbreak of tuberculosis 20 years ago selectively killed off the biggest, nastiest and most despotic males, setting the stage for a social and behavioral transformation unlike any seen in this notoriously truculent primate.

In a study appearing...in the journal *PloS Biology* (online at www.plosbiology. org), researchers describe the drastic temperamental and tonal shift that occurred in a troop of 62 baboons when its most belligerent members vanished from the scene. The victims were all dominant adult males that had been strong and snarly enough to fight with a neighboring baboon troop over the spoils at a tourist lodge garbage dump, and were exposed there to meat tainted with bovine tuberculosis, which soon killed them. Left behind in the troop, designated the Forest Troop, were the 50 percent of males that had been too subordinate to try dump brawling, as well as all the females and their young. With that change in demographics came a cultural swing toward pacifism, a relaxing of the usually parlous baboon hierarchy, and a willingness to use affection and mutual grooming rather than threats, swipes, and bites to foster a patriotic spirit.

Remarkably, the Forest Troop has maintained its genial style over two decades, even though the male survivors of the epidemic have since died or disappeared and been replaced by males from the outside. (As is the case for most primates, baboon females spend their lives in their natal home, while the males leave at puberty to seek their fortunes elsewhere.) The persistence of communal comity suggests that the resident baboons must somehow be instructing the immigrants in the unusual customs of the tribe.

"We don't yet understand the mechanism of transmittal," said Dr. Robert M. Sapolsky, a professor of biology and neurology at Stanford, "but the jerky new guys are obviously learning, 'We don't do things like that around here.'" Dr. Sapolsky wrote the report with his colleague and wife, Dr. Lisa J. Share. Dr. Sapolsky, who is renowned for his study of the physiology of stress, said that the Forest Troop baboons probably felt as good as they acted. Hormone samples from the monkeys showed far less evidence of stress in even the lowest-ranking individuals, when contrasted with baboons living in more rancorous societies.

The researchers were able to compare the behavior and physiology of the contemporary Forest Troop primates to two control groups: a similar-size baboon congregation living nearby, called the Talek Troop, and the Forest Troop itself from 1979 through 1982, the era that might be called Before Alpha Die-off, or B.A.D. "It's a really fine, thorough piece of work, with the sort of methodology and lucky data sets that you can only get from doing long-term field research," said Dr. Duane Quiatt, a primatologist at the University of Colorado at Denver and a co-author with Vernon Reynolds of the 1993 book *Primate Behaviour: Information, Social Knowledge and the Evolution of Culture.*

The new work vividly demonstrates that, Putumayo records notwithstanding, humans hold no patent on multiculturalism. As a growing body of research indicates, many social animals learn from one another and cultivate regional variants in skills, conventions, and fashions. Some chimpanzees crack open their nuts with a stone hammer on a stone anvil; others prefer wood hammers on wood anvils. The chimpanzees of the Tai forest rain-dance; those of the Gombe tickle themselves. Dr. Jane Goodall reported a fad in one chimpanzee group: a young female started wiggling her hands, and before long, every teen chimp was doing likewise.

But in the baboon study, the culture being conveyed is less a specific behavior or skill than a global code of conduct. "You can more accurately describe it as the social ethos of group," said Dr. Andrew Whiten, a professor of evolutionary and developmental psychology at the University of St. Andrews in Scotland who has studied chimpanzee culture. "It's an attitude that's being transmitted."

The report also offers real-world proof of a principle first demonstrated in captive populations of monkeys: that with the right upbringing, diplomacy is infectious. Dr. Franz B. M. de Waal, the director of the Living Links Center at the Yerkes National Primate Research Center of Emory University in Atlanta, has shown that if the normally pugilistic rhesus monkeys are reared with the more conciliatory stumptailed monkeys, the rhesus monkeys learn the value of tolerance, peacemaking and mutual hip-hugging. Dr. de Waal, who wrote an essay to accompany the new baboon study, said in a telephone interview, "The good news for humans is that it looks like peaceful conditions, once established, can be maintained," he said. "And if baboons can do it," he said, "why not us? The bad news is that you might have to first knock out all the most aggressive males to get there."

Jerkiness or worse certainly seems to be a job description for ordinary male baboons. The average young male, after wheedling his way into a new troop at around age seven, spends his prime years seeking to fang his way up the hierarchy; and once he's gained some status, he devotes many a leisure hour to whimsical displays of power at scant personal cost. He harasses and attacks females, which weigh half his hundred pounds and lack his thumb-thick canines, or he terrorizes the low-ranking males he knows cannot retaliate.

Dr. Barbara Smuts, a primatologist at the University of Michigan who wrote the 1985 book *Sex and Friendship in Baboons*, said that the females in the troop she studied received a serious bite from a male annually, maybe losing a strip of flesh or part of an ear in the process. As they age and lose their strength, however, males may calm down and adopt a new approach to group living, affiliating with females so devotedly that they keep their reproductive opportunities going even as their ranking in the male hierarchy plunges. For their part, female baboons, which live up to 25 years—compared with the male's 18—inherit their rank in the gynocracy from their mothers and so spend less time fighting for dominance. They do, however, readily battle females from outside the fold, for they, not the males, are the keepers of turf and dynasty.

The new-fashioned Forest Troop is no United Nations, or even the average frat house. Its citizens remain highly aggressive and argumentative, and the males still obsess over hierarchy. "We're talking about baboons here," said Dr. Sapolsky. What most distinguishes this congregation from others is that the males resist taking out their bad moods on females and underlings. When a dominant male wants to pick a fight, he finds someone his own size and rank. As a result, a greater percentage of male-male conflicts in the Forest Troop occur between closely ranked individuals than is seen in the control populations, where the bullies seek easier pickings. Moreover, Forest Troop males of all ranks spend more time grooming and being groomed, and just generally huddling close to troop mates, than do their counterpart males in the study.

Interestingly, the male faces in the Forest Troop may have changed over time, but the relative numbers have not. Ever since the tuberculosis epidemic killed half the adult males, the ratio has remained skewed, with twice as many females as males. Yet the researchers have demonstrated that the troop's sexual complexion alone cannot explain its character. Examining other troops with a similar preponderance of females, the Stanford scientists saw no evidence of the Forest Troop's relative amity.

Dr. Sapolsky has no idea how long the good times will last. "I confess I'm rooting for the troop to stay like this forever, but I worry about how vulnerable they may be," he said. "All it would take is two or three jerky adolescent males entering at the same time to tilt the balance and destroy the culture."

Reprinted from Natalie Angier, "No Time for Bullies: Baboons Retool Their Culture." *New York Times*, 13 April, 2004, F1, 2. Copyright © 2004 by The New York Times Company. Reprinted by permission.

ARDI AND LUCY: OUR DIRECT ANCESTORS

The great apes are our closest living ancestors, but they are not our direct evolutionary ancestors, which are proto-human lines that diverged from the primate line millions of years ago. The one we are most familiar with is Lucy, a fossil of the species *Australopithecus afarensis*. Fifteen years ago, a much older group of fossils was found in the same area in Ethiopia. The cumulative results of the intensive work on these fossils were reported in the October 2009 special issue of *Science*. The 4.4 million-year-old hominid fossils are part of a species named *Ardipithecus ramidus*, which pre-dates the Lucy line by a million years. The Ardi species lived mostly in the trees in the East African woodlands, but walked upright when on the ground. The female specimen that was most complete was about 4 feet tall, weighed 110 pounds, and had long arms, short legs, and a grasping big toe. Lucy lived on the ground and had more human-like feet. Both had small brains, like the great apes, but did not have fang-like canines in males. Ardi males were about the same size as Ardi females.

The social implications of the Ardi fossils are crucial to our understanding of human behavioral evolution. It has been argued that human teeth evolved to match dietary chewing needs, and that stone weapons replaced fangs as male instruments of aggression. According to C. Owen Lovejoy (2009), a paleoanthropologist,

> Ar. ramidus negates such hypotheses because it demonstrates that small canines occurred in hominids long before any of the dental modifications of Australopithecus or the use of stone tools. The loss of large canine teeth in males must have occurred within the context of a generalized, nonspecialized diet. Comparisons of the Ar. ramidus dentition with those of all other higher primates indicate that the species retained virtually no anatomical correlates of male-to-male conflict. Consistent with a diminished role of such agonism, the body size of Ar. ramidus males was only slightly larger than that of females.

Loss of canine weaponry and similar size mean less physical aggression among males and between males and females. If Ardi males did not have sharp canines to fight other males with or larger size to physically dominate females, how did they gain a reproductive advantage? Lovejoy says that Ardi's physical characteristics indicate a different behavioral package than a comparison with chimpanzees (who have also evolved) gives us. Walking upright allows carrying food and babies. Lovejoy suggests that the Ardi line developed pair-bonding and intensified male parental investment.

Early humans were probably not troops of aggressive alpha males and a harem of passive breeding females but rather mutually cooperative parents and their children. Unlike higher primates, human females do not have estrus—a seasonal period of sexual responsiveness during which impregnation can occur. Since hominid females were always potentially interested in sex, hominid males were likely to have been encouraged to bribe them with food and share in feeding infants as a way of gaining sexual access. According to a feminist anthropologist writing thirty years ago, "Females probably had sex more frequently with those males who were around more often, playing with offspring, helping in protection, occasionally sharing meat and foraged plants, and who were generally friendly" (Tanner 1981, 164). The Ardi fossils support that argument.

HUNTERS AND GATHERERS,
HERDERS AND FARMERS

Another theory of evolutionary adaptation argues that if modern humans are not quasi-primates, we are children of our prehistoric ancestors. This theory of evolutionary adaptation spans hundreds of thousands of years, from the time when humans lived in tribes where women gathered plant food and men hunted for meat to the present. Evolutionary psychology theory argues that the behaviors prehistoric humans required for survival are still ingrained in today's human genes. These survival adaptations are supposedly expressed in men's roaming, predation, and sexual promiscuity and in women's nesting, nurturing, and sexual loyalty. In actuality, a compilation of recent research on human genetics and culture shows changes in the human genome as recent as 10,000 to 12,000 years ago, the effects of herding and agriculture (Laland, Odling-Smee, and Myles 2010). There is genetic evidence that as food production changed from hunting and gathering to farming and herding, humans adapted with new genes for resistance to malaria, lactose tolerance, salt sensitivity, skin pigmentation, bone structure, and brain development (Gross 2006, Voight et al. 2006).

Bodies and behavior must be adaptive if a species is to survive. Success in survival involves living long enough to pass on one's genes, which will replicate successfully adapted bodies and behavior. Part of the evolutionary argument is that women have a "maternal instinct" and will put children before their careers, professions, politics, or artistic endeavors because motherhood and mothering continues the survival of the species. Voluntary childlessness or letting someone else take care of your children is thus considered "unnatural" and certainly "unwomanly."

This evolutionary theory of women's mothering assumes that it is universal and unchanging, that mothers have never evolved. But feminist anthropologists show that in the past as in the present, maternal behavior is consciously strategic and socially adaptive to changing physical and social circumstances, not instinctual. Sarah Blaffer Hrdy, an anthropologist who has studied primates and written about human evolution, claims that the idea of a universal and unchanging "maternal instinct" downplays the varied and purposeful action of mothers as they adapt to changing physical and social environments. In *Mother Nature*, Blaffer Hrdy argues that prehistorically, historically, and in the present, "every female who becomes a mother does it her way" (1999, 79). A mother's goal is not so much to get the best man's genes to pass on as to ensure the survival of her "best" children—the healthiest, liveliest, and fattest—those with the best chance of living to adulthood. To do so, she may abandon, kill, or fail to feed sickly children, twins, or deformed infants. She will certainly recruit *alloparents*—older children, other women in her kin group and community, and fathers—to help her care for and raise her children. The following excerpt from *Mother Nature* lays out Blaffer Hrdy's argument for how a female's selective behavior in procreation affects the survival of her offspring, and thus the inheritance of her own genes.

Incorporating Mothers into the Evolutionary Process

◆◆◆

Sarah Blaffer Hrdy
University of California, Davis

All through the 1970s, in the years before sociobiology fully incorporated the new view of mothers as complex, variable creatures, there was a widespread presumption that "Most adult females in most animal populations are likely to be breeding at or close to the theoretical limit of their capacity to produce or rear young…" while, by contrast, with regard to males, it was assumed that "there is always the possibility of doing better."[1]

Researchers fixated on simple measures like "counting cops"—primatologists' slang for counting the number of times each male copulates. But in species where maternal reproductive success varies a great deal, the number of matings provides only a crude and unreliable measure of any given male's reproductive success. Whether a copulation results in surviving offspring will depend on a whole range of contingencies having to do with which female a male mates with. Unless mating results in production of offspring *who themselves survive infancy and the juvenile years and position themselves so as to reproduce,* sex is only so much sound and undulation signifying nothing.[2]

Consideration of maternal effects and other underlying mysteries takes evolutionists beyond the habitual questions raised by sexual selection theory, and the staple of so many sociobiological studies: "Will she or won't she?" "Can he or can't he?" More recently, questions like "Which mother?" and "Under what circumstances?" have become more important.

Whereas males would be under heavy selection pressure to best rival after rival just to gain opportunities to copulate one more time, females have no need to compete for mates in this way. This correct generalization was often misunderstood to mean that females lacked any "preadaptation for competition" or any "genetic predisposition toward the creation of hierarchy," which was rarely true.[3] It was certainly not true if one takes into account those aspects of mothers' lives where competition matters.

Darwin's ingenious theory of sexual selection promoted a blinding hubris. If evolutionists could explain male strategies for out-competing other males and inseminating the most females, they could explain the different natures of males and females. The trouble was that this crown jewel of evolutionary theory, tailor-made as it was to explain competition between males, was poorly suited to explain the many preoccupations of females. Important sources of variance in the reproductive success of one female compared to another were overlooked.

Factors that were routinely overlooked in those early days included the female's age at first birth, the duration of the intervals between her births, social factors influencing whether her infants live or die, or even whether she reproduces at all. Nor did it always register that unless mothers gauged their reproductive effort in line with fluctuating resources and other prevailing conditions, few would manage to rear infants that survived. The poorly adapted or unlucky would die trying.

Viewing mothers the old way, no one had paid much attention to these sources of variation.[4] For example, when Jeanne Altmann first showed that high- and low-ranking baboon mothers at Amboseli differed in their probabilities of giving birth to a son versus a daughter, few knew what to make of it. Many found it hard to believe, because in order to understand what was going on one also had to take into account the social and ecological context in which each mother was operating, and to understand that baboon daughters born to low-ranking females were less likely to survive than sons were. Why? Studies of captive macaques with a similar social system provide one reason. Higher-ranking females in the same group harass mothers with daughters (the sex of offspring that will remain in the natal group and compete with her own daughters) but leave low-ranking mothers with sons alone. As a consequence, infant daughters suffer higher mortality than would sons born to mothers of the same low rank.[5]

With the support of their mothers and other matrilineal kin, daughters born to high-ranking baboon females rise in the hierarchy and, in turn, pass on the advantages of their acquired rank (along with such perks as early reproductive maturity, and greater offspring survival) to daughters. The female baboon, like most social mammals, introduces her baby into the network of social relationships she has forged. Daughters who grow up surrounded by high-ranking kin give birth at an earlier age to offspring more likely to survive. Since baboon daughters inherit their rank from their mother, these social advantages are transmitted across generations as maternal effects, and the reproductive advantages accumulate through time in her matriline. But this strange bias in production of progeny only made sense in the light of variation between females.[6] ...

Convinced that the most important variation occurs between males, some twentieth-century biologists ... still assumed that females were less evolved than males. Why? Because *variation in the reproductive success of one individual relative to another is essential for natural selection to occur.* No variation, no selection. No selection, no evolution.

The old premise that selection acts more strongly on males than females was uncritically carried forward into modern evolutionary thought. Indisputably, sexual selection weighs heavily on male traits that affect their access to mates. But competition for mates is not the only sphere where Mother Nature is at work.

Males and females pursue different reproductive strategies. Theoretically, males compete for fertilizations, trying to inseminate as many females as possible. There is a strict limit, on the other hand, to how many times a female benefits from insemination. Her reproductive success depends not on number of fertilizations but on the contingencies of her life, the qualities of the mates she chooses, and, above all, *how successful she is at keeping alive such infants as she does produce.*

This new awareness of female reproductive interests is transforming our understanding of animal mating systems. Wherever males attempt to constrain female reproductive options, we can expect selection for traits that help females to evade them. What are we to make of such far-flung solicitations and enterprising sexuality as are being documented for creatures as diverse as fireflies, langurs, and chimps? After all, applied to females, pejorative-sounding words like "promiscuous" only make sense from the perspective of the males who had been attempting to control them—no doubt the origin of such famous dichotomies as that between "madonna" and "whore." From the perspective of the female, however, her behavior is better understood as "assiduously maternal." For this is a mother doing all that she can to secure the survival of her offspring.

Whatever else these apes and monkeys are up to, it is obvious that selecting the one best male from available suitors—as Darwin imagined female choice would work—is scarcely the whole story. Females are also actively manipulating information available to males about paternity.

Is a male animal capable of remembering whether he mated with a particular female? The best experimental evidence testing the proposition that he can derives not from the langur monkeys, who first inspired the hypothesis about confusing paternity, but from European sparrows called dunnocks. A male dunnock acts as if he can not only recall *which* females he mated with, but how likely copulations at a particular time were to result in conception.

Female dunnocks live in cooperative breeding groups in which a female solicits multiple males. These males, in turn, help provision the chicks more or less in proportion to how much opportunity they had to inseminate the mother when she was last fertile. According to Nick Davies of Cambridge University, both alpha and subordinate males were significantly more likely to bring food to young they fathered, or even young they *might* have fathered. And just as the "several possible fathers" hypothesis would predict, DNA fingerprinting (which pins down paternity more precisely than human observers possibly could) revealed that males were often *but not always* accurate in their guesstimates.

Mothers in cooperatively breeding species are especially sensitive to who in their vicinity is likely either to help or hinder their reproductive endeavors. Mothers calibrate their reproductive effort according to which males, with which intentions, and which females are also present. After birth, how much a given mother invests may depend on particular attributes of her litter, its size, the ratio of sons to daughters in the litter, or even the qualities of particular offspring. Deteriorating social conditions, loss of helpful kin or a mate, or the presence of dangerous strangers can have a profound effect on maternal commitment.

Notes

1. Daly and Wilson. 1978: 59. Through two editions, Martin Daly and Margo Wilson's *Sex, Evolution and Behavior* would stand as the best available and most widely used textbook

in this area, the one I chose for my own classes. I am thus not citing a "weak link" but the standard view.

2. For one of the best recent papers on this subject see Altmann 1997. For a classic example in humans of when "counting cops" starts to break down as even a reasonable estimator of male reproductive success, sec Perusse (1993) for modern industrial populations where people use artificial birth control.

3. Cronin 1980:302. See also Abernethy 1978:129, 132.

4. Primatologists in Japan (e.g., Kawai 1958) recognized the significance of female ranking systems far earlier than their counterparts in the West perhaps because they bypassed nineteenth-century Darwinian thinking and started by observing the wild macaques in their own backyards.

5. Silk 1983 and 1988.

6. Altmann, Hausfater, and Altmann 1988.

References

Abernethy, Virginia. 1978. Female hierarchy and evolutionary perspective. In *Female Hierarchies*, Lionel Tiger and Heather Fowler, eds., 129–32. Chicago: Beresford Book Service.

Altmann, Jeanne. 1997. Mate choice and intrasexual reproductive competition: Contributions to reproduction that go beyond acquiring more mates. In *Feminism and Evolutionary Biology: Boundaries, Intersections and Frontiers*, Patricia Adair Gowaty, ed., 320–33. New York: Chapman and Hall.

Altmann, Jeanne, Glenn Hausfater, and Stuart A. Altmann, 1988. Determinants of reproductive success in savannah baboons, *Papio cynocephalus*. In *Reproductive Success: Studies of Individual Variation in Contrasting Breeding Systems*, T. H. Clutton-Brock, ed., 403–18. Chicago: Chicago University Press.

Cronin, Carol. 1980. Dominance relations and females. In *Dominance Relations: An Ethological View of Human Conflict and Social Interaction*, Donald R. Omark, F. F. Strayer, and Daniel G. Freedman, eds New York: Garland.

Daly, Martin, and Margo Wilson. 1978. *Sex, Evolution and Behavior: Adaptations for Reproduction*. North Scituate, Massachusetts: Duxbury.

Kawai, M. 1958. On the system of social ranks in a natural troop of Japanese monkeys, parts 1 and 2. Translated into English and reprinted in *Japanese Monkeys*, S. Altmann, ed. Edmonton: University of Alberta.

Perusse, D. 1993. Cultural and reproductive success in industrial societies: testing the phenomenon at the proximate and ultimate levels. *Behavioral and Brain Sciences* 16: 267–322.

Silk, Joan B. 1983. Local resource competition and facultative adjustment of sex ratios in relation to competitive abilities. *American Naturalist* 121: 56–66.

———. 1988. Maternal investment in captive bonnet macaques, *Macaca radiata*. *American Naturalist* 132(1): 1–19.

Just as mothering behavior adapts to changing environmental and social conditions, so does other human behavior. Ten thousand years ago, human cultures changed enormously from small, nomadic, hunting and foraging tribes to large settlements and cities. Writing evolved, roles were specialized and assigned to different categories of people, and ownership of land and herds created hierarchies. Hunting and gathering tribes are comparatively egalitarian, and women, as major food producers, have a high status. In the economic evolution of some human societies from foraging to agriculture, women lost status because they produced less of the food. Their main roles became child producers and child minders.

In societies that had ownership of land and other property by a few men, being able to pass on this property to biological kin became a prime factor in men's control of women's procreation; fathers wanted to be sure that it was their sons who inherited their wealth. Virginity at marriage was mandatory, as was sexual faithfulness of wives after marriage. Many patriarchal social rules that were said to emerge from supposed natural sex differences, like men's sexual promiscuity and women's maternalness, are the products of the herding and farming societies that supplanted hunters and gatherers.

A NATURE VS. NURTURE CONTROVERSY REVISITED

In the 1970s, there was a case that seemed to be an ideal accidental experiment that could test whether nature or nurture had primacy in gender development. The penis of a baby boy who was an identical twin was destroyed in the course of a botched circumcision when he was seven months old. The parents were advised to legally change the child's name and sex to "female," and to treat the child as a girl as much as possible. A vagina was surgically constructed when the child was seventeen months old. The child was feminized with frilly dresses, hair ribbons, and jewelry, and the child's exuberant and dominant behavior was squelched:

> The girl had many tomboyish traits, such as abundant physical energy, a high level of activity, stubbornness, and being often the dominant one in a girls' group. Her mother tried to modify her tomboyishness: "I teach her to be more polite and quiet. I always wanted those virtues. I never did manage, but I'm going to try to manage them to—my daughter—to be more quiet and ladylike." From the beginning the girl had been the dominant twin. By the age of three, her dominance over her brother was, as her mother described it, that of a mother hen. The boy in turn took up for his sister, if anyone threatened her. (Money and Ehrhardt 1972, 122)

You could argue that this child was a tomboy because of male genes, but the mother had also been a tomboy. Although the mother said she had learned feminine behavior poorly while she growing up as a biological female, she insisted that her physically reconstructed daughter learn well.

But when the child became a teenager and faced further surgery, lifelong hormone injections, and relegation to what had become a hated female status, the child rebelled and insisted on being returned to a male physical and social status

(Colapinto 2000). He had testosterone injections and surgical construction of a penis. He married and became a stepfather to three children. This outcome seems to clinch the argument that nature trumps nurture. But this case can be read as the rejection of a devalued gender status as much as it can the inevitable emergence of bodily and psychological hard-wiring.

In an account of the case that favored the nature argument, the teenager was referred to as Joan/John. "Joan" was described as hating being a girl. Colapinto (1997, 68) quotes Joan's identical twin brother as saying, " 'When I say there was nothing feminine about Joan,' Kevin laughs, 'I mean there was *nothing* feminine. She walked like a guy. She talked about guy things, didn't give a crap about cleaning house, getting married, wearing makeup.... We both wanted to play with guys, build forts and have snowball fights and play army.' " Enrolled in the Girl Scouts, Joan was miserable. "I remember making daisy chains and thinking, 'If this is the most exciting thing in Girl Scouts, forget it,' John says. 'I kept thinking of the fun stuff my brother was doing in Cubs.' " Is this rejection of conventional "girl things" the result of internal masculinization or the gender resistance of a rebellious child? Being a man is a preferred status in many societies, so it is not surprising when those with ambiguous genitalia prefer that gender identity (Herdt and Davidson 1988).

Joan might have been happier growing up in the pro-feminist 1980s and 1990s, playing sports and taking leadership roles. Given the surgery she had had as a child, she might have become an intersex activist. What actually happened to Joan/John and the twin brother is that they both committed suicide:

> A Winnipeg man who was born a boy but raised as a girl in a famous nurture-versus-nature experiment has died at the age of 38. David Reimer, who shared his story in the pages of a book and on the TV show Oprah, took his own life last Tuesday. His mother, Janet Reimer, said she believes her son would still be here today had it not been for the devastating gender study that led to much emotional hardship. "He managed to have so much courage," Janet told *The Sun* yesterday. "I think he felt he had no options. It just kept building up and building up." ...
>
> David recently slumped into a depression after losing his job and separating from his wife. He was also still grieving the death of his twin brother two years earlier, their mother said. A cause of death was never confirmed but Janet suspects it might have been an overdose of medication which Brian required to treat schizophrenia. Daily, David would visit his brother's grave, placing fresh flowers and pulling weeds to keep it tidy. Just last week, David told his parents that things would get better soon but they never imagined he was planning to commit suicide.
>
> Janet said she'll remember her son as 'the most generous, loving soul that ever lived." ... "He was so generous. He gave all he had." (Chalmers, 2004)

This case can be seen as induced gender dysphoria and the child as an accidental male-to-female transgendered person. The "nature" argument is that the true sex won out, but too late, and suicide was the result. But the intact twin brother also had mental problems, and also may have committed suicide. A disturbed family history, perhaps precipitated by the botched circumcision, for which the mother always felt guilty, was no doubt an element in both children's unhappiness. But more significant were the pressure and constraints of the Western sex/gender system of the mid-twentieth century. It dictated that a child without a penis could not be a boy, and that a girl had to be feminine—restrained, subdued, and dressed in frilly clothes. We are somewhat more open to a range of behavior for girls and women, but bodies are still circumscribed by rigid gender norms and expectations.

CRITICAL SUMMARY

Even though there is ample evidence to the contrary, beliefs about the biological essence of differences between girls and boys and women and men persist. For example, there has been experimental evidence since the 1930s that the so-called male and female hormones are equally important to the development of both females and males, and sex testing at sports competitions has shown that people with XY chromosomes can have female anatomy and physiology. Nonetheless, all of the research efforts in the twentieth century were geared to finding clear female-male differences, preferably with an easily identifiable physiological source. Before the intensive criticism by feminist scientists and social scientists, there was very lit- tle effort to document the social sources of masculinity and femininity in Western societies and their variety and fluidity.

Sex differences do matter in illness and aging. There is good evidence that the presence of the extra X chromosome in females that is missing in males provides protection against certain genetic diseases, since the smaller Y chromosome has fewer genes. There is also good evidence that estrogen is protective against certain illnesses, and that males and females experience the physical effects of aging dif- ferently. So there are certainly sex differences in illness risks, but the evidence for sex differences in intellectual and emotional capacities and behavior is much less solid. Life-time experiences, such as gender socialization, gendered norms and expectations, differences in educational and job opportunities, economic status, and family responsibilities have an enormous impact on men and women, and it is these social factors, we argue, that construct women and men as different in emo- tions, attitudes, and behavior.

In sum, while it is incorrect to say there is no prenatal "hardwiring" of human behavior through genetic predispositions, hormonal flooding of the fetus, brain development, or evolutionary prehistory, brains and bodies respond significantly to their physical and social environments. Sex differences are modified by gen- dered norms and expectations, opportunities over the life cycle, and by input from racial, ethnic, and social class differences. Sex differences are not fixed and unchangeable, nor do they have one cause.

If there isn't a simple or single answer to the question of whether differences between women and men are genetic, hormonal, long-term evolutionary adapta- tions, or recently learned behavior, then there isn't a simple or single way of deter- mining how much or how little can be changed by new social patterns. Rather than accepting whatever the status quo is for their time and place as natural and unchangeable, feminists have pushed for social changes. The results of feminist social change have shown that women's and men's bodies, brains, and behaviors are quite adaptable to these new social patterns.

REFERENCES AND RECOMMENDED READINGS

Bearman, Peter, ed. 2008. Exploring Genetics and Social Structure, Special Issue. *American Journal of Sociology* 114 Suppl.

Birke, Lynda. 2000. *Feminism and the Biological Body.* New Brunswick, NJ: Rutgers University Press.

Blaffer Hrdy, Sarah. [1981] 1999. *The Woman That Never Evolved.* Cambridge, MA: Harvard University Press.

———. 1999. *Mother Nature: A History of Mothers, Infants, and Natural Selection.* New York: Pantheon.

Braidotti, Rosi. 1994. *Nomadic Subjects: Embodiment and Sexual Difference in Contemporary Feminist Theory.* New York: Columbia University Press.

Butler, Judith. 1993. *Bodies That Matter: On the Discursive Limits of "Sex."* New York: Routledge.

Carey, Benedict. 2006. "Searching for the Person in the Brain." *New York Times* Week in Review, 4 February, 1, 4.

Cealey Harrison, Wendy. 2006. "The Shadow and the Substance: the Sex/Gender Debate." In *Handbook of Gender and Women's Studies*, edited by Kathy Davis, Mary Evans, and Judith Lorber. London: Sage.

Cealey Harrison, Wendy, and John Hood-Williams. 2002. *Beyond Sex and Gender.* London: Sage.

Chalmers, Katie. 2004. "Sad End to Boy/Girl Life." *WinnipegSun/News*, 10 May. http://www.canoe.ca/NewsStand/WinnipegSun/News/2004/05/10/pf-453481.html.

Coates, John M., and J. Herbert. 2008. "Endogenous Steroids and Financial Risk Taking on a London Trading Floor," *Proceedings of the National Academy of Sciences* 105: 6167-6172, Apr. 22, doi: 10.1073/pnas.0704025105.

Colapinto, John. 1997. "The True Story of John/Joan." *Rolling Stone,* 11 December, pp. 54–97.

———. 2000. *As Nature Made Him: The Boy Who Was Raised as a Girl.* New York: HarperCollins.

Cox, Michael W., and Richard Alm. 2005. "Scientists are Made, Not Born." *New York Times*, 28 February, A19.

Ermer, Elsa, Leda Cosmides, and John Tooby. 2008. "Relative Status Regulates Risky Decision Making About Resources in Men: Evidence for the Co-Evolution of Motivation and Cognition." *Evolution and Human Behavior* 29: 106–118. http://repositories.cdlib.org/postprints/2997.

Fausto-Sterling, Anne. 1985. *Myths of Gender: Biological Theories About Women and Men.* New York: Basic Books.

———. 2000. *Sexing the Body: Gender Politics and the Construction of Sexuality.* New York: Basic Books.

———. 2005. "The Bare Bones of Sex: Part 1—Sex and Gender." *Signs: Journal of Women in Culture and Society* (hereafter, *Signs*) 30: 1491-1527.

Gowaty, Patricia Adair (ed.). 1996. *Feminism and Evolutionary Biology: Boundaries, Intersections and Frontiers*. New York: Chapman and Hall.

Gross, Liza. 2006. "Clues to Our Past: Mining the Human Genome for Signs of Recent Selection." *PLoS Biology* 4 (3), 0001. DOI: 10.1371/journal.pbio.0040094.

Haraway, Donna. 1989. *Primate Visions*. New York: Routledge.

———. 1997. *Modest_Witness@Second_Millenium. FemaleMan©.Meets OncoMouse™: Feminism and Technoscience*. New York: Routledge.

Hausman, Bernice L. 2000. "Do Boys Have to Be Boys? Gender, Narrativity, and the John/Joan Case." *National Women's Studies Association Journal* 12: 114–138.

Herdt, Gilbert, and Julian Davidson. 1988. The Sambia "Turnim-Man": Sociocultural and Clinical Aspects of Gender Formation in Male Pseudohermaphrodites with 5α-Reductase Deficiency in Papua, New Guinea. *Archives of Sexual Behavior* 17: 33–56.

Hird, Myra J. 2009. "Feminist Engagements with Matter." *Feminist Studies* 35: 329–346.

Hubbard, Ruth. 1990. *The Politics of Women's Biology*. New Brunswick, NJ: Rutgers University Press.

Jacobus, Mary, Evelyn Fox Keller, and Sally Shuttleworth (eds.). 1990. *Body/Politics: Women and the Discourses of Science*. New York: Routledge.

Jordanova, Ludmilla. 1989. *Sexual Visions: Images of Gender in Science and Medicine Between the Eighteenth and Twentieth Centuries*. Madison: University of Wisconsin Press.

Kemper, Theodore D. 1990. *Social Structure and Testosterone: Explorations of the Socio-Bio-Social Chain*. New Brunswick, NJ: Rutgers University Press.

Kristof, Nicholas D. 2009. "Mistresses of the Universe," *New York Times*, February 8. http://www.nytimes.com/2009/02/08/opinion/08kristof.html

Laland, Kevin N., John Odling-Smee, and Sean Myles. 2010. "How Culture Shaped the Human Genome: Bringing Genetics and the Human Sciences Together." *Nature Reviews Genetics* 11: 137-148. doi:10.1038/nrg2734.

Leonard, Diana. 2006. "Gender, Change, and Education." In *Handbook of Gender and Women's Studies*, edited by Kathy Davis, Mary Evans, and Judith Lorber. London: Sage.

Lorber, Judith. 1993. "Believing is Seeing: Biology as Ideology." *Gender & Society* 7: 568–581.

Lovejoy, C. O. 2009. "Reexamining Human Origins in Light of Ardipithecus ramidus." *Science* 326 (no. 5949): 74, 74e1-74e8. DOI: 10.1126/science.1175834.

Money, John, and Anke A. Ehrhardt. 1972. *Man & Woman, Boy & Girl*. Baltimore, MD: Johns Hopkins University Press.

National Human Genome Research Institute. 2005. "Studies Expand Understanding of X Chromosome: NIH-Supported Research Sheds New Light on the Role of Sex Chromosomes in Health and Disease." http://www.genome.gov/13514331.

Neumann, I. D. 2008. "Brain Oxytocin: A Key Regulator of Emotional and Social Behaviours in Both Females and Males." *Journal of Neuroendocrinology* 20: 858–865.

Oudshoorn, Nelly. 1994. *Beyond the Natural Body: An Archeology of Sex Hormones*. New York: Routledge.

Roberts, Celia. 2007. *Messengers of Sex: Hormones, Biomedicine and Feminism*. New York: Cambridge University Press.

Rossi, Alice S. 1977. "A Biosocial Perspective on Parenting." *Daedalus* 106:1–31.

Roughgarden, Joan. 2004. *Evolution's Rainbow: Diversity, Gender, and Sexuality in Nature and People*. Berkeley: University of California Press.

Sapolsky, Robert M., and Lisa J. Share. 2004. "A Pacific Culture Among Wild Baboons: Its Emergence and Transmission." *PLoS Biology* 2 (4), 0534–0541. DOI: *10.1371/journal.pbio.0020106*

Science. 2009. Ardipithecus ramidus. 2 October. http://www.sciencemag.org/ardipithecus/.

Subramaniam, Banu. 2009. "Moored Metamorphoses: A Retrospective Essay on Feminist Science Studies." *Signs* 34: 951-980.

Tanner, Nancy Makepeace. 1981. *On Becoming Human*. Cambridge, UK: Cambridge University Press.

Tanner, Nancy, and Adrienne Zihlman. 1976. "Women in Evolution. Part I: Innovation and Selection in Human Origins." *Signs* 1: 585–608.

Taylor, Shelley E. 2002. *The Tending Instinct: How Nurturing is Essential to Who We Are and How We Live*. New York: Times Books, Henry Holt.

Taylor, Shelley E., Laura Cousino Klein, Brian P. Lewis, Tara L. Gruenewald et al. 2000. "Biobehavioral Responses to Stress in Females: Tend-and-Befriend, Not Fight-or-Flight." *Psychological Review* 107: 411–429.

Van den Wijngaard, Marianne. 1997. *Reinventing the Sexes: The Biomedical Construction of Femininity and Masculinity*. Bloomington: Indiana University Press.

Wizemann, Theresa M., and Mary-Lou Pardue (eds.). 2001. *Exploring the Biological Contributions to Human Health: Does Sex Matter?* Washington, DC: National Academy Press.

Voight, Benjamin F., Sridhar Kudaravalli, Xiaoquan Wen, and Jonathan K. Pritchard. 2006. "A Map of Recent Positive Selection in the Human Genome." *PLoS Biol* 4(3): 0446–0458. DOI: 10.1371/journal.pbio.004007.

Zihlman, Adrienne L. 1978. "Women and Evolution, Part II: Subsistence and Social Organization Among Early Hominids." *Signs* 4: 4–20.

CHAPTER 2

"Are You My Mother? My Father?" Gendering Procreation

Key concepts
breastfeeding, genetic engineering, heteronormativity, new technologies, patriarchal control over procreation, state and medical control of childbearing, surrogacy, valorization of sperm

One of the most significant contributions of feminist scholarship has been the social analysis of human procreation.[1] From valuing the lived experiences of a pregnant woman to examining the proliferation of high-tech innovations for getting pregnant and the medicalization of childbirth, feminism offers critical insights into the social aspects of a seemingly natural process. Through feminist analyses, we are made aware of the ironies of human procreation: it occurs in women's bodies, yet is controlled by patriarchal government interests and individual men's prerogatives.

Women as a group and as individuals generally are not the power brokers when it comes to contraceptive research, abortion policies, access to and financing maternal and child health care, or labor and delivery practices. At the same time, since procreation takes place inside a woman's body, it has been historically and cross-culturally considered a woman's responsibility to manage all its dimensions: conception, contraception, prenatal care, breastfeeding, physical care of infants and small children, and their emotional nurturance. Childbirth has also historically been women's domain, with the birthing woman attended by midwives, but since the advent of modern medicine, it has become an obstetric event, often with men doctors.

In addition to gendered power differences, human procreation provides a clear example of economic differences between industrialized and developing nations. The bodies of women of color and poor women have a history of being used for medical experimentation. The modern birth control movement, ushered in with the mass distribution of the pill, was enabled in part through pharmaceutical testing on poor and uneducated Puerto Rican women throughout the 1950s and 1960s, who were unaware that they were part of a drug trial. The demographic trends of testing contraceptive devices, sterilization, access to prenatal care, and use of expensive technologies tell us that some mothers and babies are socially valued over others. Some countries have pronatal policies encouraging women to have children by restricting access to contraception and making abortion illegal. Other countries have population restriction policies, discouraging women from having more than one or at most two children. Patrilineal family demands for sons to carry on the male line lead to multiple childbirths or selective abortions of female fetuses. Poor countries have high rates of maternal and infant mortality; rich countries spend money developing age-defying fertility treatments. Is it fair that a post-menopausal 59-year-old grandmother can give birth to triplets while an otherwise healthy 20-year-old woman dies in childbirth?

PRENATAL SEX TESTING AND SOCIAL CONSEQUENCES

Gender, racial ethnic, and class dynamics imbue the questions of who is encouraged to procreate and who is prevented, and what types of human bodies should be born. There is ample evidence to suggest a tacit preference for rich, first-world, properly sexed and gendered, male, heterosexual, attractive, White, able-bodied, genetically enhanced babies (Fogg-Davis 2001, Karsjens 2002). But how can this be guaranteed? Eugenics, meaning good genes, is the study of hereditary and genetic "improvement" of the human race by controlled selective breeding. Eugenics is today called social engineering.

Historically, eugenics has been practiced by preventing those who were regarded as having undesirable traits from passing them on to children. The Holocaust and Rwandan genocide of women, men, and children are two examples of the violent elimination of "inferior" genes by mass murder carried out by a supposedly physically and racially "superior" group. In addition to genocide, sterilization campaigns have been undertaken by governments to modify the gene pool. In the United States between 1907 and 1917, sixteen states adopted laws advocating the sterilization of the dependent poor, criminals, the "feeble-minded," and other people allegedly unfit to have children (Apple 1990, 397). In 1924, a U.S. Supreme Court decision said that state practices that routinely sterilized the "feeble minded" were constitutional. By 1937, twenty-seven states had passed variations of such laws. Under these laws, women who are poor, Black, Puerto Rican, Chicana, Native American, or mentally retarded have been sterilized either without their consent or with consent obtained under duress. For example, North Carolina's sterilization program concentrated on welfare recipients, most of whom were Black women (Schoen 2005). Often, women in active labor have been pressured to sign consent forms so that physicians could perform a tubal ligation or hysterectomy immediately after delivery. In many cases, the women spoke little or no English and did not understand what they were signing.

The advent of sonograms that show the sex of the fetus provided another way to control what kind of babies would be born. Until about 25 years ago, the first declaration made about a newly born infant was, "It's a girl!" or "It's a boy!" In many places in the world today, parents can decide to find out the sex at 16 to 19 weeks of pregnancy—at the now routinized first sonogram. Even earlier, embryos can be sorted by sex, and earlier still, sperm can be manipulated to favor X or Y chromosomes. The earlier the "sexing," the easier it is to abort fetuses of the "wrong" sex—usually female.

In addition, genetic engineering and prenatal genetic testing can be used to enhance or suppress desirable or undesirable traits in fetuses. Women who have genetic counseling are given a lot of information. They ostensibly have the autonomy to make an informed choice of whether to undergo amniocentesis and to abort if a genetic anomaly is found, but they are pressured to create socially valued fetuses (Samerski 2009). With the innovation of each new prenatal testing technology, the stakes of pregnancy rise for women. Kristen Karlberg's article describes the ways that prenatal testing serves today's eugenics.

Shaping Babies: No, Not THAT Kind! Can I Try Again?

◆◆◆

Kristen Karlberg
Purchase College, State University of New York

Kristen and John Magill adore all three of their daughters—11-year-old twins and a 5-year-old baby sister. But when they began to plan for their next—and last—child, the Magills really wanted a boy. "My husband is a 'Junior' and has a family business that he wants to continue in the family name," said Kristen, 37, of Grafton, Massachusetts. So the Magills combined a family trip to Disneyland in August with a stop at a Los Angeles fertility clinic that enables couples to pick the sex of their babies. Kristen is now expecting twin boys. "I'm excited," she said, "We always wanted a boy. We really wanted just one, but we'll be happy with two" (Stein 2004).

Pregnant Knowledge: I Can Find Out What?!

It used to be that a pregnant woman had to wait until birth to find out the sex of her child. Today many women are told the sex of their child during the pregnancy rather than at delivery, and some opt to find out at conception. The brave-new-world fantasy of being able to dictate what kind of child you want began with detecting genetic diseases and birth defects through prenatal testing and ultrasound technologies. But since the sex of the fetus is also evident in the chromosomes and on the sonograms, there is also a way of choosing sex.

The information about what "kind" of baby you will have is powerful and literally life altering. This type of knowledge is negotiated by pregnant women and their families and reinterpreted to become family knowledge, with appropriate meanings and actions. The pregnant woman is socially responsible for the type of child she produces, so she must selectively reproduce, filtering out the undesirable fetuses through abortion.

The routinization and normalization of prenatal genetic testing and sex identification effectively transform the pregnancy and its potential product—a "perfect" baby—into a medical and genetic experience. Geneticization refers to the ways in which genetic technologies are increasingly used to manage problems of "health" (Lippman 1991). A fetus' sex is arguably not a "health" issue, but "diagnosing" sex is something many pregnant women and their partners and families wish to do during the pregnancy. The sex of a fetus can be visualized as early as 12 weeks gestation using ultrasound, and is commonly revealed during the routine 16-to-19-week sonogram most pregnant women undergo in the United States. Often one of the first questions a pregnant woman now hears after, "When are you due?" is "Do you know what it is?"

Technologies are now available that design the sex of the fetus at conception. MicroSort ($2,800–$4,000 per attempt) is a patented technique where sperm carrying the X chromosome (female) are separated from sperm carrying the Y chromosome (male), resulting in a 74 percent pure sample of Y sperm and a 91 percent pure sample of X sperm. These samples are then used in artificial insemination of the woman to result in a child of the chosen sex. MicroSort only selects for sex, which the company calls "family balancing." The Genetics and IVF Institutes in Northern Virginia and Laguna Hills, California, who own the patent, are conducting a study seeking FDA approval. So far, several thousand couples have used the technique, resulting in more than 400 babies. Despite the documented preference for boys in developing countries, at this American company, 75 percent of families have been seeking girls (Stein 2004).

Potential parents with a family history of inherited disorders and older pregnant women often undergo genetic testing of the fetus. There are many different prenatal genetic testing technologies available today, amniocentesis being the most common. Amnio is conducted between 15 and 18 weeks of gestation by inserting a needle through the abdomen and into the uterus, withdrawing a small amount of amniotic fluid. The fluid is then cultured and examined to determine chromosomal makeup and, if indicated, the presence or absence of specific genes. Because amnio examines chromosomes, the sex is automatically "diagnosed" because it is dictated by the final pair of the 23 pairs of chromosomes in a human being. Chromosomal disorders, such as an absence of or extra chromosomes, are also easily detected. Down Syndrome is the most common chromosomal disorder, indicated by an extra chromosome 21.

What is often not clear to pregnant women is that amniocentesis does not automatically test for genetic disorders caused by the presence or absence of specific genes housed on chromosomes. Specific tests for specific genes must be ordered at the time the amnio is performed, and the genotypes of the biological parents must be previously obtained for comparison. When an amnio shows "normal" chromosomes, it does not guarantee a genetically "normal" child. More than 450 conditions can be diagnosed through amniocentesis, and with family pedigree and ethnicity information, about a dozen tests for genetic mutations are routinely offered to all applicable pregnant women (Harmon 2004).

In vitro fertilization, costing $10,000–$20,000 per try, in conjunction with preimplantation genetic diagnosis (PGD), is another way to try to guarantee the sex and genetic makeup of the fetus. PGD, which costs $1,000–$4,500 or more per attempt, depending on what is tested for, combines the benefit of finding out the sex of the embryo before implantation with examining it for chromosomal or specific genetic disorders. Embryos are created through in vitro fertilization, and when they reach the eight-cell stage, one cell is removed, cultured, and tested for chromosomal and, if indicated, genetic abnormalities. After the analysis is conducted on the available embryos, those with the desired sex and/or traits are implanted into the woman's uterus. PGD is banned for non-medical use in Australia, Britain, Canada, France, Germany, India, Japan, and Switzerland (Stein 2004).

Genetic Bodies and Genetic Families: Everyone Has Something

Prenatal sex identification and prenatal genetic testing equate health with the desired sex and "normal" or "good" genes, and designate the undesired sex and "deviant" or "bad" genes as illness. This process reduces individuals to their genes, just as the question, "Do you know what it is?" reduces the future baby to its sex. In this perspective, genetics is permeated with conceptions of normality and deviance, resulting in socially constructed "genetic bodies." Those being tested for deviations in genes or chromosomes become "genetic bodies" when they are found to have "bad" or "good" genes or the "right" or "wrong" sex chromosomes. This definition could encompass all individuals, because all bodies have potential genetic information discoverable through genetic testing.

Women's bodies are inherently multiply defined because of their capacity to produce other bodies through their own. The current constructions of flawed genomes and bodies are predominantly represented as dwelling within the female body, which is layered with gendered experiences and meanings. One of these gendered experiences is pregnancy. A pregnant woman's body is potentially two genetic bodies simultaneously—hers and the fetus's—and they both belong to a genetic family.

Genetics magnifies the links among blood relatives, even as the new procreative technologies have the potential for severing biological from social parenting in ways that go beyond adoption. The traditional understanding of "parent" now has been generally subcategorized into "biological" and "social," with the "genetic" parent as a facet of the biological parent. If one blood relative possesses a genetic trait, it is extremely likely that another blood relation has that trait. Thus, the genetic body is not one's own when viewed through the lens of familial heredity. Genetic bodies belong to genetic families—those where a member has experienced some type of genetic testing that explicitly identifies genetic information about the family. A genetic family does not have to have a genetic anomaly to be "marked;" it must have merely been examined through the lens of genetics. Once this genetic information is "in the family," the genetic family will forever be marked by that genetic knowledge, be it benign or dangerous. A genetic family does not have to be blood-related to be affected by this information. Same-sex partners, adopted children, donor-egg and donor-sperm children are all implicated in the genetic family. The genetic family I refer to here is one fashioned by genetic technologies to produce the desired kind of family, be it composed of one boy and one girl, or with children free of genetic disease or a genetic condition, such as deafness.

The uniqueness of genetic families is their multiple social realities. They may be traditional and often nuclear in the blood and marital relation of members, yet they are technological and biomedical through obtaining genetic information. Genetic families also may be formed through donor insemination utilizing screening of the egg, sperm, or embryo, with no blood relations among members. No matter what their structure, genetic families are postmodern because they are defined through biotechnological capabilities and/or genetic linkages.

Genetic Responsibility to Shape Families: It's Women's Work

Pregnant women are the center of genetic families. They are in the tenuous position of mediating the needs and desires of individual families in relation to the social acceptability and social demands of modern society in the twenty-first century. The parental responsibility to produce a healthy child is taken very seriously today. It is assumed that a pregnant woman will undergo testing to guarantee genetic health. The genetic stigmatization of certain detectable genetic disorders can be viewed as a bridge to the potential label of genetic irresponsibility. Women who have children with Down syndrome are queried as to whether they had a prenatal test to detect the disorder. The query implies that if they did not, they failed in their parental responsibilities to the future child. If they did, and kept the baby, they may be criticized for the added burden on their family or society, or praised as exemplary mothers.

Practice guidelines from the American College of Obstetricians and Gynecologists recommend that all pregnant women be offered or referred for genetic screening, and those over 35 should be offered or referred for amniocentesis. If doctors do not provide information about testing to pregnant women, they can be held liable for births of children that parents argue would not exist if they could have detected the disorders prenatally and aborted the fetuses (Cleaver 2002; Marteau 1996).

These types of testing offer no cure for the "wrong" sex or genotype. If something undesirable is detected after the fetus is implanted in the uterus, the only way to prevent a baby with that genetic trait being born is to have an abortion. The assumption that defects can be repaired through surgery *in utero* is grossly mistaken. Fetal surgery is in clinical trials and currently available at four hospitals in the United States, and for only four congenital malformations, all of which are detected through ultrasound and are not considered genetic conditions (Wilson 2002). Postnatal surgical repair is a viable option for many congenital malformations of the gastrointestinal tract, lungs, and heart, but genetic conditions are usually multifaceted syndromes and are not curable through surgeries.

The responsibility for what kind of fetus will develop into an acceptable baby to fit within a family lies primarily with the pregnant woman (Karlberg 2004). Pregnant women and their partners construct families through their shared meanings of genetic fitness or desired sex for that particular family. The Western cultural hegemony of the nuclear family is a thing of the past. The unit "man, woman, child" is dismissed through biotechnological solutions and personal definitions for various groupings of kin, including same-sex parents.

What is "Normal?": Controversies and Conflicts

Shaping families, whether through prenatal genetic testing and ultrasound with abortion or through assisted reproductive technologies allowing choice of type of embryo to be inserted into the uterus, is a controversial issue. Sex selection is more clear-cut than selecting on genetic diagnoses, but both conjure images of "designer babies." Jeffrey Steinberg, director of Fertility Institutes, which has offices in Las Vegas and Los Angeles that offer sex selection says, "These are grown-up people expressing their reproductive choices. We cherish that in the United States. These people are really happy when they get what they want" (Stein 2004). Ralph Kazer, a Northwestern University fertility doctor, offers a contrasting opinion. He says, "My job is to help people make healthy babies, not help people design their babies. Gender is not a disease" (Stein 2004).

Research at the Genetics and Public Policy Center at Johns Hopkins University found that 60 percent of Americans are uncomfortable with sex selection for non-medical reasons. (A medical reason would be a potentially lethal sex-linked trait.) What is disturbing about prenatal sex selection is that worldwide, the ratio of infant boys to girls is far off balance. The normal ratio of newborns is approximately 106 boys for every 100 girls. In China, the ratio is a numbing 120.5 boys to 100 girls (Li 2007), and in Vietnam, 112 boys to 100 girls (Clark 2009). In India in 2001, the ratio was as high as 129.8 boys to 100 girls in some regions (Guilmoto 2007). The most basic outcome of a gender-unbalanced society is that there are not enough adult women to partner with adult men, but some propose that a higher proportion of unpartnered men bodes more than a lack of heterosexual partners. Some social scientists suggest that crime and social disorder are more likely in societies with "surplus males" (Glenn 2004). The preference for boys worldwide makes the option of sex selection extremely disturbing in the light of the persistence of patri-archy and male dominance.

While prenatal sex selection is obviously not socially acceptable to many in the United States, the question of where to draw the line with genetic disorders is less clear. Prenatal genetic testing results often come in statistics, and numbers are confusing when trying to apply them to quality of life. Is a 40 percent chance of mental retardation too high? What about a 1 in 90 chance for Down syndrome? Do you allow a baby to be born with a disorder that is "incompatible with life," like anencephaly (the brain does not develop)? Is a life expectancy of 35 for a baby born with cystic fibrosis too short? Would a person with achondroplasia (dwarf-ism) be accepted in the family? What if there is a family member with the disorder diagnosed in the fetus? Is a cleft palate severe enough to terminate? Is a missing limb reason to abort? The levels of acceptability vary by family, but time and again, in my research with pregnant women who had prenatal genetic testing I heard, "I'm just grateful for the opportunity to find out and prevent it if I can" (Karlberg 2004).

Women's feelings about their experiences of pregnancy have been altered by prenatal genetic testing. Anxiety around the testing, both whether to have testing and what to do with the information it provides, has been extensively studied. The most notable finding is that women attempt to withhold attachment to the devel-oping fetus until the results are available. Diane Beeson (1984) termed this "sus-pension of pregnancy" while Barbara Katz Rothman (1986) called it "the tentative pregnancy." Rayna Rapp's (1999) decade of ethnographic research in the prenatal genetic testing arena supports their findings. Studies that have examined women's experiences of a selective termination following a genetic diagnosis found that many women suffer severe emotional consequences, sometimes impacting every-day activities and lasting as long as a year after the abortion (Green and Statham 1996) and sometimes as severe as "pathological levels of posttraumatic stress symptoms" (Korenromp 2009).

Pregnant women are at the forefront of the decision-making process, and they are the ones most implicated because being pregnant one day and not the next without a baby born involves questions about what happened. The answers to those questions are filtered through personal preferences and beliefs about abor-tion, religion, and disability, among others. Some argue that the mere availability of prenatal testing implies that the goal is to prevent births of children with disabil-ities. Some doctors believe women will opt for abortion if something is detected prenatally, with studies showing that 72.5 percent of women diagnosed with cen-tral nervous system anomalies in their fetuses opted for termination (Schechtman et al. 2002), while 88 percent of the cases of Down syndrome diagnosed prenatally were aborted (Boyd 2008). The yearning to have a child free of genetic abnor-malities has been explored in a body of research that found that women who have had exposure to people living with a particular genetic disease are generally less inclined to consider abortion of a fetus with that disorder (Beeson and Duster 2002). Yet the desire to have a "healthy" child is pervasive, and even if one opts to continue a pregnancy known to have a genetic abnormality, the support of disabled individuals and their families varies so much that it makes it extremely difficult to opt to have a disabled child (Saxton 1984; Rapp 1999).

Some disability activists have protested the assumption that their lives are not worth living (Shaksepeare 2006). What is unique about abortion as a result of diagnosis through prenatal testing is that the action is taken to prevent the birth of a human being who will have undesired characteristics, as opposed to other types of disability prevention and medical treatment (Asch 2002). Some doctors express concern over women terminating pregnancies for reasons the doctors do not believe are worthy of abortion (Harmon 2004; Karlberg 2004).

The issues are never easy, and the pregnant woman bears the brunt of the decision. She is the representative of the action taken, her body bears the scars, and she deals with the emotional ramifications of the decisions.

And I know we were lucky to be able to lose Ezra the way we did, even though that entailed making the hardest decision of our lives. My husband, Jake, says that the decision to terminate a pregnancy that had gone seriously awry just past the legal limits of abortion in our state makes him feel like there is a hole in his soul. For me, it is a more specific hole. I remember sitting in the clinic in Wichita, Kansas—one of the two places in the western hemisphere and Europe where a woman can get an abortion after twenty-four weeks, regardless of the condition of the fetus—feeling Ezra kick, and thinking that he wanted to be with us. For weeks afterwards, I think about that kicking. Small muscle twinges, even elsewhere in my body, remind me of that small but insistent presence, and I fall into the huge hole of this loss, Ezra's absence (Bell 2003).

References

Asch, Adrienne. 2002. "Prenatal Diagnosis and Selective Abortion," in *The Double-Edged Helix: Social Implications of Genetics in a Diverse Society*, edited by J. S. Alper, C. Ard, A. Asch, J. Beckwith, P. Conrad, and L. N. Geller. Baltimore: Johns Hopkins University Press.

Beeson, Diane. 1986. "Technological Rhythms in Pregnancy: The Case of Prenatal Diagnosis by Amniocentesis," in *Cultural Perspectives on Biological Knowledge*, edited by T. Duster and K. Garrett. Stamford, CT: Ablex.

Beeson, Diane, and Troy Duster. 2002. "African American Perspectives on Genetic Testing," in *The Double-Edged Helix: Social Implications of Genetics in a Diverse Society*, edited by J. S. Alper et al. Baltimore: Johns Hopkins University Press.

Bell, Ida. 2003. "Fireflies: Another Kind of Lucky." *Brain, Child* Spring 2003: 54–56.

Boyd, P.A., C. DeVigan, B. Khoshnood, M. Loane, E. Garne, and H. Dolk. 2008. "Survey of Prenatal Screening Policies in Europe for Structural Malformations and Chromosome Anomalies, and Their Impact on Detection and Termination Rates for Neural Tube Defects and Downs Syndrome." *British Journal of Obstetrics and Gynecology* 115: 689–696.

Clark, Helen. 2009. "Vietnam: Sex Selection Skews Sex Ratio." IPS News, 21 August. http://ipsnews.net/news.asp?idnews=48166.

Cleaver, Hannah. 2002. "German Court Award for Disabled Child Creates Controversy." www.medscape.com/viewarticle/436943.

Glenn, David. 2004. "A Dangerous Surplus of Sons?" *Chronicle of Higher Education* 50 (34), 30 April, A14.

Green, Josephine, and Helen Statham. 1996. "Psychosocial Aspects of Prenatal Screening and Diagnosis," in *The Troubled Helix: Social and Psychological Implications of the New Genetics*, edited by T. Marteau and M. Richards. Cambridge, UK: Cambridge University Press.

Guilmoto, Christophe. 2007. "Characteristics of Sex Ratio Imbalance in India, and Future Scenarios." Presented at the 4th Asia Pacific Conference on Reproductive and Sexual Health and Rights, Hyderabad, India, October 29–31.

Harmon, Amy. 2004. "In New Tests for Fetal Defects, Agonizing Choices." *New York Times* 20 June, 1, 22.

Karlberg, Kristen. 2004. Genetic Bodies and Genetic Families: Social and Material Constructions of Prenatal Genetic Testing. Ph.D. Dissertation, University of California, San Francisco.

Katz Rothman, Barbara. 1986. *The Tentative Pregnancy: Prenatal Diagnosis and the Future of Motherhood*. New York: W. W. Norton.

Korenromp, M. J., Page-Christiaens, G. C., van den Bout, J., Mulder, E. J., and Visser, G. H. 2009. "Adjustment to Termination of Pregnancy for Fetal Anomaly: A Longitudinal Study in Women at 4, 8, and 16 Months." *American Journal of Obstetrics and Gynecology* 201(2): 160.e1–160.e7.

Li, Shuzhuo. 2007. "Imbalanced Sex Ratio at Birth and Comprehensive Intervention in China." Presented at the 4th Asia Pacific Conference on Reproductive and Sexual Health and Rights, Hyderabad, India. October 29–31.

Lippman, Abby. 1991. "Prenatal Genetic Testing and Screening: Constructing Needs and Reinforcing Inequities." *American Journal of Law and Medicine* 18 (1-2): 15–50.

Marteau, Theresa and Elizabeth Anionwu. 1996. "Evaluating Carrier Testing: Objectives and Outcomes," in *The Troubled Helix: Social and Psychological Implications of the New Genetics*, edited by T. Marteau and M. Richards. Cambridge, UK: Cambridge University Press.

Rapp, Rayna. 1999. *Testing Women, Testing the Fetus: The Social Impact of Amniocentesis in America*. New York: Routledge.

Saxton, Marcia. 1984. "Born and Unborn: The Implications of Reproductive Technologies for People with Disabilities," in *Test-Tube Women*, edited by R. Arditti, R. Deulli-Klein and S. Minden. Boston: Routledge and Kegan Paul.

Schechtman, K. B., D. L Gray., J. D Baty. and S. M. Rothman. 2002. "Decision-Making for Termination of Pregnancies with Fetal Anomalies: Analysis of 53,000 Pregnancies." *Obstetrics and Gynecology* 99: 216–222.

Shakespeare, Tom. 2006. *Disability Rights and Wrongs*. Abingdon, UK: Routledge.

Stein, Rob. 2004. "A Boy for You, A Girl for Me: Technology Allows Choice." *Washington Post*, 14 December, A01.

Wilson, R. D. 2002. "Fetal Therapy: Current Status and Future Prospects." Invited Session, 52nd Annual Meeting of the American Society for Human Genetics, Baltimore, MD. *Original article commissioned for this book.*

NEW TECHNOLOGIES: BOON OR BANE?

When bodies do not procreate the way they should, both men and women confront a social stigma for infertility. In childless couples, both masculinity and femininity may be questioned; men are ridiculed for "shooting blanks," and women are labeled "barren." Regardless of the cause, much of the treatment for infertility takes place inside women's bodies. Even if a woman is fertile, but her male partner is subfertile, she is the one to undergo physical traumas.

The variety of options for technologically assisted human procreation sever genetic, gestational, and parental links. Donor insemination (DI) involves the use of semen from a man not the woman's partner. It is usually resorted to in cases of male factor infertility. DI also enables lesbians and single women to reproduce without a male partner. Men with genetic predispositions to diseases, or men exposed to chemotherapy or other toxins that kill or damage semen can become the social fathers of the children their partners bear after donor insemination. A newer technique for male factor infertility is intracytoplasmic sperm injection (ICSI), which enables subfertile men to participate in genetic procreation: a single sperm cell is injected into an ovum with a microscopic needle.

In cases where either the woman or the man is subfertile but the woman has an intact womb, in vitro fertilization (IVF) joins their egg and sperm in a petri dish or test tube in a laboratory; if an embryo grows, it is placed inside the uterus. The woman must take hormones to induce production of multiple ova and to help sustain the pregnancy. The average cost of IVF is $10,000–$20,000 per cycle. Many women undergo multiple cycles of IVF, as the success rate is still roughly 30 percent. IVF is also used with egg, sperm, and embryo donation. Where a woman does not have a viable uterus, her male partner's sperm can be used to impregnate a surrogate, who gestates the fetus for the commissioning couple.

There are two types of gestational surrogacy. Partial surrogacy involves the surrogate mother as the genetic mother of the child, where conception usually occurs by insemination using the commissioning father's sperm. Full surrogacy involves the commissioning couple as the genetic parents of the child. Conception uses the commissioning mother's ovum and the commissioning father's sperm, and the embryo is gestated in the surrogate's womb. One research study of 34 surrogate mothers found no psychological problems as a result of the surrogacy arrangement (Jadva 2003). However, some feminists claim that gestational surrogacy is a form of prostitution or slavery, exploitation of the poor and needy by those who are better off (Ber 2000). Or, surrogacy can be seen as a way poor women can earn substantial amounts of money. In the United States, surrogacy provides business opportunities for lower middle-class White women. Web sites contain multiple listings from potential surrogates, giving detailed fee schedules for intended parents and whether the surrogate has medical insurance to cover part of the cost (see, for example, http://www.surromomsonline.com). Potential surrogates also describe their pregnancy rates and live births for their own family and for commissioning couples. Many of these ads also provide photographs of the surrogate and assure the "buyers" of her healthy lifestyle.

The costs of surrogacy, IVF, and other reproductive technologies are high, frequently mounting to $20,000 to $30,000 per attempted pregnancy. Those with medical insurance or economic resources are able to consider procreation if they are infertile, unmarried, and as they age, to delay procreation until they are in their 40s and sometimes even in their 50s and 60s. Low-income infertile women are unlikely to be able to tap into any of these medicalized sources of becoming a mother (Bell 2009).

Through the practices of sperm, oocyte, embryo donation, and surrogacy, the taken-for-granted assumption that procreation of human bodies occurs in genetically coherent lineages is disrupted. While women may experience giving birth and men support their partners through full-term pregnancies, their genetic connection to offspring may be nonexistent. Biological "clocks" and the notion of "women of procreative age" are no longer relevant: women with premature ovarian failure as well as postmenopausal women may become pregnant and give birth through egg donations and IVF.

Through these new technologies and contractual relationships with donors, it is possible for a baby to have five different individuals involved in its creation—an egg donor (genetic mother), a sperm donor (genetic father), a gestational mother (carrier through pregnancy), and a commissioning mother and father. The legal and social issues of who is the "real parent" often reflect patriarchal bargaining, with men often holding more social power to claim a child in disputed cases (Katz Rothman 2000, 15–26).

PREGNANCY AND CHILDBIRTH: RESPONSIBILITY AND POWERLESSNESS

Becoming pregnant, maintaining a pregnancy, and vaginally birthing a full-term baby are rites of passage into normative womanhood. In images and representations of normal motherhood, conception, pregnancy, and childbirth should come naturally to female bodies, since that is what it is believed women are born to do—they are made to be mommies. But not all mommies are rewarded for achieving this cultural rite of passage: unmarried mothers, teen mothers, mothers with disabilities, and poor mothers are labeled burdens to society and criticized for having children. Clearly, these women should have prevented the pregnancy through abstinence or contraception or given the child to a prosperous heterosexual couple, and certainly should not have chosen to become pregnant in the first place (Hertz 2006).

Pregnancy and childbirth are so wrapped up with being "a natural woman" that we don't see the extent to which governments and Western medical systems control both. Most women in Western societies do not experience pregnancy or childbirth as a natural phenomenon. Rather, they must interact with midwives, nurses, physicians, and other professionals, and abide by government rules and regulations. In becoming pregnant for the first time, many women are confronted with new vocabularies, products, and procedures—ovulation predictor kits, genetic screening, sonograms, amniocentesis, alpha-fetal protein screening, gestational diabetes, episiotomies, epidurals, fetal monitors, forceps, caesarean sections, saving cord blood, neo-natal intensive care units, lactation consultants. They are expected to become mothering experts, even as they are assumed to have an inborn "maternal instinct."

Women's bodies are always and everywhere viewed and treated as potentially pregnant. Walk into a local bar, and you will see multiple postings that state: WARNING, DRINKING ALCOHOL DURING PREGNANCY HAS BEEN LINKED TO BIRTH DEFECTS AND IS THE LEADING KNOWN PREVENTABLE CAUSE OF MENTAL RETARDATION. In at least two states, South Carolina and Wyoming, women have been arrested for drinking while pregnant (Roth 2000). When taken to an emergency room, women are routinely asked if they are pregnant to limit their exposure to harmful x-ray transmissions.

During March 2001, the U.S. Supreme Court heard arguments in a case considering the constitutionality of a governmental policy of surreptitiously drug testing pregnant women in a South Carolina hospital and then reporting positive cocaine results to law enforcement officers. In this case, the Supreme Court ruled that the policy violated the Fourth Amendment restriction against unlawful searches. Despite rulings to protect them, pregnant women, particularly women of color, are continuously watched and punished for supposedly harming their fetuses. While drug use during pregnancy is known to lead to negative outcomes for mother and fetus, testing pregnant women punishes them and their families. When pregnant women fear they will be prosecuted for drug use, they do not seek prenatal care, choose to deliver at home, and do not have access to drug treatment programs for themselves or their babies (Roberts 1998). Additionally, testing pregnant women is a racist practice. In a 1990 study, researchers found that 15.4 percent of White women and 14.1 percent of African American women used drugs during pregnancy. African American women, however, were ten times more likely than White women to be reported to authorities (Chasnoff et al. 1990).

Women's bodies are valued for their procreative possibilities, but at the same time, women are deemed untrustworthy and dangerous to the potential life they carry. Recent social policies have emerged to "protect" women's bodies from harmful environments, but at the same time, they control women. Increasingly, women's rights are seen as subordinate to the fetal rights of the unborn or not-even-conceived entity (Casper 1998). The potential for pregnancy has justified discriminatory practices in employment against women, even though male fertility is equally vulnerable to toxic environments. On the positive side, the U.S. Pregnancy Discrimination Act of 1978 was passed to provide security for working women under federal laws similar to laws for people with disabilities.

The Medicalization of "Natural Childbirth"

In childbirth, too, women in industrialized Western countries are not in charge of their own bodies. Birth in every society is attended and ritualistic. In most societies, the attendants are women, usually those who have themselves experienced childbirth, and the rituals are performed to ease the birthing woman's pain. With the professionalization of medicine, male obstetricians replaced women midwives in many Western countries. Childbirth was medicalized, transforming pregnancy into an illness and delivery into a traumatic, surgical event.

Barbara Katz Rothman, a sociologist who studies birth in America, defines two models of pregnancy and birth management, the patriarchal biomedical model and the woman-centered midwifery model (2000, 15–26). One outcome of the medicalization of childbirth has been the increasing rates of caesarean sections in many Western hospitals. Another common procedure is episiotomy, cutting the skin between the anus and the vagina. In the United States, episiotomies have been routine since the 1930s, as they have been believed to be better for postbirth repair, but according to a recent review of outcomes over the past 50 years, they may cause more pain and physical trauma. The conclusion of the report published in the *Journal of the American Medical Association* stated, "Evidence does not support maternal benefits traditionally ascribed to routine episiotomy. In fact, outcomes with episiotomy can be considered worse since some proportion of women who would have had lesser injury instead had a surgical incision" (Hartmann et al. 2005, 2148).

The "natural childbirth" movement grew in resistance to the medicalization of childbirth. It has been most popular with women who wanted to experience birth "awake and aware." The theory of natural childbirth proponents is that lessons in breathing during contractions and the help of a supportive and knowledgeable coach would enable a woman to give birth without so much pain that she would need to be medicated. In actuality, the process has been co-opted to the needs of the medical system, subverting its intent of empowering women and their partners (Mardorossian 2003).

IS BREASTFEEDING BEST?

Breastfeeding is another area where women are exhorted to live up to social expectations. Pulled between the desire to be a good mother and breastfeed for at least a year, many women who work outside the home have turned to pumping and storing their breast milk (Slade 1997). Disliking the pump, other mothers have felt coerced by the social pressures and public health campaigns for breastfeeding, and several recently bucked good-mother norms to complain in the mass media (Lepore 2009, Rosin 2009, Warner 2009).

Breastfeeding has positive physiological effects on mothers' bodies and some well-documented benefits for infants' physical and psychological development. The controversial aspects involve the difficulties of breastfeeding in workplaces and public places in most developed countries. There is also a question of whether bottle-feeding pumped breast milk offers the same psychological warmth and physical closeness as breast feeding.

In the following encyclopedia article, Linda Blum and Jennifer Esala provide a comprehensive overview of current breastfeeding issues.

Breastfeeding

◆◆◆

Linda M. Blum
Northeastern University

Jennifer J. Esala
University of New Hampshire

Infancy is the first and most vulnerable stage of the life course of the child and a significant passage in the life course of the mother. Because they occur at this critical juncture, decisions about infant feeding reflect concerns about optimizing infant and child health but also about dividing familial roles and resources and negotiating the cultural norms for what constitutes a good mother. Although current medical opinion unanimously endorses breastfeeding over bottle feeding, social researchers, who view breastfeeding as a sociocultural as well as biological process, disagree about the importance of breastfeeding in contemporary society for both mothers and children.

Historical Background

Historically, breastfeeding often symbolized a mother's moral duty to her child and to the larger society. In the eighteenth and nineteenth centuries, for example, maternal breastfeeding was part of new democratic values and was thought to instill strength and virtue in the nation's future citizenry. Nonetheless, alternative practices such as wet nursing (hiring a woman other than the baby's biological mother to breastfeed the infant) and bottle feeding with animal milk or other foods continued because circumstances could make maternal breastfeeding difficult or impossible but also because some groups, particularly in the affluent classes, retained strong cultural preferences against it (Fildes 1986).

By the early twentieth century, however, cultural prescriptions for the good mother shifted and breastfeeding rates declined as public sanitation, hygienic water and supplies of cow-milk, and the prestige of science made physician-prescribed infant formulas the more appealing, modern practice (Apple 1987).

The late twentieth century marked the revival of breastfeeding prescriptions, a turnaround in rates, and, somewhat paradoxically, the extension of medical authority over what had been the less medicalized, less modern practice. Authority over other aspects of childbearing and child rearing had shifted a century earlier, particularly for the middle class, from kin and religious leaders to medical professionals for the final word on what was best for child and mother. Christian groups aiming to strengthen the traditional family against scientific authority first embraced natural birth and breastfeeding in the 1940s and 1950s, but resistance to medicalization grew with the 1960s back-to-nature ethos and feminist demands for woman-centered health care (Blum 1999). With increased scientific understanding of the immunological properties of human milk, the partial incorporation of feminist demands into hospital birthing, and the involvement of the U.S. government in breastfeeding promotion, medical authority became predominant.

Thus, social research on breastfeeding is an outgrowth of the critical feminist response. However, although there is a shared sociocultural perspective, the recent surge in social research on breastfeeding is divided on the validity of medical claims, the role of government, and whether breastfeeding among all mothers should be prioritized by feminists and sociologists.

A Side Note on Global Issues

The movement toward breastfeeding in the United States, Britain, and other developed nations spurred controversy over the use and rampant promotion of formula in developing nations. The severe risks to infants and children in forgoing breastfeeding amid poverty, contaminated water, and unsanitary conditions have led to repeated international protests against formula producers as well as international agreements under the auspices of the World Health Organization and the United Nations Children's Fund (UNICEF) to promote breastfeeding and restrict the marketing of substitutes (Dykes 2007).

However, social scientists point out that breastfeeding is not free or without consequences (Blum 1999; Carter 1995; Smith 2004). In conditions of scarcity lactation can compromise mothers' nutritional status and ability to perform household and paid work, and this can put the entire family and the nursing baby at risk. Breastfeeding is always more than its product, human milk; it is a social practice involving trade-offs of women's time and activities.

Medical Research: Is Breast Best?

The health risks to children of advanced nations in forgoing human milk are less clear, leaving social research divided. The current American Academy of Pediatrics recommendation, which is supported by other medical professionals, is that mothers should breastfeed for a minimum of one year (i.e., using no formula or other milks), the first six months exclusively, as the only source of infant nutrition (AAP 2005). The U.S. government promotes this standard, as it has set steadily increasing national goals. The goals for 2010 are for a 75 percent initiation rate, 50 percent at six months, and 25 percent at one year (U.S. Department of Health and Human Services 2003).

Rates over time have responded to such campaigns but continue to fall below targets. Initiation rates in the first decade of the twenty-first century were about 70 percent, with just over a third of mothers still breastfeeding at six months, and less than 20 percent at one year. Moreover, many mothers rely on formula; by three months 30 to 40 percent of breastfeeding mothers are supplementing (in addition to the 30 percent who never breast-fed), and at six months less than 15 percent report relying on breast milk alone (Centers for Disease Control and Prevention 2007). This rapid turn to formula supplementation indicates that most mothers attempt to breastfeed, but for a number of reasons, the standard of using breast milk exclusively is unrealistic. Rates for the United Kingdom and Australia are similar, with high drop-off and supplementation rates (Bartlett 2005; Lee 2007; Murphy 1999).

The most well-established benefits of human milk include decreased risk for common ear, respiratory, and gastric-diarrheal infections among infants and young children (Centers for Disease Control and Prevention 2007; U.S. Department of Health and Human Services 2003). The evidence for more dramatic claims—reduced risk of childhood cancers, sudden infant death syndrome, diabetes, and lifetime obesity, along with a higher IQ—is equivocal.

Although many social researchers appear to accept medical claims without skepticism, several have raised important criticisms. The sociologist Linda Blum, as part of a larger ethnographic study, examined 30 years of late-twentieth-century infant-feeding advice, finding that it oversimplifies complex results and thus exaggerates the benefits of breastfeeding. She also noted that because breastfeeding rates are correlated strongly with income, education, and race, the distinct contribution of breast milk to infant and child health is difficult to determine even with advanced statistical techniques because researchers do not yet understand the myriad ways in which social advantage is health-enhancing (Blum 1999).

Jules Law (2000) found that much medical research is flawed because unexamined normative assumptions favoring the gendered division of caregiving are conflated with breastfeeding. Some research on breast versus formula feeding has used infant hospitalization as an outcome variable, ignoring the tendency of physicians to assess breast-fed babies with full-time mothers as better cared for and thus better off at home compared with formula-fed babies with other caregivers. Thus, formula feeding may be associated with higher rates of hospitalization but not higher rates of illness.

Such circular studies also have claimed that breastfeeding leads to mother–child bonding when it is used as both an outcome and a presumptive indicator of bonding. Though retained by breastfeeding advocates, this notion of bonding—of a critical early stage in which separation from the mother causes children's pathology—was based on questionable analogies from studies of war orphans and monkeys and was discredited by subsequent research (Blum 1999; Eyer 1992).

Public Health: Should Mothers Be Manipulated?

The sociologist Joan Wolf (2007) has shown that medical journals are riddled with conflicting findings on breastfeeding; she demonstrated how this equivocal research may be misused by breastfeeding promotion campaigns under government sponsorship. The American Public Health Association Code of Ethics states that public health, in its tapping of public resources and intent to change behavior, should address only fundamental causes of disease. However, formula feeding in advanced nations has not been shown to be a primary cause for any known disease; therefore, according to Wolf, it should not be interpreted as a danger to children.

Other social researchers also take issue with the public health approach, citing its role in creating unnecessary guilt on the part of bottle-feeding mothers for the implied lack of care for their children (Dykes 2007). In a longitudinal qualitative study the British sociologist Elizabeth Murphy found that the obligation to follow expert advice is profoundly moral, heightened by the maternal imperative to place children's interests first; thus, bottle-feeding mothers experience stigmatized, deviant identities (Murphy 1999). In a related survey, Ellie Lee found a large minority of mothers reporting guilt, failure, uncertainty, and worry about the harm done by formula feeding; mothers who had planned to breastfeed but found it difficult after complicated births reported the most distress (Lee 2007).

Murphy, Lee, and Wolf built on the sociology of risk, which has shown that even well-informed publics misunderstand risk calculation and probabilistic statements of likelihood, translating imperfect options such as bottle versus breast into absolutes of "hazard or safety" (Wolf 2007, 613). Moreover, "bombarded with [expert] advice about how to reduce their risk of everything," most take personal, individual responsibility for problems with persistent social roots (Wolf 2007, 612).

Social researchers largely agree that most obstacles to breastfeeding are social and that such obstacles should be changed to avoid blaming individual mothers. Changing workplace policies that limit mothers' ability to combine labor force participation and infant care are a clear priority, particularly in the United States with its lack of nationally guaranteed paid family leave. For some, such reforms should aim to enlarge the range of positive caregiving choices for mothers and families rather than increase breastfeeding rates; but others argue for policy change primarily so that more mothers will breastfeed.

Should Breastfeeding Be the Priority?

Two Australian political economists have contributed significantly to policy arguments. Judith Galtry argues for policies based on the International Labor Organization's Maternity Protection Convention; in addition to paid leave, this includes flexible work programs and paid breastfeeding breaks during the workday. Comparing the high, moderate, and low breastfeeding nations of Sweden, the United States, and Ireland through a review of quantitative studies, Galtry discovered that only Sweden's generous paid leaves, along with its many gender equity measures, raise both breastfeeding initiation and duration rates (Galtry 2003).

Julie Smith argued somewhat differently for changed incentive structures, calculating that if human milk were given a market value that included mothers' labor and consumption costs, mothers no longer would be compelled to choose the ostensibly cheaper formula (Smith, 2004). However, Galtry ignored larger factors that contribute to "Sweden's enviable child health statistics" (Galtry 2003, 174), notably generous antipoverty and universal health care measures. Smith echoed manipulative, fear-inciting rhetoric with her contention that "artificial [i.e., formula] feeding is the tobacco of the 21st century" (Smith 2004, 377).

Contemporary cultural studies scholarship on breastfeeding similarly argues for prioritizing breastfeeding, exaggerating its contribution to infant and child health and the risks posed by bottle feeding. Such studies analyzing popular culture, however, add that priority be given to breastfeeding for mothers to increase their sensual pleasure, empowerment, and resistance to having their bodies thought of as sex objects (Bartlett 2005).

Following earlier sociological work (Blum 1999; Carter 1995), cultural studies confirm that norms for women's sexual bodies pose another major obstacle to breastfeeding. That is, contemporary norms of heterosexuality define breasts as objects of display for the male gaze. Though infant-feeding advice trivializes mothers' embarrassment and counsels learning to nurse discreetly, numerous instances of mothers being sanctioned for public breastfeeding demonstrate that the conflict between maternal breasts and sexualized breasts is an obstacle with social, not individual, roots.

Laws in several nations protect public breastfeeding, removing it from categories of lewd and lascivious or indecent conduct, yet the sight of maternal breasts continues to threaten strongly held cultural norms (Bartlett 2005; Blum 1999, 2005). Thus, cultural scholars argue for breastfeeding as a "creative corporeal model" for women's empowerment (Bartlett 2005, 178).

Race and Class Differences?

Cultural scholars who contend that breastfeeding can be empowering and pleasurable for all mothers often write about their own experience, noting but discounting the fact that they mother within privileged social locations (Bartlett 2005; Hausman 2004). Many sociologists, in contrast, question whether breastfeeding is objectively the best choice for all mothers and their children (Blum 1999; Carter 1995; Law 2000; Lee 2007; Murphy 1999).

Qualitative studies consistently find that institutional and cultural obstacles loom larger in the lives of lower-income mothers who confront more stressful lives, competing health and family needs, rigid workplaces, and scarce privacy, with single mothers being particularly vulnerable. Middle-class women also find breastfeeding difficult, chaotic, and autonomy-compromising (Blum 1999; Carter 1995; Dykes 2007; Lee 2007; Murphy 1999).

Nonetheless, public health officials repeatedly assume that less-privileged mothers must be ill-informed in light of their lower propensity to breastfeed (Centers for Disease Control and Prevention 2007; U.S. Department of Health and Human Services 2003). Ethnographic studies strongly suggest that this assumption is false; Blum (1999) and Carter (1995) demonstrated that working-class mothers are just as informed and concerned with what is best for their children as middle-class mothers.

In addition to these obstacles, Blum found that African-American low-income mothers often chose not to breastfeed to resist racist legacies that cast them as close to nature, ostensibly oversexed, and in need of monitoring (Blum 1999). Bartlett has argued similarly for Australian aboriginal women, who, particularly when migrating to urban areas, confront racialized stereotypes and scrutiny of their mothering practices, leading to lower rates of breastfeeding (Bartlett 2005).

Future Research: At the Breast or at the Pump?

For many mothers in contemporary society, infant feeding at the breast has been melded with experience with the pump, a manual or electric device to speed the expression of breast milk. Breast pumps are ubiquitous in advice and public health literature, portrayed as a handy tool for mothers returning to the workplace and other everyday activities while providing the very best for their babies. The limited research on their use suggests that most women find breast pumping unpleasant, time-consuming, physically draining, and professionally compromising (Blum 1999; Dykes 2007). Blum noted the irony of public discussion increasingly collapsing the natural practice of feeding at the breast with mothers at the pump.

Future research should focus more centrally on this phenomenon, which challenges depictions of breastfeeding as a creative corporeal model of womanly empowerment as well as of intimacy and attachment between mother and child. Breast pumping may offer a positive option for partners who share parenting (Dykes 2007); however, Blum found that African-American mothers who relied on kin networks tended to reject breastfeeding because of reliance on this unpleasant practice (Blum 1999).

Future research also might expand on Galtry's cross-national comparisons of infant-feeding norms and practices. Although it is important to compare developing nations to ameliorate high infant mortality, comparing advanced nations may shed greater light on the efficacy of varied forms of policy support for diverse families and care-giving arrangements.

Social movement researchers also might compare breastfeeding activism within advanced nations. Although voluntary organizations dedicated to breastfeeding support have been scrutinized (Blum 1999), little attention has been paid to recent breastfeeding demonstrations, the public "nurse-ins" of U.S. "lactivists" (Blum 2005) and Australian "breastfests" (Bartlett 2005). Equally compelling are questions of why breastfeeding activism in other advanced nations focuses more centrally on antiglobal, anticorporate efforts.

Social research on breastfeeding reflects continuing concerns for children's health and well-being. However, it also reflects concerns about changing gendered divisions of care-giving and questions about which women can be good mothers who contribute to the nation's future.

References

American Academy of Pediatrics. (2005). Breastfeeding and the use of human milk. Retrieved May 2, 2008, from http://www.aappolicy.aappublications.org

Apple, R. D. (1987). *Mothers and medicine: A social history of infant feeding, 1890–1950.* Madison: University of Wisconsin Press.

Bartlett, A. (2005). *Breastwork: Rethinking breastfeeding.* Sydney, Australia: UNSW Press.

Blum, L. M. (1999). *At the breast: Ideologies of breastfeeding and motherhood in the contemporary United States.* Boston: Beacon Press.

Blum, L. M. (2005). "Breast versus bottle in the 'real world' or what I did last summer." SWS Network News, 22(4), 5–6. Retrieved May 5, 2008, from http://www.socwomen.org/newsletter/QuarkDec05.pdf.

Carter, P. (1995). *Feminism, breasts, and breastfeeding.* New York: St. Martin's Press.

Centers for Disease Control and Prevention. (2007). Breastfeeding trends and updated national health objectives for exclusive breastfeeding—United States, birth years 2000–2004. Retrieved May 29, 2008, from http://www.cdc.gov/mmwr/preview/mmwrhtml/mm5630a2.htm.

Dykes, F. (2007). *Breastfeeding in the hospital: Mothers, midwives, and the production line.* New York: Routledge.

Eyer, D. (1992). *Mother-infant bonding: A scientific fiction.* New Haven CT: Yale University Press.

Fildes, V. A. (1986). *Breasts, bottles, and babies: A history of infant feeding.* Edinburgh, UK: Edinburgh University Press.

Galtry, Judith. (2003). "The Impact on Breastfeeding of Labour Market Policy and Practice in Ireland, Sweden, and the USA." *Social Science & Medicine* 57: 167–177.

Hausman, B. L. (2004). "The feminist politics of breastfeeding." *Australian Feminist Studies* 19: 273–285.

Law, J. (2000). "The politics of breastfeeding: Assessing risk, dividing labor." *Signs* 25: 407–450.

Lee, E. (2007). "Health, morality, and infant feeding: British mothers' experiences of formula use in the early weeks." *Sociology of Health and Illness* 29: 1075–1090.

Murphy, E. (1999). "'Breast is best': Infant feeding decisions and maternal deviance." *Sociology of Health and Illness* 21: 187–208.

Smith, J. (2004). "Mothers' milk and markets." *Australian Feminist Studies,* 19: 369–379.

U.S. Department of Health and Human Services. (2003). HHS blueprint to boost breast-feeding. Retrieved May 29, 2008, from http://www.fda.gov/fdac/features/2003/303_baby.html

Wolf, J, B. (2007). "Is breast really best? Risk and total motherhood in the national breastfeeding awareness campaign." *Journal of Health Politics, Policy and Law* 32: 595–636.

SPERM AND INSEMINATION: REPRESENTATIONS OF MASCULINITY

Just as human bodies are not solely biologically created, ova, sperm, embryos, and fetuses are not simply biological entities. Rather, through processes of discovering, understanding, and learning about the basics of human procreation, we attribute gendered characteristics to them, as if they were boys and girls, or men and women, instead of parts of procreation. Thus, we are taught "truths" about how gendered bodies behave through the most rudimentary exploration of the behavior of human cells.

Human procreation narratives follow traditionally gendered scripts, where the married mother and father, who love each other, consciously decide to procreate through penis-vagina heterosexual intercourse. Nine months later, the baby is birthed from the mother's body, and infant and mother quickly settle into a natural relationship of sustenance, nurturing, and protection. This script is an idealization that omits single motherhood, lesbian and gay parenting, adoption, use of procreative technologies to conceive, surrogate mothers, and other variations on the Western heterosexual nuclear family.

The reason for the idealized "how babies are made" script is *heteronormativity*. Western cultural expectations of sexuality and procreation are predicated on the supremacy of heterosexuality as natural and superior to any other sexual expression. These normative cultural expectations create a social environment that regulates sexuality and family structure. Heteronormativity creates the processes by which heterosexual relations are represented as the only natural way to have sex and make babies: biological boys who become men pair up with biological girls who become women.

One of the ways that heteronormativity is constructed and reinforced is through children's books. Children learning "how babies are made" are also learning how to be "normally" masculine and feminine. The procreative narratives in children's books are not descriptions of biological facts; rather, they are prescriptions of properly gendered sexuality. Lisa Jean Moore's article shows how

depictions of sperm in children's books show proper and unacceptable characteristics of "masculinity."

Sperm, the Lovable Character in Facts-of-Life Books

◆◆◆

Lisa Jean Moore
Purchase College, State University of New York

Many of our intimate dealings with semen are shrouded in secrecy or confiden-
tiality, such as books read with our mothers, secrets shared in a coatroom, and wet
dreams hidden in our beds. Our knowledge about human procreation often starts
with facts-of-life books, which are produced and marketed within the context of
capitalist, patriarchal, and heteronormative socio-cultural norms. Information
about human procreation is "processed" and "distilled" for the young—it is made
sterile and idealized. The stylized and sterilized representations are then narrated
to children in order to teach them about *"where they have come from."* Similar
to how research scientists and health-care providers sanitize and sterilize medical instruments for their work, knowledge about human procreation must be
scrubbed, washed, massaged, and homogenized for consumption by the young.
As these biological actions are illustrated for the young audience, so too are heteronormative values imparted to reproduce social hierarchies. Humans, then, are
both biologically and materially reproduced by the circulation of sperm while
simultaneously socially reproduced by images and narratives about the circulation
of sperm.

Children's culture is both a fantastic and a dangerous space to explore sperm's
discursive and representational constructions. "When we want to prove that
something is so basic to human nature that it cannot be changed, we point to its
presence in our children" (Jenkins 1998, 15). Both children and sperm are constructed as some form of pre-socialized creatures that exist as biological and thus
remain unmediated, animalistic, primitive, and naïve. The truth of human nature
is embodied in children and sperm cells. And we often lament that social forces
corrupt children as they get older.

Even though it is an interactive event that requires seemingly endless social
negotiation and power transfer, human procreation is assumed to be some innate
biological drive that furthers progressive human evolution. The surrounding
social interaction is erased when the naïve child's body, similar to the imagined
sperm cell, is shown as naturally heterosexual, monogamous, procreative, gendered. Reading children's facts-of-life books, we are bombarded with fabrications
of "universal truths."

Traditional fairy tales are moral fables teaching children proper ways to live. Many contemporary Western stories about human procreation emerge from a scientific context but are similar to fairy tales with their hidden moral discourse. These books rely on biology and anatomy, and authors and illustrators use scientific terminology, such as "sperm," "egg," "ovum," and "conception." Furthermore, the images, whether rendered through photography, cartooning, or painting, are based on scientific technologies, such as electron microscopes, dissection, and x-rays. This scientific context is important to acknowledge because it is the children's books' reliance on science that bolsters the claim that their contents are objective and truthful.

According to these scientific narratives, our cells, the very building blocks of our bodies, are gendered in very predictable ways. These cells perform gender in the very ways they build new human bodies. But just because there is a claim of scientific relevance and objectivity does not mean that these stories are not also fantastic and rooted in prevailing moral and social imperatives. Indeed, what is remarkable about these books—published over a 40-year span—is the homogeneity of social messages reiterated through a child-appropriate scientific lens.

"We Was Robbed": Spermatic Hierarchy

Children's books are only one enterprise that produces representations and meanings of human sperm. Sperm is almost universally viewed as the bringer of life within children's books. These books neglect to mention that sperm can also be the bringer of sexually transmitted diseases and death.

In children's books, not all sperm are created equal. Embedded in sperm imagery from cartoon books are smiling, competitive, or befuddled sperm talking to one another and presumably the audience. These sperm evaluate themselves and others based on their ability to follow directions, swim quickly, navigate the difficult terrain, and eventually merge with the egg. In children's books, the measure of the better sperm is loosely based on motility (speed), not morphology (shape). From secular books that anthropomorphize sperm, we learn that sperm have desire, are in a race, and are competitive. There will be one and only one winner, so there is a sense of entitlement and empowerment, but also unfairness.

Sperm are depicted with racing stripes and numbers on them, and state "Gotcha!" and "We was robbed!" as they are racing to the egg (Cole 1993, 24). There is also a sense of male bonding in that sperm cheer each other on. "Come on, boys!" appears in three of the books as a rallying cry from the masses of sperm in pursuit of the egg (Cole 1993; Smith 1997, 5). But there can be only one "winner," and out of the millions and millions of sperm that exist in a male body, the one that aggressively "swims" to join with the egg is exceptional. This distinction of being *the* sperm that gets to inseminate the egg is noted almost universally (Andry and Schepp 1968). Hierarchies among men are thus naturalized: as with sperm, competitions based on physical strength, endurance, and speed are the natural—and adaptive—way to figure out hierarchies among boys and men.

The Egg Plays a Part, Too

All the emphasis on the sperm cell has led to a very diminutive, passive, and unrecognized role of the egg in conception. Children's books are not generally revised to take into account the advances or changes in scientific explanations of conception and fertilization. For example, children's books rarely describe how the egg also must manage a journey from the ovaries, through approximately 15 centimeters of fallopian tubes to reach the uterus. Furthermore, medical researchers have determined that eggs may release molecules similar to bourgeonal (a chemical agent that causes cells to migrate toward other cells) which are sperm-attracting compounds and trigger odor receptors on the sperm cell. Children's books would look quite different if eggs were represented as having an active role in journeying to the location of conception as well as being active participants in the moment of conception.

Alternative Narratives of Conception

Children's books do not often consider alternative ways that sperm and eggs might come together. Assisted procreative technologies have created multiple opportunities to transform human being's fertility—transformations that do not require a heterosexual connection. Sperm and egg cells might be joined in the laboratory by medical technicians who select particular sperm cells and particular egg cells. These cells are injected into one another and then cultured in a lab setting to be placed in the woman's body later. A child can have more than one "mother" (egg provider, gestator, social parent) and more than one "father" (sperm donor, social parent). With multiple possibilities for conceiving children, stories of "where I came from" must adjust.

More books are needed that depict variations of origin stories featuring adoption, foster families, single parenting, sperm donation, assisted procreative technologies, and blended families. But more than that, an alternative method is needed to separate out the stereotypical gender roles that are inscribed into human reproductive cells. Stories matter, and stories we tell children are especially salient. Children's books are powerful, as they are socialization in action. These books are not just stories that answer the question, "Where do babies come from?" They also answer the implicit questions, "Who am I?" "How did I get here?" And, "What kind of person am I?" Implicit in the answers are a whole host of assumptions about gender, sex, sexuality, marriage, and health that need to be considered. Having "new" or other understandings of masculinity and femininity in procreation expands the stories of who we are. If the egg and sperm were degendered (Lorber 2005) and not directly linked to a gendered concept of parenting (i.e., passive yet nurturing mothers, and strong yet competitive fathers), children might be more accepting of fathers as primary parents, single parents, and families where both parents are the same gender.

References

Andry, Andrew, and Schepp, Steven. 1968. *How Babies are Made.* Boston: Little Brown.

Cole, Babette. 1993. *Mommy Laid an Egg: or, Where do Babies Come From?* San Francisco, CA: Chronicle Books.

Jenkins, Henry. 1998. "Introduction," in *The Children's Culture Reader,* edited by Henry Jenkins. New York: New York University Press.

Lorber, Judith. 2005. *Breaking the Bowls: Degendering and Feminist Change.* New York: W.W. Norton.

Mayle, Peter. 1977. *Where Did I Come From? The Facts of Life Without Any Nonsense and with Illustrations.* Secaucus, NJ: Carroll Publishing Group.

Smith, Alistar. 1997. *How are Babies Made?* London: Usborne.

Adapted for this book from Lisa Jean Moore, "Billy, the Sad Sperm with No Tail: Representations of Sperm in Children's Books." *Sexualities* 6: 279–305, 2003, and Lisa Jean Moore, *Sperm Counts: Overcome by Man's Most Precious Fluid.* New York: New York University Press, 2007.

CRITICAL SUMMARY

Human procreation has the potential to be a joyous experience. However, in a vast majority of the world, individual men and male-dominated institutions have control over who has babies, when they have them, and who claims ownership of those babies. Women's procreative bodies are kept under strict control through social norms, laws, and biomedicine. For example, today most women live in cultures where they are considered the property of their fathers (they are given their father's last name) until they are married off to husbands (they usually take their husband's last name). From early ages we teach children to see male superiority and heterosexuality as naturally ingrained in sperm. We instruct children to be mommies and daddies in gender-specific ways and then reward them for the "correct" performance. But as children age, we do not provide them with adequate tools to protect their bodies from pregnancy and sexually transmitted diseases. If they procreate in ways that are not mandated, they are stigmatized and punished. When their bodies do not procreate, they are also stigmatized, and if they have the resources, they pursue expensive and complicated technologies to achieve pregnancies and produce particular types of babies. Gendered power dynamics infiltrate the labor and delivery experience and complicate breastfeeding.

In addition to the greater social power of men in procreation and normative beliefs about gender and sexuality, processes of medicalization have dominated our procreative knowledge and practices. Medicalization establishes biomedical and technological meanings and interpretations of procreation as the most legitimate. Through medicalization, the nexus of pharmaceutical, biotechnological, economic, and professional interests dominate prevention of pregnancy, fertility, pregnancy itself, and childbirth. As a result, the costs of procreation have escalated in Western industrialized countries, while women in poor countries lack medical help in difficult pregnancies or births. For example, in pregnancies in pre-teen women whose bodies are not fully developed, the baby may get stuck because the birth canal is too narrow. These births often cause tears of the bowel and urinary tract, medically referred to as fistulas. Even though there are simple surgeries that can repair fistulas, many women face a lifetime of leaking urine and feces and accompanying ostracism (Miller et al. 2005; Wall et al. 2005). In Western countries, long and difficult labors can produce similar problems, but their incidence is much smaller. While we fully encourage continued investigation into cultural, biomedical, and holistic knowledge and practices of human procreation aimed at retaining the life-affirming values of the experiences of parenthood, we must also acknowledge the gross inequities in access to medical and surgical options where they are most needed.

NOTE

1. We prefer to say "procreation" rather than "reproduction" because human beings don't reproduce or replicate like copying machines. What we are talking about is the whole process of egg and sperm joining, gestation through pregnancy, and childbirth. That process is "procreation."

REFERENCES AND RECOMMENDED READINGS

Agigian, Amy. 2004. *Baby Steps: How Lesbian Alternative Insemination is Changing the World*. Middletown, CT: Wesleyan University Press.

Almeling, Rene. 2007. "Selling Genes, Selling Gender: Egg Agencies, Sperm Banks, and the Medical Market in Genetic Material." *American Sociological Review* 72: 319–340.

Apple, Rima. 1990. *Women, Health and Medicine: A Historical Handbook*. New Brunswick, NJ: Rutgers University Press.

Becker, Gay. 2000. *The Elusive Embryo: How Women and Men Approach New Reproductive Technologies*. Berkeley: University of California Press.

Beckett, Katherine. 2005. "Choosing Cesarean: Feminism and the Politics of Childbirth in the United States." *Feminist Theory* 6: 251–275.

Bell, Ann V. 2009. "'It's Way Out of My League': Low-Income Women's Experiences of Medicalized Infertility." *Gender & Society* 23: 688–709.

Ber, R. 2000. "Ethical Issues in Gestational Surrogacy." *Theories of Medical Bioethics* 21: 153–169.

Boswell-Penc, Maia, and Kate Boyer. 2007. "Expressing Anxiety? Breast Pump Usage in American Wage Workplaces." *Gender, Place, and Culture* 14: 551–567.

Bumiller, Kristin, Molly Shanley, and Anna Marie Smith (eds.). 2009. Thematic Issue: Reproductive and Genetic Technologies. *Signs* 34: 735–1027.

Casper, Monica. 1998. The Making of the Unborn Patient: A Social Anatomy of Fetal Surgery. New Brunswick, NJ: Rutgers University Press.

Chasnoff, I., H. Landress, and M. Barrett. 1990. "Prevalence of Illicit Drug or Alcohol Use During Pregnancy and Discrepancies in Mandatory Reporting in Pinellas County, Florida." *New England Journal of Medicine*. 322: 1202–1206.

Chatterjee, Nilanjana, and Nancy E. Riley. 2001. "Planning an Indian Modernity: The Gendered Politics of Fertility Control." *Signs* 26: 811–845.

Clarke, Adele. 1998. *Disciplining Reproduction: Modernity, American Life Sciences, and the "Problem of Sex."* Berkeley: University of California Press.

Cooper, Susan, and Ellen Glazer. 1998. *Choosing Assisted Reproduction: Social, Emotional and Ethical Considerations.* Indianapolis, IN: Perspectives Press.

Davis-Floyd, Robbie E. 1992. *Birth as an American Rite of Passage.* Berkeley: University of California Press.

Ettore, Elizabeth. 2002. *Reproductive Genetics, Gender and the Body.* New York: Routledge.

———. 2010. "Bodies, Drugs, and Reproductive Regimes," in *Culture, Bodies, and the Sociology of Health,* edited by Elizabeth Ettore. Surrey, UK: Ashgate.

Fogg-Davis, Hawley. 2001. "Navigating Race in the Market for Human Gametes." *Hastings Center Report.* 5: 13–21.

Franklin, Sarah, and Celia Roberts. 2006. *Born and Made: An Ethnography of Preimplantation Genetic Diagnosis.* Princeton, NJ: Princeton University Press.

Fujimura, Joan H. 2006. "Sex Genes: A Critical Sociomaterial Approach to the Politics and Molecular Genetics of Sex Determination." *Signs* 32: 49–82.

Furstenberg, Frank F. 2007. *Destinies of the Disadvantaged: The Politics of Teen Childbearing.* New York: Russell Sage Foundation.

Gerodetti, Natalia, and Véronique Mottier (eds.). 2009. Special Issue, Feminist Politics of Reproduction. *Feminist Theory* 10: 147–244.

Ginsburg, Faye, and Rayna Rapp (eds.) 1995. *Conceiving the New World Order: The Global Politics of Reproduction.* Berkeley: University of California Press.

Grady, Denise. 2010. "Lessons at Indian Hospital About Births." *New York Times,* 6 March. http://www.nytimes.com/2010/03/07/health/07birth.html.

Greenhalgh, Susan. 2001. "Fresh Winds in Beijing: Chinese Feminists Speak Out on the One-Child Policy and Women's Lives." *Signs* 26: 847–886.

———. 2008. *Just One Child: Science and Policy in Deng's China.* Berkeley: University of California Press.

Gutiérrez, Elena R. 2008. *Fertile Matters: The Politics of Mexican-Origin Women's Reproduction.* Austin: University of Texas Press.

Hänsch, Anna. 1997. "The Body of the Woman Artist: Paula Modersohn-Becker and Rainer Maria Rilke on Giving Birth and Art." *European Journal of Women's Studies* 4: 435–449.

Hartmann, Katherine, Meera Viswanathan, Rachel Palmieri, Gerald Gartlehner, John Thorp, Jr., and Kathleen N. Lohr. 2005. "Outcomes of Routine Episiotomy: A Systematic Review." *Journal of the American Medical Association* 293: 2141–2148.

Hertz, Rosanna. 2006. *Single by Chance, Mothers by Choice.* New York: Oxford University Press.

Jadva, Vasanti, Clare Murray, Emma Lycett, Fiona MacCallum and Susan Golombok, 2003. "Surrogacy: The Experiences of Surrogate Mothers." *Human Reproduction* 18: 2196–2204.

Karsjens, Kari L. 2002. "Boutique Egg Donations: A New Form of Racism and Patriarchy." *DePaul Journal of Health Care Law* 5: 57–89.

Katz Rothman, Barbara. [1982] 1991. *In Labor: Women and Power in the Birthplace.* New York: W.W. Norton.

———. 2000. *Recreating Motherhood: Ideology and Technology in a Patriarchal Society,* 2nd ed. New Brunswick, NJ: Rutgers University Press.

Lepore, Jill. 2009. "Baby Food." *The New Yorker,* 19 January, 34–39.

Longhurst, Robyn. 2007. *Maternities: Gender, Bodies and Space.* New York: Routledge.

Mamo, Laura. 2007. *Queering Reproduction: Achieving Pregnancy in the Age of Technoscience.* Durham, NC: Duke University Press,

Marantz Henig, Robin. 2004. *Pandora's Baby: How the First Test Tube Babies Sparked the Reproduction Revolution.* New York: Houghton Mifflin.

Mardorossian, Carine M. 2003. "Laboring Women, Coaching Men: Masculinity and Childbirth Education in the Contemporary United States." *Hypatia* 18: 113–134.

Markens, Susan. 2007. *Surrogate Motherhood and the Politics of Reproduction.* Berkeley: University of California Press.

Martin, Emily. 1991. "The Egg and the Sperm: How Science Has Constructed a Romance Based on Stereotypical Male-Female Roles." *Signs* 16: 485–501.

———. 1992. *The Woman in the Body: A Cultural Analysis of Reproduction.* Boston, MA: Beacon Press.

Miller, S., F. Lester, M. Webster, and B. Cowan. 2005. "Obstetric Fistula: A Preventable Tragedy." *Journal of Midwifery and Women's Health* 50: 286–294.

Moore, Lisa Jean. 2007. *Sperm Counts: Overcome by Man's Most Precious Fluid.* New York: New York University Press.

Nordqvist, Petra. 2008. "Feminist Heterosexual Imaginaries of Reproduction: Lesbian Conception in Feminist Studies of Reproductive Technologies." *Feminist Theory* 9: 273–292.

O'Brien, Mary. 1981. *The Politics of Reproduction.* New York: Routledge.

Oudshoorn, Nelly. 2003. *The Male Pill: A Biography of Technology in the Making.* Durham, NC: Duke University Press.

Plotz, David. 2005. *The Genius Factory: The Curious History of the Nobel Prize Sperm Bank.* New York: Random House.

Reed, Richard K. 2005. *Birthing Fathers: The Transformation of Men in the American Rites of Birth.* New Brunswick, NJ: Rutgers University Press.

Rich, Adrienne. 1976. *Of Woman Born: Motherhood as Experience and Institution.* New York: Bantam Books.

Roberts, Dorothy. 1998. *Killing the Black Body: Race, Reproduction, and the Meaning of Liberty.* New York: Vintage.

———. 2009. 'Race, Gender, and Genetic Technologies: A New Reproductive Dystopia?" *Signs* 34: 783-804.

Rosin, Hanna. 2009. "The Case Against Breastfeeding." *The Atlantic,* April, 64-70.

Roth, Rachel. 2000. *Making Women Pay: The Hidden Costs of Fetal Rights.* Ithaca, NY: Cornell University Press.

Rothschild, Joan. 2005. *The Dream of the Perfect Child.* Bloomington: Indiana University Press.

Rousseau, Nicole. 2009. *Black Woman's Burden: Commodifying Black Reproduction.* New York: Palgrave Macmillan.

Samerski, Silja. 2009. "Genetic Counseling and the Fiction of Choice: Taught Self-Determination as a New Technique of Social Engineering." *Signs* 34: 735–761.

Saul, Stephanie. 2009. "21st Century Babies." *New York Times,* 11 October, 1, 26-27; 12 October A1, 14.

Simonds, Wendy, Barbara Katz Rothman, and Bari Meltzer Norman. 2006. *Laboring On: Birth in Transition in the United States.* New York: Routledge.

Slade, Margot. 1997. "Have Pump, Will Travel: Combining Breast-Feeding and a Career," *New York Times*, 14 December, Section 3, 12.

Spar, Debora L. 2006. *The Baby Business: How Money, Science, and Politics Drive the Commerce of Conception*. Cambridge, MA: Harvard Business School Press.

Teman, Elly. 2010. *Birthing a Mother: The Surrogate Body and the Pregnant Self*. Berkeley, CA: University of California Press.

Thompson, Charis. 2005. *Making Parent: The Ontological Choreography of Reproductive Technologies*. Cambridge: MIT Press.

Wall, L.L., S.D. Arrowsmith, N.D. Briggs, A. Browning, and A. Lassey. 2005. "The Obstetric Vesicovaginal Fistula in the Developing World." *Obstetrical and Gynecological Survey* 60 (7 Suppl 1): S3-S51.

Warner, Judith. 2009. "Ban the Breast Pump." *New York Times*, 2 April, http://warner.blogs.nytimes.com/2009/04/02/why-i-dumped-the-pump/.

Wertz, Richard W., and Dorothy C. Wertz. 1989. *Lying-in: A history of Childbirth in America* (expanded edition). New Haven, CT: Yale University Press.

Yalom, Marilyn. 1997. *A History of the Breast*. New York: Knopf.

Zvi, Karen. 2005. "Contesting Motherhood in the Age of AIDS: Maternal Ideology in the Debate over Mandatory HIV Testing." *Feminist Studies* 31: 347–374.

CHAPTER 3

Eve, Venus, and "Real Women"

Constructing Women's Bodies

Key concepts
cosmetic surgeries, eating disorders, female sexuality, mastectomy,
medicalization, menstrual politics, ritual genital cutting

In the summer of 2004, Dove, a company that markets body lotions and other products for women, ran a series of advertisements that featured what it called "real women." They were a bit plump—some even more than a bit—ethnically and racially diverse, and they flaunted their bodies joyfully, even sexually. From a feminist perspective, the ongoing Dove Campaign for Real Beauty is a refreshing departure from a fantasy world of young, thin, airbrushed, cosmetically enhanced female models.

The standards of beauty for women tend to be sexually appealing to heterosexual men and produce idealized versions of Western and White women's faces and bodies. Dominant cultural norms are powerful influences, especially since what's considered beauty appears in the movies, on television, in the photos accompanying celebrity stories in magazines, and in advertisements everywhere. The extent to which lighting, makeup, clothes, and remade photos manufacture these images is rendered invisible.

Emulating these images, women exercise, diet, and have surgical procedures to look pubescent, with prominent breasts, narrow waists, rounded hips, and tight buttocks and thighs. Breasts are enhanced through surgical implants, tummies are tucked, and cellulite is suctioned from abdomens and thighs. Face-lifts and Botox injections are popular methods for looking young, and skin bleaches are often used to look whiter. Noses and eyelids are reshaped to erase racial and ethnic distinctiveness. One type of diet after another is taken up and discarded. Some girls and women make themselves ill with anorexic and bulimic fat control.

Many women choose to go along with fairly conventional norms and expectations of femininity as important to their identity and self-esteem; they see it as their choice, not as succumbing to oppressive norms. Other women defy or resist the pressure of the norms, flaunting hefty bodies as sexy and strong, refusing to have breast reconstruction after a mastectomy or a face-lift when wrinkles appear.

What version of women is "real"? Because women are culturally defined by their bodies, it is crucial that they have some power to do the defining. In this chapter, we look at the ways women make decisions that reflect prevailing social expectations but which they feel are important to their self-identity. We also discuss the ways that they resist and rebel against norms of beauty and femininity.

THE UNATTAINABLE VENUS: COSMETIC SURGERIES

Elective cosmetic surgery—breast implants or reshaping, face-lifts, liposuction to remove fat deposits, Botox injections to smooth wrinkles and enlarge lips—are extremely popular in Western societies. From a feminist perspective, there is on the one hand, a sense that people who have elective procedures to alter their faces and bodies are hapless conformists to culturally imposed ideals of youth and beauty, and on the other, there is recognition of choice and autonomy in women's decisions to have cosmetic surgery. Of course, the choices are considerably narrowed by the cost of these procedures. There are also medical issues; the surgeries may be cosmetic, but they are still surgeries. In the following article, Victoria Pitts-Taylor, a sociologist, explores the way that medicalization, which turns a social issue into a medical problem, legitimizes the use of cosmetic surgeries.

The Surface and the Depth: Medicalization, Beauty, and Body Image in Cosmetic Surgery

◆◆◆

Victoria Pitts-Taylor
Queens College and the Graduate Center, City University of New York

One of the reasons why feminists have been so opposed to cosmetic surgery is that the practice medicalizes norms of appearance, making it seem as if only beautiful people are healthy. What is a social issue—idealization of certain looks and their economic and social rewards—is turned into a supposedly objective medical issue. Any deviation from a standardized ideal then becomes a curable illness. The too-long nose can be shortened, the too-short chin can be lengthened, protruding ears can be flattened, and bags under the eyes can be removed. The wrinkles and laugh lines of age can be erased, and fat deposits can be liposuctioned away. Breasts can be made larger or smaller, vaginas can be tightened, and penises can be lengthened.

The standards by which these features are measured are certainly racialized, classed and gendered—in other words, they are expressions of primary power relationships in society. In fact, much of the history of cosmetic surgery can be seen as the history of "passing," where devalued ethnic groups and recent immigrants came to plastic surgeons for remedies for their physical signs of "otherness," in the hope that economic and social success would follow (Gilman 1999). Male and female American Jews, African-Americans, and Irish immigrants were targeted candidates for cosmetic surgery in the nineteenth and early twentieth century.

In the twentieth century, cosmetic surgery became more gendered, particularly with the advent of breast implants in the 1960s. Eventually, cosmetic surgeons began to promote a female body that was not so much normalized as technologized, with bodily proportions unlikely to be found outside of the surgeon's office. For instance, in addition to the enormous popularity of breast implants, we have seen the advent of rib removals to create a tiny waistline and foot reshaping to allow fitting into narrow, pointy-toed shoes. Procedures like these allow the creation of female bodies that seem to transcend the ordinary aging process, that adhere to current standards of beauty, and sometimes, that fulfill the most spectacular heteronormative imaginaries of enormous breasts, tiny waists, and seemingly ageless skin.

The medicalization of beauty masks social norms with the scientific language of objectivity, making less visible the political implications of the dominance of Anglo-Saxon ideal faces and thin, busty bodies. Even so, cosmetic surgery has always been controversial among doctors and the larger public, partly because it is highly commercialized, and partly because it operates on (and thus puts in some risk) healthy bodies. To buttress their medical legitimacy, cosmetic surgeons have relied on psychological theories like Alfred Adler's "inferiority complex" to establish a medical basis for the gains of cosmetic surgery. The inferiority-complex argument suggested that patients would improve their self-esteem, unburden themselves from the stigma of abnormality, and alleviate their long-term feelings of inferiority by undergoing cosmetic surgery. Thus, if scientific medicalization of the body's surface was not enough to convince people of cosmetic surgery's medical worth, then the medicalization of the body's depth—its psyche—might accomplish it (Pitts-Taylor 2007).

In recent years, however, with the unprecedented explosion of popular interest in cosmetic surgery, surgeons have become less defensive about their practices. Now surgeons are much more willing to operate on people who have normal features, to perform multiple operations on a single patient, and to design bodily transformations that were unthinkable only one or two decades ago. There is a much greater market for cosmetic surgery than ever before, and cosmetic surgery has responded by embracing its new role with enthusiasm and market savvy. Surgeons have begun to use more aggressive direct-to-consumer advertising, and they have participated in television reality shows on cosmetic surgery. Some surgeons now even advertise their own "extreme makeovers"—packages of multiple surgeries performed during one operation—for prospective patients.

In a number of ways, cosmetic surgeons mix medical with aesthetic indications, blurring the line between them to be able to do more than one lucrative procedure at a time and to negotiate medical insurance payments. For instance, patients seeking help for drooping eyelids that are interfering with eyesight may be persuaded to also have bags under their eyes removed, surgery that medical insurance will not pay for alone. Patients who want to improve the appearance of their noses have been diagnosed with deviated septums, which they might not otherwise have had corrected, so that they can get insurance coverage for rhinoplasty. In the United Kingdom and the Netherlands, even cosmetic surgeries like breast reductions and implants have been paid for by national health programs when the patients' bodies have met certain guidelines that allowed the procedures to be deemed medically necessary.

In addition, some surgeries are touted as good for physical health. Until recently, when published studies began to show otherwise, liposuction was touted as a quick and easy surgical response to the health problems caused by obesity. Studies now suggest that losing weight through liposuction offers none of the health benefits of losing weight through exercise and diet (Klein et al. 2004). Genital cosmetic surgeries for women are being advertised as reconstructions for sexual health: vagina-tightening surgery to restore women to their pre-childbirth naturally "healthy" state. So-called "mommy makeovers," which combine breast lifts and implants with abdominoplasty and liposuction, are sold to women as a form of post-childbirth self-care.

The pathologization of the effects of aging and childbirth and any deviations from narrow norms of beauty are deeply worrying to feminists. Virginia Blum argues that women will "become surgical": after their first cosmetic surgery they will begin to see their bodies as cosmetic surgeons do, as infinitely repairable (Blum 2003). Kathryn Pauly Morgan identified a "technological imperative" that coerces women into seeing themselves from the perspective of "fix-up" technologies (1991; see also Wijsbek 2000). Other feminists argue that cosmetic surgery defines women's looks by the "male gaze" that objectifies and sexualizes them. In this sense, cosmetic surgeons, most of whom are men, are replicating and reinforcing the way male-dominated Western culture views women. If women are dissatisfied with their bodies, they are viewing themselves through men's eyes. Kathy Davis argues that women are using cosmetic surgery to alleviate the psychological suffering that attends women's concern with appearance (2003, 41). She suggests that women who choose cosmetic surgery are making rational choices, but they are doing so out of a sense of bodily self-hatred and in a context of enormous cultural pressure to look young and normatively beautiful.

The medicalized, high-tech male gaze not only assumes that all women want to appeal sexually to heterosexual men, but it also makes women's bodies into objects that need constant maintenance and improvement. The female body is measured against the airbrushed images presented in celebrity culture, advertising, and pornography, and an increasing range of women's body parts are subject to surgical "improvement" modeled after idealized images. One recent addition to the offerings by cosmetic surgeons is labiaplasty, in which women's vaginal lips are cut and reshaped to look prettier and more erotically appealing. The surgical "beautification" of female genitalia, as transparently heteronormative and gendered as the project may be, proceeds like all cosmetic surgeries under the auspices of medical authority and legitimacy. In addition to beautification, all women are promised better self-esteem, better sexual relations with their partners, and enhanced sexual sensation through removal of skin that may cover the clitoris. Women living in cultures that demand virginity at marriage are also offered "hymen repair" as a way to "restore" virginity.

Body Image "Disorder"

Ironically, the use of cosmetic surgery itself is being turned into a medical disorder—body dysmorphic disorder (BDD), or distortion of body image. While psychological theories have long been used in cosmetic surgery discourse to promote its benefits, the vast rise in the number of cosmetic surgery patients in the past twenty years has been accompanied by a psychiatric assessment of "appropriate" criteria for its use. Cosmetic surgery patients are now being sorted as "good" and "bad" through tests of their body-self attitudes. There are formal and informal screenings for BDD, a relatively new psychiatric diagnosis formally recognized by the *Diagnostic and Statistical Manual of Mental Disorders* in 1997 (Arthur and Monnell 2005). It is now being applied to some cosmetic surgery patients who appear obsessed with their bodies.

In the mass media, BDD is discussed as a new social problem. It is accompanied by efforts from some psychiatrists—specialists in BDD—to publicize the disorder through the proliferation of books, Web sites, and television shows that educate the public on appropriate expectations for cosmetic surgery. There is even a cosmetic surgery self-help culture that teaches prospective patients which reasons for cosmetic surgery are legitimate and which are illegitimate, and which kinds of patients are normal and which might be pathological. For example, "flags" for psychological problems "in dealing with your body image" include having surgery in the same area more than several times; being under treatment for anxiety, depression, or sleep disorder; having a drug or alcohol problem; being in the "middle of a life crisis"; and having "concerns regarding gender/sexual identity issues" (Ganny and Collini 2000, 41).

These developments are especially problematic for women for several reasons. First, women are the primary targets of the cosmetic surgery industry. Although men increasingly undergo cosmetic surgery, the vast majority who do so are women (91 percent in 2007, according to the American Society of Plastic Surgeons [ASPS]). Women are also far more likely to be diagnosed with mental disorders and as such, may be more vulnerable to the normalizing effects of medicalization (Busfield 1996). Thus, women now face a double-edged sword: they are both intensely targeted as consumers of cosmetic surgery and also heavily scrutinized when they do so. There is an imperative to choose surgery, but such a choice can be seen as a sign of irrationality at best, and at worst, mental illness.

For women of color, the situation is even more difficult. So-called "ethnic" women and men (non-White) now make up almost 25 percent of cosmetic surgery patients, according to the ASPS. While cosmeticians have long been criticized for "whitening" the faces of people of color, cosmetic surgeons now offer people of color surgeries tailored to alter ethnic and racial variations in appearance. Undergoing those surgeries opens people of color to accusations of racial ethnic self-hatred, as Nikki Sullivan (2004) showed in her account of Michael Jackson's cosmetic surgeries. People of color considering cosmetic surgery are told by the industry that they are "honoring" their racial heritage, but they also risk violating social norms related to racial or ethnic identity.

Taming the Cosmetic Surgery "Frankenstein"

The diagnoses of BDD and surgery addiction, the development of screening practices for surgeons, and the framing of body-image dissatisfaction and too much cosmetic surgery as social problems are ways the medical profession is trying to socially manage the virtual explosion of cosmetic surgery in the United States. Now that it is more affordable and socially acceptable, doctors and the lay public are attempting to establish new normative boundaries for cosmetic surgery. What kinds of surgeries, and which kinds of patients, will we culturally, medically, and legally accept? What are the acceptable and unacceptable reasons for cosmetic surgery? Who are the acceptable and unacceptable patients? The answers to these questions will set new norms for surgical body modification and healthy body images.

References

American Society of Plastic Surgeons, "2007 Statistics," www.plasticsurgery.org.

Arthur, Gary K., and Kim Monnell. 2005. "Body Dysmorphic Disorder." Emedicine, 29 June. www.emedicine.com/med/topic3124.htm.

Blum, Virginia. 2003. *Flesh Wounds: The Culture of Cosmetic Surgery.* Berkeley: University of California Press.

Busfield, Joan. 1996. *Men, Women, and Madness.* New York: New York University Press.

Davis, Kathy. 2003. *Dubious Equalities and Embodied Differences: Cultural Studies on Cosmetic Surgery.* New York: Rowman and Littlefield.

Ganny, Charlee, and Susan J. Collini. 2000. *Two Girlfriends Get Real About Cosmetic Surgery.* Los Angeles: Renaissance Books.

Gilman, Sander. 1999. *Making the Body Beautiful: A Cultural History of Aesthetic Surgery.* Princeton, NJ: Princeton University Press.

Klein, Samuel, Luigi Fontana, V. Leroy Young, et al. 2004. "Absence of an Effect of Liposuction on Insulin Action and Risk Factors for Coronary Heart Disease." *New England Journal of Medicine* 350: 2549–2957.

Nash, Joyclyn. 1995. *What Your Doctor Can't Tell You About Cosmetic Surgery.* Oakland, CA: New Harbinger Publications.

Pauly Morgan, Kathryn. 1991. "Women and the Knife: Cosmetic Surgery and the Colonization of Women's Bodies." *Hypatia* 6: 25–53.

Pitts-Taylor, Victoria. 2007. *Surgery Junkies: Wellness and Pathology in Cosmetic Culture.* New Brunswick, NJ: Rutgers University Press.

Sullivan, Nikki. 2004 " 'It's as Plain as the Nose on his Face': Michael Jackson, Modificatory Practices, and the Question of Ethics." *SCAN: Journal of Media, Culture, Arts* 1 (3). http://scan.net.au.

Wijsbek, Henri. 2000. "the Journal of Medical Ethics The Pursuit of Beauty: The Enforcement of Aesthetics or a Freely Adopted Lifestyle?" *Journal of Medical Ethics* 26: 454–458

Original article commissioned for this book.

BREASTS AND BODY IMAGE

Given the social importance of breasts in modern Western gendered societies, the incidence of both breast augmentation and breast reduction have skyrocketed with the increasing popularity of cosmetic surgeries in the last 20 years. During the same period, mammograms and self-examinations have led to a rise in the number of women who find they have breast cancer. So, on the one hand, we have elective cosmetic surgery on breasts to enhance sexual attractiveness to men, and on the other, we have women faced with losing a breast in a society that equates breasts with femininity.

According to the Centers for Disease Control (2009), aside from non-melanoma skin cancer, breast cancer is the most common form of cancer in women in the United States. In 2005 (the most recent year numbers are available), 186,467 women were diagnosed with breast cancer, and 41,116 died from it. Breast cancer is the second most common cause of cancer death in White, Black, Asian/Pacific Islander, and American Indian/Alaska Native women. The primary cause of cancer deaths for these groups is lung cancer. For Hispanic women, the statistics are reversed, with breast cancer the primary cause of cancer death, but the margin between lung and breast cancer for this group are very small.

Treatment choices today are combinations of chemotherapy, radiation, hormonal therapies, breast-conserving surgery (removal of the cancerous lump), and mastectomy (removal of the entire breast). The course of treatment is supposedly governed by type and stage of the cancer, risk and benefit statistics, and prognosis, but as with so much about the body, social, cultural, and power issues enter into the choices. Less invasive surgery (lump removal) conserves the breast but entails undergoing radiation. Complete breast removal is usually followed by a course of chemotherapy.

For women with breast cancer, the choice of type of treatment (lump removal versus removal of the entire breast and reconstruction) is heavily influenced by their body image. Many doctors advocate less invasive surgery, but studies have shown that patients make their decision based on body image as well as assessment of risks and their medical and financial resources (Figueiredo et al. 2004). Their feelings about their bodies also influence whether they will undergo the additional surgery for breast reconstruction (Kasper 1995). In general, breast-conserving surgery is chosen more often by younger, wealthier, urban women treated in larger teaching hospitals, with lower use by African Americans (Katz 2005; Nattinger 2005). The researchers conclude that women of all ages should be given a range of treatment choices and that their feelings about their body image should be taken seriously by their doctors. As one woman said:

> The physical reconstruction and the emotional well-being are two separate things. I don't see it just because now I have a reconstructed breast, I'm whole again. It's something I have to work out for myself, cognitively, emotionally, instead of just looking in the mirror and seeing another breast there. (Kasper 1995, 212)

In 2009, Muriel Sims, an independent women's studies scholar, was diagnosed with breast cancer. On her blog, she posted a poignant reverie on her relationship to her breasts throughout her life, and how she felt about their imminent loss.

Me and My Breasts

◆◆◆

Muriel L. Whetstone Sims
Independent Women's Studies Scholar, Fort Worth, TX

I dreamed about them again last night. I dreamed about their beginnings. I dreamed about how they've existed parallel to my life, serving and exposing me, reflecting my rebellion, betraying my trust. When I awoke, my breasts were sore and achy, probably due to my monthly cycle. But it doesn't take much creative muscle to imagine that my brain has let slip the fate that awaits them in just a couple of days.

I was an early bloomer, at least eight years old when they made their debut on my flat chest. One of the first in my class to sprout, I was at first ashamed of them. The source of pointing and giggles from the other little girls, they were subject to be grabbed and pinched by pubescent boys. Mother noticed my frisky adolescent curves, too, and ceremoniously presented me with a girdle.

From the beginning, my breasts seemed to exist parallel to my life. They grew peacefully upon my chest, and I did my best to ignore them. Then when I turned 10, they became more interesting as I noticed how interested middle school boys are in girls with perky bosoms. Suddenly, they had a purpose.

The period between 10 and 15 years old—1969 to 1974—my breasts became for me symbols of conjured up courage and imitated maturity. Teenage boys assumed I was much older than I actually was, while couldn't-care-less men approached me boldly. I learned to embrace the power of my bouncy boobies, to appreciate the attention I got because they were on my chest.

I was particularly fond of strutting up and down my working-class Chicago neighborhood outfitted in playfully sexy halter tops and rump-revealing hot pants.

Naturals were popular then, and my own was always perfectly coiffed. Sleeveless triangular material that tied around the back and again at the back of the neck, my favorite halter tops loosely covered my braless breasts, while my shoulders, upper back, and midriff were bare and exposed. Breasts weren't so bad after all. I was liberated by the attention.

On television, at the movies, on the covers of *Ebony* magazine, all around me liberation of one sort or another was being proclaimed and claimed—in an overall rise in youth culture, a national demand by Blacks for civil rights, and second-wave feminism. James Brown recorded and released in 1971 the hit single, "Hot Pants," which played in heavy rotation on the city's all-Black radio stations.

> *Thinkin' of loosin' that funky feelin' don't!*
> *Cause you got to use just what you got*
> *To get just what you want*
> *Hot pants make ya sure of yourself—good Lord*
> *You walk like you got the only lovin' left*

I was a young teenager, a virgin barely kissed, my own liberation dormant, untested. Yet, I attracted and reveled in the rootless affection the soft roundness of my breasts attracted, and instinctively I knew the Godfather of Soul was singing about me.

Then the babies arrived, a daughter when I was 17, and a son at 19. As my belly grew, so did my breasts until they were so big and full of milk I didn't recognize them. I remember staring at myself, thinking I looked like someone had taken me by the mouth and blown me up to resemble a human cow. Whenever it was time to feed my babies, or when they simply cried, the fullness in my chest could bring tears to my eyes. The leakage through my clothes made me turn from mirrors in disgust.

So in spite of my mother-in-law's pestering, I reclaimed my body. Stocked up on formula and glass baby bottles, and stubbornly refused to breastfeed. I was not yet 20 years old. The health benefits of breastfeeding were not as well known. Young and hot, I was not interested in latching babies to my breasts. More than 30 years later it seems my mother-in-law, bless her soul, was right all along as studies now show that breastfeeding appears to protect against breast cancer, probably by affecting levels of estrogen in a woman's body.

Raising the children through their middle years, I went through an early period during the 1980s where I deliberately hid my breasts and any hint of femininity under layers of mannish styled clothing. From somewhere I got my hands on an old discarded army jacket that I wore everywhere except to work. I was most often seen with a cap on my head. When hatless, I wore my chemically straightened hair brushed back flat against my head.

I remember now that I felt betrayed by my womanhood. At home I was wife and mother, and thus, primary manager of my young family. I look back at photographs of myself, and I am clearly depressed; although I was not yet 30, I look every bit of 40 years old. During those years there was nothing about being a woman that I wanted much to do with.

I was in my 20s, and had by then experienced a few unfortunate experiences. Incidences when my attractiveness and inexperience nearly got me raped or assaulted. Instead of welcoming the attention of men, I began looking for invisibility, corners to hide in. I spent an entire winter hidden under clothes that silenced the hecklers, and made strangers ignore me. Without raising my voice above a whisper, I silently protested the unfairness of being female in America.

The end of the '80s brought with it a determination to nurture myself in a way I had never done before. The children were teenagers, the marriage was over all except the walking out, and I wanted something better for myself. Four months before my 30th birthday I enrolled in college where I earned my degree in magazine journalism.

Those three years in school were so liberating! In the company of encouraging professors my intelligence was fed, and my self-confidence bloomed. After graduation, I cut my hair and began wearing it naturally again. I revamped my wardrobe, and unearthed my sassiness. Pictures taken during this season of my life show a smiling, contented woman, her silky legs unfurled under short skirts, her plump breasts bursting out of her blouses like crocuses in springtime.

Goodbye

Since discovering cancer in my left breast, and deciding a double mastectomy is the right thing for me to do, I find myself unconsciously massaging them. Holding them I try to burn in my memory how they feel to my touch, how they feel when they are touched. Last week I stood in the bathroom mirror and took snapshots of them with my cell phone camera. Goodness, are they ever droopy, ravished by pregnancy, age and gravity, racing one another to my lap. I attempt to cheer myself by reminding myself that thanks to implants, I'll be 80 with the bouncy bosom of a 20-year-old.

On Tuesday, September 15, 2009, I will lie down and when I raise up again my body will be absent the breasts that have reflected so much of my life back to me. We've been through a lot together, me and my breasts, and while I didn't ask for them, we've grown attached. Never knew how much until I had to contemplate losing them. But if nothing else, my breasts have taught me a lot about how society defines me as a woman. And they've helped me to grow into my womanhood as they became a reflection of both my strength and my vulnerability.

It was a wild ride, but soon we will part company. And even though no one looking from the outside in will be able to tell the difference, I will know they're gone, and I will miss them.

Reprinted from Muriel Lenore, "Good-Bye," posted at www.floridasdaughter.wordpress.com on September 13, 2009. Reprinted by permission of Muriel L. Whetstone Sims.

CONTROLLING BODY SIZE

Dieting to control weight is so common among women that it seems to be a perennial topic of dinner-table conversation, at least among older women. Younger women are more likely to resort to extreme dieting, and to hide their not eating or eating and throwing up from their family and friends, going online for support. *Anorexia* (self-starvation) and *bulimia* (binge eating and induced vomiting) are extreme ways to lose weight in order to meet Western cultural standards of beauty and to maintain control over one's body (Bordo 2005; Brumberg 1988, 1998; Gremillion 2002). Medical measurements of "obesity" are based on idealized averages for height, weight, and gender, but body imagery as "fat" or "thin" or "perfect" emerges from cultural influences. Racial ethnic and social class eating patterns and views of healthy weight combine with available food and ideals of feminine beauty to make some women prone to obesity and to developing eating disorders (Markey 2004).

Young, White, heterosexual, middle-class college women who are dissatisfied with their body image are particularly vulnerable to eating disorders (Cooley and Toray 2001). Heterosexual women are subject to pressure from the media and the significant men in their lives to stay thin to be sexually attractive. Women are critical of their own and other women's body size; often policing each other regarding their weight (Fallon and Rozin 1985). Lesbians, whose views of beauty are not influenced by men's opinions, are heavier than comparable heterosexual women, more satisfied with their bodies, and less likely to have eating disorders (Herzog et al. 1992).

A different rationale for eating problems was found in intensive interviews with women who were heterogenous on racial group, class, and sexual orientation (Thompson 1994). For these African-American, Latina, and White women, binge eating and purging were ways of coping with the traumas of their lives— sexual abuse, poverty, racism, and prejudice against lesbians. Eating offered the same comfort as drinking, but was cheaper and more controllable. Rather than a response to the culture of thinness, for these women, anorexia and bulimia were responses to injustice.

More personalized factors have emerged in cult-like positive views of anorexia and bulimia as demonstrations of the power to control one's body and even to have a transcendental "out-of-body" experience (Lintott 2003). Not eating or getting rid of what one has eaten becomes a way of life, a crusade for self-control (Hornbacher 1998). Eating disorders, in this view, are a triumph of mind over body:

> Eating disorders involve the view of one's body as "other," as something that can be dominated. In order to view the body and its needs as a natural force that can be overcome, there must be something responsible for the overcoming. ... The eating-disordered individual locates her self in that part of her that is able to contemplate objects immense in size and to resist forces that threaten to destroy her: her hunger and desire for food. ... (Lintott 2004, 75)

In this sense, eating disorders are not seen as giving in to oppressive norms of beauty or thinness, but going beyond the body entirely.

MENSTRUAL POLITICS

Another arena where women seek to gain control over their bodies is menstruation. Biologically, menstruation is the end result of hormonal preparation of the uterus for pregnancy after ovulation. If a fertilized ovum is not implanted in the uterus, the lining sloughs off—and that is menstruation. When a woman's ovaries stop maturing and releasing eggs, the cycle ceases—and that is menopause. These cycles are imbued with cultural and social significance in many societies. Menstruation, as a mark of becoming a woman, is often celebrated. In modern Western societies, a girl's first period (menarche) is not ritualized. Rather, it begins a monthly worry about showing blood and the danger of getting pregnant. Worse, the "condition" has become somewhat shameful and stigmatizing—something to be hidden.

In a famous political fantasy in *Ms. Magazine*, Gloria Steinem asked:

> What would happen … if suddenly, magically, men could menstruate and women could not? The answer is clear—menstruation would become an enviable, boast-worthy, masculine event. Men would brag about how long and how much. Boys would mark the onset of menses, that longed-for proof of manhood, with religious ritual and stag parties. … Military men, right-wing politicians, and religious fundamentalists would cite menstruation ["*men*-struation"] as proof that only men could serve in the Army ["you have to give blood to take blood"], occupy political office ["can women be aggressive without that steadfast cycle governed by the planet Mars?"], be priests and ministers ["how could a woman give her blood for our sins?"]. … In short, if men could menstruate, the power justifications could probably go on forever. If we let them. (1978, 110)

The equation of menstruation with high or low status, Steinem said, depends on the status of women. Whether women have high or low status in a society determines whether menstruation is celebrated publically or hidden in menstrual huts, whether it confers a sacred aura or one of pollution that needs to be "sanitized," and whether it is medicalized as a pathological condition or handled as a proud part of womanhood.

These questions underpin the current feminist debate about menstrual suppressants, such as Lybrel and Seasonale, which suppress ovulation and menstruation for months or a year at a time. Despite lingering fears about their long-term safety, these "lifestyle pills for healthy bodies" use a marketing ploy that produces "associations between cleanliness and femininity, between freedom of movement and women's bodies, and between limited menstrual flow and natural embodiment" (Mamo and Fosket 2009, 931). The marketing for the extended-use pills informs women that the "period" originally introduced in the three-week dosage of older birth-control pills was never a menstrual period, since these pills suppress ovulation, but a "pill period" which might just as well be foregone completely. The end result is a mature female body that is not vulnerable to pregnancy and messy periods, but is always available for heterosexual sex (Mamo and Fosket 2009).

Menopause, biological cessation of menstruation and fertility, has also been medically manipulated to suppress the effects of estrogen fluctuations. It has even been countered by procreative technologies to prolong fertility. Thus, women's procreative cycles can be medically manipulated at either end of the age spectrum. Does this make their bodies more pliant to cultural and social demands, or is it a form of control in women's hands?

For the last 35 years, feminists have called into question the safety of these drugs and deplored the pharmaceutical companies' profits off the bodies of women. They have criticized the elevation of the non-menstruating, non-pregnant, and non-aging woman as ideal. These are legitimate questions, but for any individual woman, the debate over the feminist implications of menstruation as "dirty" and menopause as a mark of aging may be irrelevant. Body control may be just what she wants.

WOMEN'S SEXUALITY: DISCOVERING THE CLITORIS

Body control extends to sexuality, and, as with other areas where women's choices are at stake, knowledge of one's body is crucial.

Until the eighteenth century, Western philosophers and scientists believed that there was one sex and that women's internal genitals were the inverse of men's external genitalia (Laqueur 1990). To them, the womb and vagina were the penis and scrotum turned inside out. The clitoris, if it was mentioned at all, was described as a small penis. It couldn't have been totally ignored, because it was also believed that a woman could not conceive unless she had an orgasm, so some men must have known where to find the clitoris and stimulate it. This knowledge about the location and purpose of the clitoris, though, keeps getting lost. Judging from questions to a sex-information hot line, the clitoris is hard to find, and its purpose is mysterious. If we examine some of the Western "experts" who have produced meanings about female bodies and sexualities, it is clear that the clitoris is a very elusive, dangerous, and complicated organ.

In the biomedical textbooks of the 1900s through the 1950s, the clitoris was depicted and described as homologous to the penis, that is, as formed from the same anatomical tissue. In 1905, Sigmund Freud, the father of psychoanalysis, published essays that argued for a differentiation of clitoral and vaginal orgasms. To Freud, clitoral orgasms were immature; as women became properly socialized into their mature sexual orientation of heterosexuality, he believed they should experience orgasm only in their vaginas. Sexologists of the 1930s and 1940s read female genital physiology as evidence of their sexual experiences, often citing an enlarged clitoris as proof of prostitution or lesbianism. To them, the clitoris revealed a woman's transgression against patriarchal sexual norms.

In 1953, Kinsey's *Sexual Behavior in the Human Female* used interviews with 5,940 women as its database. Kinsey and his colleagues interpreted this data to define the clitoris as the locus of female sexual sensation and orgasm. Despite this scientific evidence culled from women's descriptions of their sexual experiences, the clitoris virtually disappeared from anatomical textbooks from the 1950s to the 1970s. A survey of lay and medical dictionaries found that definitions of the clitoris referred to the male body as a template or norm from which the female body is somehow derived (Braun and Kitzinger 2001). This definition often implied that the clitoris was inferior to the penis. Basing one's knowledge on historical anatomical rendering and dictionary definitions of the time would have led one to believe that the clitoris was a small, purposeless organ.

During the 1970s, consciousness-raising groups of women equipped with plastic vaginal speculums, mirrors, and flashlights taught one another how to explore their sexual and procreative organs. These groups of women created fertile ground for feminist reformation of anatomical texts. The self-examinations and group meetings revolutionized existing descriptions and renderings of the clitoris (Federation 1981). A study that also challenged the conventional denigration of the clitoris, the *Hite Report* on female sexuality, published in 1976, was based on data from 1,844 anonymous questionnaires distributed to American women between 14 and 78 years old. Although many questioned the methodological rigor of this study, the project amassed significant and compelling data about the importance of clitoral stimulation for female orgasm.

These feminist insurgencies were met with great resistance from mainstream medicine. Throughout the 1980s and 1990s, the backlash to feminism reasserted that women's sexual response was linked exclusively to procreation. Certain anatomical texts of this time seemed to purposefully render the clitoris as useless or unnecessary (Moore and Clarke 2001). More recently, videos, CD-ROMs, and Web sites have joined medical texts and pornography as modes of viewing genital anatomy. But the new ways of accessing images and descriptions of the clitoris did not necessarily change the definition of the clitoris: "Continuities with previous textual anatomies abound in new visual and cyber forms, such as the heterosexual requirement, the female body as reproductive not sexual, and the biomedical expert as the proper and dominant mediator between humans and their own bodies" (Moore and Clarke 2001, 87).

Feminist research on women's genital anatomy, such as that of Rebecca Chalker (2002), a pioneer of the self-help health movement, has established that the clitoris is made up of 18 distinct and interrelated structures. Biometric analysis of a diverse sample of female genitals has shown the variation in women's genital dimensions, including clitoral size and labial length (Lloyd et al. 2005). However, mapping, representing, and defining the clitoris is not just a matter of genital anatomy; it is a political act.

The clitoris has many competing and contradictory narratives that vary depending upon personal, cultural, political, and historical circumstances. Based on who is defining the clitoris, it can be classified as an inverted and diminutive penis, a small erectile female sex organ, a love button, an unhygienic appendage to be removed, a site of immature female sexual expression, a key piece of evidence of sexual perversion, a vibrant subject of pornographic mediations, or an important part of female sexual experience.

Ritual Genital Cutting

The relationship between genital anatomy and sexuality has led Western women to use elective genital surgery to make the vaginal labia look "pretty" and to enhance clitoral sensitivity, yet they condemn ritual genital cutting in Africa. African feminists have claimed that "Western eyes" only see cultural oppression and subordination of women in these practices, calling it mutilation, whereas they themselves are not so condemnatory. In the following excerpt, Wairimũ Ngaruiya Njambi, a women's studies and sociology professor, describes the Kenyan ritual of *irua ria atumia,* a circumcision coming-of-age ceremony for girls, from an African perspective.

Telling My Story

◆◆◆

Wairimũ Ngaruiya Njambi
Florida Atlantic University

My intent in this section is not to provide yet another universal account of how female circumcision should be viewed, or even a comprehensive or "authentic" view of Gĩkuyũ practices, but rather to demonstrate the situatedness of bodies in relation to such practices, all the while recalling Haraway's point that "Location is also partial in the sense of being *for* some worlds and not others" (1997, 37, emphasis in original). Additionally, I see myself as a post-colonial product; a hybrid; raised as a Catholic in a rural peasant family in central Kenya, now living and teaching in the US—with all ambivalences about cultural practices that such a mixture can produce. Such a story matters to me first of all because it is rendered invisible and unimportant by anti-FGM discourse.

In Gĩkuyũ context, culture and bodies are not held separately, and they are historically tied very closely to circumcision, for both women and men. The oral history I encountered while growing up presented *irua ria atumia* (female circumcision) as a ritual that was appropriated by the Gĩkuyũ women, from a neighbouring ethnic group, as a way of introducing a celebration of "womanhood" to a culture that only celebrated "manhood." Yet this empowering image was reconfigured within Christianity. As Edgerton notes, "for reasons that remain obscure, the church did not object to the [Gĩkuyũ] practices of circumcising teen-aged boys, but it regarded the circumcision of adolescent girls as barbaric" (Edgerton 1989, 40). To me this reflects a common Judeo-Christian assumption that circumcised male bodies are normal and acceptable, and even that painful passage to manhood is desirable. On the other hand, the same tradition upholds a presumption that female bodies are innately passive and should be protected from such pain. Contrary to missionary concern, for Gĩkũyũ women, as for men, enduring pain bravely is also integral to the passage of womanhood, as Kratz (1994) observed. Additionally, given the dominant view that men transcend nature while women remain nature-associated, it is possible to suggest that *irua* offers a clear case in which women disrupt such a paternalistic dualism as a way of marking their entry into culture.

While the cultural significance of female circumcision has been waning in the past few decades, due mainly to church pressures, its cultural importance was still strong enough during my youth that I saw it as a necessity. It may seem ironic, given the tales of "flight from torture" told in the media, but my parents refused to allow me to be circumcised, as it was against Catholic teachings. I had to threaten to run away from home and drop out of school before my parents relented and allowed me to be circumcised. The procedure was performed with a medical scalpel in a local clinic run by a woman who was a trained nurse in the western sense, and also a relative of an important Gĩkũyũ female medical healer and powerful leader of the early 20th century, Wairimũ Wa Kĩnene. During the operation, the hood of the clitoris was cut through its apex which caused the hood to split open and the clitoris to become more completely exposed. Such exposure has been associated with sexual enhancement. However, any generalization here might be unwise as it is likely that women's experience of *irua* varies, perhaps significantly.

Performed in a time of many social transformations in the 1970s, my circumcision was not the communal experience it would have been in earlier decades, an event that would have tied me forever to other women and men of my "age-set" *(riika)*. However, despite shifting cultural forms, circumcision still continued to be fundamentally important in that those who were circumcised were inscribed with the status and privilege of "womanhood." Usually performed on girls aged 14–16, Gĩkũyũ female circumcision, like many other forms, does not involve holding young women down so that they cannot escape their "torture" from "mutilating villains." Rather, it is a chance for teenage girls to demonstrate their bravery by unflinchingly accepting their moment of pain, as mentioned in some Gĩkũyũ songs.

Prior to my circumcision, my circumcised age-mates still considered me (16, at the time) a child. With their newly acquired "womanhood," they wore a new "no nonsense" attitude that demanded the attention of most adults around. I was not allowed to join the more serious conversations about topics such as menstrual cycles, pregnancy, and sexual fantasies. I could not talk to other adults without having to worry about the words I chose to employ, without having to worry about interrupting someone. I was required, with all the other little kids (!), to cover my ears with my hands whenever grown-ups made sexual jokes with one another that children were not allowed to hear. All the uncircumcised girls (Irĩgũ) and boys (Ihĩĩ), seen as childish and immature, were required to respect and to give up their seats when requested. In fact, the most profoundly humiliating insult that one can level at a Gĩkũyũ adult is to accuse them of acting like an "uncircumcised" boy or girl. Today, however, as the importance of female circumcision declines, this insult has less power over women than it does over men, for whom circumcision remains a must.

By completing my *irua*, I became a Gĩkuyũ woman. And even though the concept of "age-set" had been disrupted by the time of my circumcision, I entered a category whose pleasures and benefits were previously denied to me. As a 16-year-old girl, I just wanted to become a woman like many other Gĩkuyũ girls, problematically or unproblematically....

Far from maliciously torturing women, circumcision not only gave Gĩkuyũ women some access to social, political and economic power in an undeniably patriarchial society, but it also allowed them to be keepers of Gĩkuyũ history, a valuable responsibility. Furthermore, apart from their obvious gendered differences in relation to the surgical operation and cultural expectations associated with each, there was little difference in the ceremonial aspects of female and male circumcision. Both women and men were circumcised on the same day, they wore the same ceremonial clothing, they both were secluded in the forest (for educational instructions) for the same time period.

For the Gĩkuyũ, the circumcision initiation did not stand by itself, but was integrated with other social activities, such as *ngwĩko*, a communal sexual practice for newly circumcised women and men after the healing period. According to my grandmother (Njoki), *ngwĩko* itself was accompanied by a series of long dances that took place throughout the day after which, as the night approached, groups of women and men were paired and moved together into a *kĩrĩrĩ* (women's hut), or a *thingira* (men's hut). During this time, both women and men were expected to engage in sexual activity where both would take multiple sexual partners in a one-night session....

A Reflexive Look at *Irua Ria Atumia*

My intention here is not to suggest that *irua* for the Gĩkuyũ is better or any less problematic than other cultural practices that mark women's bodies in one way or another. And probably no amount of critical reflexivity will protect me here from those who, when criticized for imperialist and arrogant representations of "Others," are quick to dismiss such criticism as nothing more than a mindless defence of tradition. However, far from blindly celebrating the Gĩkuyũ *irua ria atumia* and my experience of it, I am perfectly aware that it is never possible for any cultural practice, no matter how small, powerful, acceptable or desirable, to be non-problematic. For values and interests only exist in competition with other values and interests. Consider that, to some extent, the deployment of circumcision rituals is part of an attempt to galvanize an essential "Gĩkuyũ identity" in relation to neighbouring ethnicities and later to colonial intrusions. In 2003 a contemporary Gĩkuyũ social movement called *Mũngiki* is engaged in what one would call a dangerous form of revivalism, even fundamentalism, of "Gĩkuyũ culture" in the face of social change. Embracing female circumcision as an important component of this revival, some *Mũngiki* members are reported in the Kenyan media to have resorted to violence against some Gĩkuyũ women who resist this reinscription. As Edward Said makes clear in *Culture and Imperialism,* one danger here lies in the assumption that there is such a thing as one uncontaminated (Gĩkuyũ) "identity" or "culture" that exists "out there" in the first place—and into which some would automatically (or forcibly) be included while others are excluded.

At the same time, to re-emphasize a question I raised earlier, in the presence of so many religious and other cultural disputes over practices of female circumcision, is it possible to say that the decision to refrain from such practices is not equally a product of specific values and interests? For example, should we say that those in my village who refrained from practices of female circumcision but who chose Christianity instead (like those who assert "science" as on their side) cleverly and safely managed to escape the markings of culture? Are their bodies any less culturally marked than those whose bodies underwent practices of female circumcision? To answer "yes" to these questions allies one with common fixations (feminist or otherwise) on dichotomies of bodily oppression (via circumcision) versus freedom (via eradication). I instead would like to move the dialogue to rethink this idea that bodies exist outside of cultural performativity, and to look at multiple and heterogeneous ways in which not only cultures, bodies, and sexualities emerge in contextualized entanglements, but also the kinds of negotiations and ambiguities that are involved in such processes. For instance, while circumcised women are at times invited to describe its impact on their sexuality or their ability to achieve orgasm, there is no interrogation of the constructions of "sexuality" and "orgasm" upon which the discussion is based.

Also, it is important to point out that all genital operations (like all other physical operations) come with the risk of infections and bleeding, and *irua* is not an exception to such problems. This is especially the case in places where the healing practices that once accompanied *irua* have been discontinued and the new healing procedures are expensive, or have not been adopted due to fear of prosecution in places where circumcision is outlawed. My question is how do we situate the potential for infections associated with female circumcision in the context of similar risks with the multitude of other body modifications practised by people worldwide?

Besides those of female circumcision, consider similarities with abortion practices, which, when driven underground, routinely result in serious health problems and even death for women and girls. Yet our consistent call is for "safe and legal" abortions, rather than their eradication, on the basis that women should control their own bodies. Also consider the host of legal and fashionable body modifications (in the US especially) such as tattooing, piercing, penis/clitoris slicing, tongue slicing, and cosmetic procedures (including Botox injections, liposuction, breast implants, and female genital trimming) that escape the "mutilation" label. How is it determined which of these practices leads to a risk that warrants the emergence of a global eradication movement? How do we discuss these issues without creating an imperialistic impression that only those with some social, political, and economic power and who live in the west have rights to take risks with their bodies?

References

Edgerton, R. B. 1989. *Mau Mau: An African Crucible*. New York: The Free Press.
Haraway, D. J. 1997. Modest_Witness@Second_Millennium.FemaleMan©_Meets_ *OncoMouseTM; Feminism and Technoscience*. New York: Routledge.
Kratz, C. A. 1994. *Affecting Performance: Meaning, Movement and Experience in Okiek Women's Initiation*. Washington and London: Smithsonian Institution Press.
Said, Edward. 1994. *Culture and Imperialism*. London: Vintage.

Western feminists commenting on Njambi's article noted that a society's views of women's bodies are socially constructed, shaped by power relations, changeable over time, and not necessarily accepted by everyone in that society. Western feminists, therefore, can ally with African feminists opposed to ritual genital cutting and support their efforts at education and development of rituals that do not involve genital cutting.

CRITICAL SUMMARY

In the social construction of women's bodies, a good touchstone is, "Don't take anything for granted." First, there's no such thing as a "real woman." All women's bodies are made in conformity or resistance or inventive adaptation to social norms and expectations. Second, the lines between agency and submission to social pressures are not so clear. A woman who conforms to heteronormative standards of beauty by undergoing cosmetic surgery may feel liberated and empowered by her choice. A woman with breast cancer has to come to terms with a new body image and a realization that no surgery will return her to "normal." A woman with an eating disorder may see herself as triumphantly transcending her body, just as a woman who has had a face-lift may see herself as conquering age.

Feminists are divided on many of these body issues. Third-wave feminist menstrual activists are reclaiming their bodies from medicalization and industrialization and freeing themselves from taboos and shame (Bobel 2010). They reject the biologically centered goddess imagery of radical feminism, but they end up making menstruation a major part of their lives, in a way that many second-wave feminists long put behind them. The politics of the anti-genital cutting movement produces friction between African and Western feminists.

From one point of view, elective cosmetic surgery to enhance one's looks and sexuality is autonomous, but from another, it is a choice within a cultural atmosphere of the importance of heteronormative admiration. Undergoing surgery to look young, thin, and sexy conforms to the prevailing pressures on heterosexual women to attract a man.

Eating disorders and obesity are another problematic issue. Feminists may claim that women should be able to do whatever they want with their bodies, whether it is conforming or rebellious. But obesity is not just a matter of eating too much—there are racial ethnic, social class, and environmental public health issues implicated in "fat as feminist issue" (Yancey, Leslie, and Abel 2006). Extreme dieting can be seen as a reaction to the stigmatization of fatness or an autonomous choice. But, like pride in a fat body, cosmetic surgery, and other body manipulations, extreme dieting is a way to literally take one's life into one's own hands, since they all increase the chances of ill health.

The social pressures on women to construct an ideal body and face combine powerful institutions in Western society—medicine and heterosexuality. Fitness regimes, dieting, eating disorders, and cosmetic surgery are all legitimized as part of physical and psychological health. Yet underneath the health message is the older traditional assumption that a women's body is for making babies. For heterosexual women, procreation may be tied up with having a male partner, so sexual attractiveness is another set of body expectations. Lesbian women and single mothers by choice don't have to succumb to the male gaze to get pregnant, although they are medicalized through male-dominated institutions and thus may also be regulated by powerful ideologies of bodily presentation.

Beauty is a social construction with hegemonic and heteronormative values—women are supposed to attract powerful, rich men and impress their female peers. Beauty is also a profitable big business. Yet there is also pleasure for one's self in creating an image of beauty that validates one's own self-identity (Leeds Craig 2006). By choice, that image may be constructed through culturally conforming, time-consuming, and costly routines. But one's presentation of self can just as well be quirky, individualized, and gender-bending. Assuming you live in a society where how you look, dress, and use your body is under your control, and not subject to punishment for non-conformity, you have a lot to play with. Whatever you do with your body, you'll be a "real woman."

REFERENCES AND RECOMMENDED READINGS

Ahmed, Sara. 2007. "A Phenomenology of Whiteness." *Feminist Theory* 8: 149–168.

Boston Women's Health Book Collective. 2005. *Our Bodies, Ourselves: A New Edition for a New Era.* New York: Touchstone/Simon & Schuster.

Davis, Kathy. 1995. *Reshaping the Female Body: The Dilemma of Cosmetic Surgery.* New York: Routledge.

———. 2007. *The Making of Our Bodies, Ourselves: How Feminism Travels Across Borders.* Durham, NC: Duke University Press.

Dellinger, Kirsten, and Christine L. Williams. 1997. "Makeup at Work: Negotiating Appearance Rules in the Workplace." *Gender & Society* 11: 151–177.

Dove Campaign for Real Beauty. http://www.dove.us/#/cfrb/.

Dworkin, Shari L., and Faye Linda Wachs. 2009. *Body Panic: Gender, Health, and the Selling of Fitness.* New York: New York University Press.

Felski, Rita, and Claire Colebrook (eds.). 2006. Special Issue on Beauty. *Feminist Theory* 7: 131–282.

Gimlin, Debra L. 2002. *Body Work: Beauty and Self-Image in American Culture.* Berkeley: University of California Press.

Glenn, Evelyn Nakano. 2008. "Yearning for Lightness: Transnational Circuits in the Marketing and Consumption of Skin Lighteners." *Gender & Society* 22: 281–302.

Haiken, Elizabeth. 1999. *Venus Envy: A History of Cosmetic Surgery.* Baltimore: Johns Hopkins.

Hobson, Janell. 2005. *Venus in the Dark: Blackness and Beauty in Popular Culture.* New York: Routledge.

Jeffreys, Sheila. 2005. *Beauty and Misogyny.* Hove, UK: Routledge.

Jones, Meredith. 2008. *Skintight: An Anatomy of Cosmetic Surgery.* New York: Berg.

Inckle, Kay, 2007. *Writing on the Body? Thinking Through Gendered Embodiment and Marked Flesh.* Newcastle, UK: Cambridge Scholars Publishing.

King-O'Riain, Rebecca Chiyoko. 2006. *Pure Beauty: Judging Race in Japanese American Beauty Pageants.* Minneapolis: Minnnesota University Press.

Kwan, Samantha, and Mary Nell Trautner. 2009. "Beauty Work: Individual and Institutional Rewards, the Reproduction of Gender, and Questions of Agency." *Sociology Compass* 3: 49–71.

Laqueur, Thomas. 1990. *Making Sex: Body and Gender from the Greeks to Freud.* Cambridge, MA: Harvard University Press.

Leeds Craig, Maxine. 2002. *Ain't I a Beauty Queen? Black Women, Beauty, and the Politics of Race.* New York: Oxford University Press.

———. 2006. "Race, Beauty, and the Tangled Knot of a Guilty Pleasure." *Feminist Theory* 7: 159–177.

Murphy, Michelle. 2004. "Immodest Witnessing: The Epistemology of the Vaginal Self-Examination in the U.S. Feminist Self-Help Movement." *Feminist Studies* 30: 115–147.

Off Our Backs. 2004. Special Feature on Body Image. 34 (11/12), November-December: 13–69.

Pitts, Victoria. 2003. *In the Flesh: The Cultural Politics of Body Modification,* New York: Palgrave.

Reaves, Sheila, et al., 2004. "If Looks Could Kill: Digital Manipulation of Fashion Models." *Journal of Mass Media Ethics* 19: 56–71.

Rhode, Deborah L. 2010. *The Beauty Bias: The Injustice of Appearance in Life and Law.* New York: Oxford University Press.

Roach Anleu, Sharyn. 2006. "Gendered Bodies: Between Conformity and Autonomy," in *Handbook of Gender and Women's Studies,* edited by Kathy Davis, Mary Evans, and Judith Lorber. London: Sage.

Rooks, Noliwe M. 1996. *Hair Raising: Beauty, Culture, and African American Women.* New Brunswick, NJ: Rutgers University Press.

Weitz, Rose. 2009. *The Politics of Women's Bodies: Sexuality, Appearance, and Behavior,* 3rd edition. New York: Oxford University Press.

Wingfield, Aida Harvey. 2009. *Doing Business With Beauty: Black Women, Hair Salons, and the Racial Enclave Economy.* Lanham, MD: Rowman & Littlefield.

Wolf, Naomi. 1991. *The Beauty Myth: How Images of Beauty are Used against Women.* New York: William Morrow.

Aging

Calasanti, Toni M., and Kathleen F. Slevin (eds.). 2006. *Age Matters: Realigning Feminist Thinking.* New York: Routledge.

Cruikshank, Margaret. 2003. *Learning to be Old: Gender, Culture, and Aging.* Lanham, MD: Rowman & Littlefield.

Lynch, Annette, Marybeth C. Stalp, and M. Elise Radina. 2007. "Growing Old and Dressing (Dis)gracefully," in *Dress Sense: Emotional and Sensory Experiences of the Body and Clothes,* edited by Donald Clay Johnson and Helen Bradley Foster. Oxford, UK: Berg Publishers.

Morganroth Gullette, Margaret. 2004. *Aged by Culture.* Chicago: University of Chicago Press.

Off Our Backs. 2005. Special Feature on Women and Aging. 35 (9/10), September-October: 22–50.

Rosenfeld, Dana. 2009. "Heteronormativity and Homonormativity as Practical and Moral Resources: The Case of Lesbian and Gay Elders." *Gender & Society* 23: 617–638.

Body Size

Bordo, Susan R. [1993] 2005. *Unbearable Weight: Feminism, Western Culture, and the Body.* Berkeley: University of California Press.

Brumberg, Joan Jacobs. 1988. *Fasting Girls: The Emergence of Anorexia Nervosa as a Modern Disease.* Cambridge, MA: Harvard University Press.

———. 1998. *The Body Project: An Intimate History of American Girls.* New York: Vintage.

Cooley, E., and T. Toray. 2001. "Body Image and Personality Predictors of Eating Disorder Symptoms During the College Years." *International Journal of Eating Disorders* 30: 28–36.

Fallon, April E., and Rozin, Paul. 1985. "Sex Differences in Perceptions of Desirable Body Shape." *Journal of Abnormal Psychology.* 94: 102–105.

Gremillion, Helen. 2002. "In Fitness and in Health: Crafting Bodies in the Treatment of Anorexia Nervosa." *Signs* 27: 381–414.

Herzog, David B., Kerry L. Newman, C.J. Yeh, and Meredith Warshaw. 1992. "Body Image Satisfaction in Homosexual and Heterosexual Women." *International Journal of Eating Disorders* 11: 391–396.

Hornbacher, Marya. 1998. *Wasted: A Memoir of Anorexia and Bulimia.* New York: HarperCollins.

Kirkland, Anna. 2008. *Fat Rights: Dilemmas of Difference and Personhood.* New York: New York University Press.

Lintott, Sheila. 2003. "Sublime Hunger: A Consideration of Eating Disorders Beyond Beauty." *Hypatia* 18: 65–86.

Lovejoy, Meg. 2001. "Disturbances in the Social Body: Differences in Body Image and Eating Problems among African American and White Women." *Gender & Society* 15: 239–261.

Markey, Charlotte. 2004. "Culture and the Development of Eating Disorders: A Tripartite Model." *Eating Disorders: Journal of Treatment and Prevention* 12: 139–156.

Miller M.N., and A.J. Pumariega. 2001. "Culture and Eating Disorders: A Historical and Cross-Cultural Review." *Psychiatry* 64: 93–110.

Rothblum, Esther D., and Sondra Solovay (eds.). 2009. *The Fat Studies Reader.* New York: New York University Press.

Shaw, Gina. 2005. "Pro-Anorexia Web Sites: The Thin Web Line." http://www.webmd. com/content/Article/109/109381.htm

Thompson, Becky W. 1994. *A Hunger So Wide and So Deep: American Women Speak Out on Eating Problems.* Minneapolis: University of Minnesota Press.

Wann, Marilyn. 1998. *Fat! So? Because You Don't Have to Apologize for Your Size.* Berkeley, CA: Ten Speed Press.

Yancey, Antronette K., Joanne Leslie, and Emily K. Abel. 2006. "Obesity at the Crossroads: Feminist and Public Health Perspectives." *Signs*: 31: 425–443.

Breast Cancer

Centers for Disease Control. 2009. U.S. Cancer Statistics Working Group. United States Cancer Statistics: 1999–2005 Incidence and Mortality Web-based Report. Atlanta, GA. http://www.cdc.gov/uscs

Figueiredo, M. I. et al. 2004. "Body Image Important for Older Women in Choosing Surgery." *Journal of Clinical Oncology*, 1 October. www.breastcancer.org/research_ surgery_113004.html

Gagné, Patricia, and Deanna McGaughey. 2002. "Designing Women: Cultural Hegemony and the Exercise of Power among Women Who Have Undergone Elective Mammoplasty." *Gender & Society* 16: 814–838.

Hartman, Stephanie. 2004. "Reading the Scar in Breast Cancer Poetry." *Feminist Studies* 30: 155–177.

Hobler Kahane, Deborah. 1995. *No Less a Woman: Femininity, Sexuality and Breast Cancer,* 2nd rev. ed. Alameda, CA: Hunter House.

Kasper, Anne S. 1995. "The Social Construction of Breast Loss and Reconstruction." *Women's Health Research on Gender, Behavior, and Policy* 1: 197–219.

Kasper, Anne S., and Susan J. Ferguson (eds.). 2000. *Breast Cancer: Society Shapes an Epidemic.* New York: St. Martin's Press

Katz, Steven J., Paula M. Lantz, Nancy K. Janz, et al. 2005. "Patient Involvement in Surgery Treatment Decisions for Breast Cancer." *Journal of Clinical Oncology* 23 (24): 5526–5533.

Klawiter, Maren. 2008. *The Biopolitics of Breast Cancer: Changing Cultures of Disease and Activism.* Minneapolis: University of Minnesota Press.

Lorde, Audre. 1980. *The Cancer Journals.* San Francisco, CA: Aunt Lute Books.

Nattinger, Ann B. 2005. "Variation in the Choice of Breast-Conserving Surgery or Mastectomy: Patient or Physician Decision Making?" *Journal of Clinical Oncology* 23 (24): 5429–5431.

Price Herndl, Diane. 2006. "Our Breasts, Our Selves: Identity, Community, and Ethics in Cancer Autobiographies." *Signs* 32: 221–245.

Yalom, Marilyn. 1997. *History of the Breast.* New York: Knopf.

Genital Cutting

Abusharaf, Rogaia Mustafa. 2001. "Virtuous Cuts: Female Genital Mutilation in an African Ontology." *Differences* 12: 112–40.

Frueh, Joanna. 2003. "Vaginal Aesthetics." *Hypatia* 18: 137–158.

Gruenbaum, Ellen. 2000. *The Female Circumcision Controversy: An Anthropological Perspective.* Philadelphia: University of Pennsylvania Press.

Hernlund, Ylva, and Bettina Shell-Duncan. 2007. *Transcultural Bodies: Female Genital Cutting in Global Context.* New Brunswick, NJ: Rutgers University Press.

Mahklouf Obermeyer, Carla. 1999. "Female Genital Surgeries: The Known, the Unknown, and the Unknowable." *Medical Anthropology Quarterly* 13: 79–106.

Njambi, Wairimū Ngaruiya. 2004. "Dualisms and Female Bodies in Representations of African Female Circumcision." *Feminist Theory* 5: 281–303. Responses by Kathy Davis (305–311), Claudia Castañeda (311–317), Millsom Henry-Waring (317–323), and reply, 325–328.

Rahman, Anika, and Nahid Toubia. 2000. *Female Genital Mutilation: A Guide to Laws and Policies Worldwide.* London: Zed Books.

Shell-Duncan, Bettina, and Ylva Hernlund (eds.). 2000. *Female "Circumcision" in Africa: Culture, Controversy, and Change.* Boulder, CO: Lynn Reinner.

Wade, Lisa. 2009a. "Defining Gendered Oppression in U.S. Newspapers: The Strategic Value of 'Female Genital Mutilation.'" *Gender & Society* 23: 239–314.

———. 2009b. The Evolution of Feminist Thought about Female Genital Cutting. Sociologists for Women in Society Fact Sheet. *SWS Network News* XXVI, No. 3, Fall, 26–31.

Walker, Alice. 1992. *Possessing the Secret of Joy.* New York: Harcourt, Brace, Jovanovich.

Webber, Sara. 2003. "Cutting History, Cutting Culture: Female Circumcision in the United States." *American Journal of Bioethics* 3: 65–66.

Menstrual Politics

Bobel, Chris. 2010. *New Blood: Third Wave Feminism and the Politics of Menstruation.* New Brunswick, NJ: Rutgers University Press.

Buckley, Thomas, and Alma Gottlieb (eds.). 1988. *Blood Magic: The Anthropology of Menstruation.* Berkeley: University of California Press.

Chrisler, Joan C., and Ingrid Johnston-Robledo (eds.). 2002. Special Issue: Behavioral Science Research on Menstruation and Menopause. *Sex Roles* 46 (1/2): 1–59.

Fingerson, Laura. 2006. *Girls in Power: Gender, Body, and Menstruation in Adolescence.* New York: SUNY Press.

Kelly, Jennifer. 2005. *Zest for Life: Lesbians Experience Menopause.* Melbourne, Australia: Spinifex Press.

Knight, Chris. 1991. *Blood Relations: Menstruation and the Origins of Culture.* New Haven, CT: Yale University Press.

Laws, Sophie. 1990. *Issues of Blood: The Politics of Menstruation.* London: Macmillan.

Lee, Janet. 1996. *Blood Stories: Menarche and the Politics of the Female Body in Contemporary U.S. Society.* New York: Routledge.

Lock, Margaret, and P. Kaufert. 2001. "Menopause, Local Biologies and Cultures of Aging." *American Journal of Human Biology* 13: 494–504.

Mamo, Laura, and Jennifer Ruth Fosket. 2009. "Scripting the Body: Pharmaceuticals and the (Re)Making of Menstruation." *Signs* 34: 945–949.

Steinem, Gloria. 1978. "If Men Could Menstruate—A Political Fantasy." *MS. Magazine* (October): 110.

Winterich, Julie. 2003. "Sex, Menopause, and Culture: Sexual Orientation and the Meaning of Menopause for Women's Sex Lives." *Gender & Society* 17: 627–642.

Winterich, Julie, and Debra Umberson. 1999. "How Women Experience Menopause: The Importance of Social Context." *Journal of Women and Aging* 11: 57–73.

Sexuality

Braun, Virginia, and Celia Kitzinger. 2001. "Telling It Straight? Dictionary Definitions of Women's Genitals." *Journal of Sociolinguistics* 5: 214–233.

Carpenter, Laura M. 2005. *Virginity Lost: An Intimate Portrait of First Sexual Experiences.* New York: New York University Press.

Chalker, Rebecca. 2002. *The Clitoral Truth: The Secret World at Your Fingertips.* New York: Seven Stories Press.

Federation of Feminist Women's Health Centers. 1981. *A New View of the Woman's Body.* New York: Simon and Schuster.

Freud, Sigmund. [1905] 1962. *Three Essays on the Theory of Sexuality,* trans. James Strachey. New York: Basic Books.

Hite, Shere. 1976. *The Hite Report: A Nationwide Study on Female Sexuality.* New York: Macmillan.

Jackson, Stevi. 2006. "Gender, Sexuality and Heterosexuality: The Complexity (and Limits) of Heteronormativity." *Feminist Theory* 7: 105-121.

Johnson, Merri Lisa, ed. 2002. *Jane Sexes It Up: True Confessions of Feminist Desire.* New York: Four Walls Eight Windows.

Kamen, Paula. 2000. *Her Way: Young Women Remake the Sexual Revolution.* New York: New York University Press.

Kinsey, Alfred C. et al. 1953. *Sexual Behavior in the Human Female.* Philadelphia: W. B. Saunders.

Laqueur, Thomas W. 2003. *Solitary Sex: A Cultural History of Masturbation.* New York: Zone Books.

Lloyd, Jillian, Naomi S. Crouch, Catherine L. Minto, Lih-Mei Liao, and Sarah M. Creighton. 2005. "Female Genital Appearance: 'Normality' Unfolds." *British Journal of Obstetrics and Gynaecology* 112: 643–646.

Lloyd, Elisabeth A. 2005. *The Case of the Female Orgasm: Bias in the Science of Evolution.* Cambridge, MA: Harvard University Press.

Moore, Lisa Jean, and Adele E. Clarke. 1995. "Clitoral Conventions and Transgressions: Graphic Representations of Female Genital Anatomy, c1900–1991." *Feminist Studies* 21: 255–301.

Stein, Arlene. 2006. *Shameless: Sexual Dissidence in American Culture.* New York: New York University Press.

CHAPTER 4

Adonis, Don Juan, and "Real Men"
Constructing Male Bodies

Key concepts
bear bodies, digital rectal exams, Don Juan and male sexuality, hegemonic
masculinity, the male circumcision controversy, male body image,
masculine identity and prostate cancer, metrosexuals

"He's so hot!" she exclaimed while thumbing through *People* magazine's 50 Most Beautiful People issue (or was it the Sexiest Man Alive issue?). Is this woman's remark based on some personal idiosyncratic preference for a particular male body? It is difficult to decipher her preference for one man over the next when the pictures in page after page seem to show the same male body, slightly modified by hair color, clothing, or gestures. This body is usually tall, muscular, sexy, and the face is handsomely "chiseled" into White or White-looking features—an Adonis. In Greek mythology, Adonis was a handsome young man loved by the goddess Venus. In our own society, an Adonis is a model of male beauty.

The standards for beauty are so narrow that one good-looking man in a magazine very much resembles others. What explains the uncanny similarity all these beautiful men have to one another? Do the editors of *People* magazine only see and choose one "look"? Knowing what the preferred look is, do models, actors, and movie stars have some template of a body that they make themselves into, so that they emerge molded into a precise male form? Is this young woman's remark, like so many of our own, part of a process of socially producing and consuming representations of the ideal male body? We praise individuality, but do we admire and valorize the human body in all its shapes, sizes, and capacities, or are we overwhelmingly encouraged to develop preferences for certain bodies over others? And what do these preferences tell us about the social power, status, and virtue we attribute to the individuals inside these bodies?

ADONIS: THE IDEAL MASCULINE BODY

Similar to the ideal female body, the ideal male body is constructed by dominant social institutions and depicted through frequently reproduced images.

From art, sculpture, television, films, the Internet, newspapers, and magazines, we are always reminded of the ideal male body through a constant parade of virile, young, able-bodied men. But ideal bodies do not emerge from a vacuum. Clearly, ideal images of human bodies must be historically and socially situated to be understood. In Western contemporary cultures, a sampling of popular images would suggest that the ideal male body is over six feet tall, 180–200 pounds, muscular, agile, with straight white teeth, a washboard stomach, six-pack abs, long legs, a full head of hair, a large penis (discreetly shown by a bulge), broad shoulders and chest, strong muscular back, clean-shaven, healthy, and slightly tanned if White, or a lightish brown if Black or Hispanic. Asian Adonises are rarely seen. With such imagery all around them, boys and men in Western societies are encouraged to emulate this perfection. Their "audience" of girls, women, and older men judge their bodies—and their characters—by these standards. Even though it is not openly admitted, tall, strong-looking men have the advantage over short, flabby men in business careers and politics, not just in the realm of romance. The other side of the secret evaluation of men's looks as indicative of their worth is that money and political power go a long way to compensate for less than ideal height, weight, and age.

Coming to understand the contours of the ideal male body and its ability to garner social power requires ongoing child and adult socialization. Boys (and girls) are not born thinking that their bodies are mechanisms to increase their social standing. They learn from their peers, through ritualistic teasing and name-calling, and from adults through praise and rewards, what bodies have the best payoff. In the case of boys and men, certain physical attributes, such as height, are not easily modified, and they must come to terms with what it means to be short in societies that value taller men. As this personal narrative by science writer Stephen Hall attests, being less-than-average height has deep effects on one's self-esteem, sense of safety and belonging, and social acceptance.

Size Matters

◆◆◆

Stephen S. Hall

When I was 11 years old, attending the sixth grade in a small mill town in Massachusetts, the boys would gather in the schoolyard before classes started, to play games and work off energy, much as schoolchildren do today. The play sometimes got rough, especially when we engaged in a brutal Darwinian contest of survival sometimes known as British bulldog.

The rules, as best I can recollect, went like this: all but one of the boys lined up at one end of an outdoor basketball court, while the remaining boy stood in the middle of the court. At an agreed-upon signal, the mass of boys dashed toward the opposite end while the lone boy in the middle attempted to grasp, tackle, snag, impede, trip, dragoon, or otherwise wrestle to the ground one of the dozens of boys barreling across the court. Once a boy was tackled, he joined the growing group in the middle attempting to tackle the remaining participants. With each rush from end to end, more and more boys would get tackled and wind up in the middle. When there was no one left to tackle, that round of the game ended. And then it would start all over again—with the first boy tackled in the previous round standing alone in the middle.

The distilled, stylized aggression of this game resembled a minimalist football game in which there were only fullbacks and linebackers, all colliding and scrapping and plowing through the snow.

In retrospect, I realize that this brute-force exercise crystallized for me the parlous transition from boyhood to manhood. Like many games, it informally codified the cultural insistence on physical aggression (even violence) for boyhood "success." It ritualized, and elevated to mass entertainment, the serial ostracisms of the One, for each round of the game established the lowest-ranking member in the physical (but also, inevitably, social) pecking order. It thrived on the animating tension of isolation and exclusion, singling out one boy for ignominy (and thus inadvertently accentuating the loneliness many boys feel on the cusp of adolescence). And of course this daily rite of passage was built around a mindless set of rules, legislated by children and enforced in the absence of adults. It was also, I hasten to add, a great deal of fun. Boys do like to collide.

But the game always left me feeling chagrined for a completely different reason. The fundamental lesson I learned on the playground, rightly or wrongly, was that size matters.

Children are acutely aware of who among them is "bigger." In earliest childhood, this instinctual grasp of social hierarchy primarily involves age (that is, who's older), not size. But for most of childhood, and especially during puberty and adolescence, this consciousness evolves into self-consciousness, an excruciatingly diligent examination of differences in physical size, pubertal maturation, shape, strength, and appearance. I remember this elementary school gauntlet-of-the-fittest so vividly because in this particular school population, two boys were notably smaller than the rest, and consequently were always the first to be tackled. Indeed, they usually took turns trying to tackle each other when each new game started—a kind of inside game of humiliation and desperation that satisfied the demands of schoolboy aesthetics, which call for entertainment seasoned with cruelty.

One of the boys, Albert Destramps, was much smaller than all the other boys, with almost delicate, doll-like features. He endured the usual razzing, names such as shrimp and shorty, and I confess I probably lent my voice to the chorus of insults a time or two. His size, however, didn't seem to diminish his zest for participation or the stream of acid, often witty insults he habitually spewed.

To be tackled by Albert on this particular playing field was the height of preadolescent humiliation, and the desperation on the faces of those in danger of being brought down by this diminutive motor mouth remains etched in my memory still. The terrorized boys who found themselves even partially in his clutches had the look of farm animals striving to escape a burning barn, wide-eyed, thrashing, as if they were about to die—of embarrassment. An inability to tackle Albert, conversely, became an empty-handed trophy of failure. Thus are echelons of respect and fear, hierarchies of dominance, and psychological strategies of behavior incorporated into the deepest marrow of boyhood. It's a particularly intense form of emotional education, and each day's lesson was completed before the bell rang for the first class.

It became something of a ritual in this primal exercise that Albert, because he was such an easy target, would always be grabbed, tackled, and smothered at the start of each game (if he wasn't in the middle himself) by the next-smallest boy in the school. That boy was me.

Albert was the only kid I could pick on, the only kid over whom I could exercise even a nanosecond of physical mastery, and so, without regret and indeed almost with relief, that's what I did. I wasn't the only one to pick on him, of course, but I should have known better. Albert and I tormented each other down there on the lower rungs of the pecking order—and believe me, he gave as good as he got. But it was our shared destiny and bad fortune to be physically smaller than the rest of the boys at a time in male development when size becomes a prominent, even dominant, factor in status and self-esteem.

The fact that I so vividly remember the casual humiliations of those frigid Massachusetts mornings after more than four decades attests to the raw power of such childhood encounters. Many male friends to whom I've mentioned my interest in size, including the tall ones, have unburdened themselves of similar tales of size-related tribulations (if not traumas), which suggests that a child's experience of size disparity—and the sense of otherness it cultivates in the developing mind, the feeling of involuntary and unwanted citizenship in a despised land—is enduring, resilient, deep, almost universal. The playground, the lavatory, the cafeteria, the locker room, the hallways: to children during their formative years, and to boys in particular, these are fields of random cruelty, corridors of fear, chambers of dread. They are makeshift arenas of physical confrontation, where incidents we forever remember from our childhood and adolescent years become incorporated, like knots in tree bark, into the adults we will become. Wherever boys play games, as on the playing fields of nature, where predation and aggression have shaped animal behavior for tens of millions of years, sheer size makes a difference. You won't find that fact in many textbooks, but it may be the single most important lesson of unsupervised schoolboy existence.

The way those feelings of beleaguerment, insecurity, and behavioral adaptation live on in adult psychology has been insightfully captured by the cartoonist Garry Trudeau, the creator of Doonesbury. In a lovely 1996 essay called "My Inner Shrimp," Trudeau admits that "for the rest of my days, I shall be a recovering short person" with "the soul of a shrimp." Trudeau, unlike some of us, benefited from a delayed but explosive growth spurt that propelled his final height to over six feet.

But it's the feelings he experienced at age fourteen, when he was the third-smallest kid in his high school class, that still perfuse his adult soul. Trudeau sometimes pondered going to a high school reunion to show off all those postpubertal inches. But the Little Man Inside nixed the idea.

"Adolescent hierarchies," he writes, "have a way of enduring; I'm sure I am still recalled as the Midget I myself have never really left behind."

"Stature" is one of those beautiful words that has a narrow meaning—in this case referring to physical height—but that easily expands to much larger, even metaphoric, dimensions when it refers to less quantifiable but more important human qualities that we admire, aspire to, and devote so much life energy to attaining. Turning the concept inward, "stature" also refers to how we view ourselves in the mirror as well as in that private chamber of self-identity where we really undress our hopes, fears, vanities, insecurities, and self-appraisals.

If Garrison Keillor's Lake Wobegon is that mythical place where "all the children are above average," I have lived most of my life way south of Wobegon. At any stage of physical development and growth, from infancy to adulthood, in any country on the planet—and we could be talking here about the Netherlands, where the average Dutch citizen is taller than the average height anywhere else on earth, or those parts of equatorial Africa where pygmies still gather and hunt—about half of us are, by definition, below average in height for our particular tribe. That's not to suggest that this half of the population is abnormal. But in a social context that focuses on physical appearance and celebrates physical performance, size is an aspect of our identity on which we are constantly measured throughout life, even though the quantity measured lies almost totally outside our control. In ways subtle and blunt, physical stature affects who we are and who we become: the way people treat us, the activities we pursue, the games we play, the spouses we choose, the respect we command, even the salaries we receive.

Although many men who were small as children or adolescents reach average or above-average height, the fear of remaining forever below average carves one of the deepest furrows in the otherwise hardscrabble surface of a man's emotional and psychological life. From a parent's point of view, size becomes one of the earliest areas in which we compare, as we all do, our own children against other children. They're all beautiful, of course, but we carry around in our heads our children's percentile positions on the growth chart just as proudly as we carry their photos in our wallets. Their height represents the signature of our genes scribbled, however briefly, on the unfurling scroll of human events. During adolescence, a child's deep emotional frustration about being short can yank parents down into the disturbing world of teenage anguish and pain and remind us of our own limitations as parents. Trudeau recalls the night he fell sobbing into his father's arms: "We both knew," he writes, "it was one problem he couldn't fix." The inability of parents to fix the "problem" of small stature, and the sense of betrayal that helplessness incurs in their offspring, can color, often darkly, the relations between parents and children.

Having lived this experiment, I know the feeling. Of all the childhood terms of endearment I endured—shrimp, runt, peewee, pip-squeak, punk, peanut, bug, mouse, gnat, midget, Mr. Peabody—I had a particular favorite: squirt. It might seem odd to embrace an insult, but I loved the short, explosive burst of energy the word captured. Though intended to diminish me, it was at the same time subversive, irrepressible, and relentless, perhaps even avenging. Nonetheless, all the nicknames were diminutives; on the phylogenetic ladder of adolescence, I was down there with mice and mascots. When I was a high school freshman, my height placed me in what would be the first percentile on today's standard growth chart. I didn't need a chart, however, to be reminded that 99 percent of my male peers were taller than I was. They reminded me every day, with teasing, taunts, and occasionally physical assault.

Since then I've inched upward to a fairly respectable smaller-than-average adult size. However, physical size was the most consuming emotional issue of my youth, especially during adolescence—more consuming than, but not unrelated to, peer acceptance, dating, bullying, classroom performance, sexual maturation, and almost anything else considered essential to adolescent self-image, not to say self-loathing. And I gather I'm not alone. I've been surprised at how widespread and intense this lingering obsession about developmental size is among perfectly normal, seemingly well-adjusted adults whenever the topic comes up. I think we never entirely outgrow the sensation of being small, of being different, of being physically vulnerable. The emotional impulses we learn, usually as a matter of day-to-day survival in the difficult, formative times of adolescence, are like the reptilian brain, deep inside, surrounded by more civilized tissue but never totally disconnected, just waiting for the right conditions—perhaps a sufficiently stressful situation—to emerge.

The human life cycle relentlessly reinforces the dominant role of physical size in our personal development. I have been in the delivery room when a ruler was first laid against the fat, writhing masses of my newborn children. I've been the last boy picked for sports games. I sent away for my Charles Atlas booklet when I was a scrawny 12 year old. As an adolescent with delayed puberty, I stood in front of the mirror searching—even praying—for the first visible hint of sexual maturity. I stood on tiptoes to kiss a high school date. And I grew increasingly impatient with and distrustful of my parents' repeated assurances that I would undergo a growth spurt—which, when it finally arrived, seemed too little and too late. I have spent a lifetime being asked by photographers to sit in the front row—except the photographer at my own wedding, who nonchalantly asked my wife to sit in a chair while I stood behind her, so that the disparity between my height and hers (about three inches) would not be so apparent.

At another level, though, size becomes a visual shorthand for the fundamental difference among us. With the possible exception of gender and skin color, our physical size is probably the first thing other people notice about us, especially if we vary significantly in any direction from the mean, whether short or tall, thick or thin. We are socialized to value cultural factors such as intelligence, creativity, empathy, and perseverance, but the society of children does not always embrace those values—especially when the adults are not looking. Kids are keenly aware of big and small, short and tall, strong and weak. Indeed, these categorizations are among the earliest organizing principles in how children see the world and their place in it. Before we even utter a word, other people think they know something about us. And, in a way, they are right, because size matters.

It matters from the moment we are born, for size at birth is of great importance. Babies whose birth weights are unusually low are at risk for a lifetime of inferior health. Indeed, provocative recent research suggests that low birth weight predicts serious adult health problems such as diabetes and cardiovascular disease. Size also matters to the parents of an infant, who—whether they admit it or not— thrill or fret, depending on which quartile of the growth chart their child inhabits. Size matters to the presocialized child, whose infantile impulses governing territoriality and aggression precede the civilizing influence of education. Children who are bigger than their peers quickly learn how to get their way. Physical aggression in humans actually peaks between ages two and three, according to one prominent researcher who has recently begun conducting experiments to prevent aggressive behavior, such as bullying, by intervening with pregnant women through counseling before the child is born.

Size matters in sports throughout childhood. As one of those Saturday-morning soccer dads, I've been struck by how physical size often—not always, but often—translates into physical superiority and athletic dominance, and how greater size can trump, or at least neutralize, greater athletic skill in a smaller child. Size matters especially during adolescence and even into adulthood, because it clearly has an impact on social perceptions, romantic interactions, workplace hierarchies, and our self-perception long after we've stopped growing. To hear some researchers tell it, adult stature may determine everything from our earning power to our happiness.

HEGEMONIC MASCULINITY

Our culture, like most throughout the world, stratifies individuals based on phenotypic variables—color of the skin, size of the body, and the presentation of gender and heterosexuality—and on achieved qualities—economic wealth, political power, and influence or authority over others. Ironically, these are linked: the right physical attributes advantage people in achieving power, prestige, and wealth, and those at the top of the social ladder can use their assets for cosmetic surgery, personal training, and sexual enhancement. More insidiously, the standards of beauty are modeled on what those at the top prefer.

Dominant men not only have social power, they have cultural power. This combination is called *hegemony*. Hegemonic men are economically successful, from racially and ethnically privileged groups, and visibly heterosexual; they are well educated or excel in their careers and work at the most prestigious and lucrative occupations. Some may be of poor or working-class or immigrant origins, but most have overcome their humble beginnings and have professional or managerial careers, pursue athletic goals, or go into politics. Their hegemonic status is produced and legitimated by these valued attributes: Whiteness, wealth, social position, heterosexuality.

One of the paradoxical effects of patriarchal systems of domination is that even though men have dominance over women, men are not a monolithic group. In addition to being gendered, men are differently raced, differently abled, and differently classed. They can be gay, straight, bisexual, transgender. In many cultures, these sexual and social differences are used to stratify groups of men into different categories of privilege and power. Each man's ability to wield and benefit from patriarchal power is thus different. The ranking of culturally desirable male bodies mirrors their social standing.

Raewyn Connell, who coined the term, defined hegemonic masculinity as "the configuration of gender practice which embodies the currently accepted answer to the problem of the legitimation of patriarchy, which guarantees (or is taken to guarantee) the dominant position of men and subordination of women" (1995, 77). By describing the historical and social processes that put certain men at the top of the patriarchal hierarchy and make others complicit in supporting their position, Connell and other scholars in masculinity studies challenge the assumption that the characteristics of masculinity arise from natural male bodies. In contemporary Western society, the characteristics of hegemonic masculinity are embodied in an "ideal type" exhibiting the potential for physical power and violence, but acting with total rationality and control of emotion. It is an artificial image, based on cultural icons, such as successful tycoons, movie actors, and sports figures, and does not reflect the reality of most men's actual behavior. These icons, though, are powerful models, and they influence the behavior of men of many social classes and racial ethnic groups.

METROSEXUALS AND BEARS

Just as women and girls have body projects, men in pursuit of hegemonically male bodies are encouraged to modify their bodies to fit the ideal type. Psychological research studies have determined that men's media exposure is significantly associated with rising concern about their own physique, in particular their weight, muscularity, and general fitness. The more films and men's magazines the research subjects consumed, the greater their preoccupation with muscularity, and the more they dieted, exercised, and used beauty products (Hatoum and Belle 2004). Other social psychological research indicates that through the life span, boys' and men's self-concepts of their bodies change.

Indeed, research shows that today's college men are reporting greater levels of body dissatisfaction, and this is true for both gay and heterosexual men. Men associate their attractiveness with increased muscle definition, and are concerned about body *shape* (as opposed to weight) and increasing their muscle mass (Ridgeway and Tylka 2005). Eating disorders in males typically involve a constant competition to stay more defined than other men. Gay and heterosexual men have equivalent levels of body esteem, satisfaction with body shape, and desired levels of thinness (Yelland and Tiggemann 2003). In addition, the male body is increasingly being objectified and sexualized in popular print ads. For example, advertisements promoting weight lifting, exercise products, and underwear present the model as dehumanized (the gaze of the male model is not at the viewer), and the body is objectified (bodies are shown in parts, such as from the shoulders down). Additionally, the naked male body is increasingly portrayed in magazines targeted towards women and gay men. The viewing and purchasing of muscle and fitness magazines was associated with body dissatisfaction in both gay and heterosexual men (Duggan and McCreary 2004).

Some men turn to medications to maintain an "authentic" and virile masculinity. They face the world armed with prescriptions for Rogaine or Propecia for hair growth, Viagra or Cialis for firm and lasting erections, or they buy under-the-counter illegal substances like steroids for muscle mass and amphetamines for nervous energy. But men need not visit the doctor, the gym, or a dealer in order to participate in the increasingly expensive world of body perfection—body grooming tools are available over the counter or at the local salon. Enter the metrosexual:

> So what makes a metrosexual man? He's been defined as a straight, sensitive, well-educated, urban dweller who is in touch with his feminine side. He may have a standing appointment for a weekly manicure, and he probably has his hair cared for by a stylist rather than a barber. He loves to shop, he may wear jewelry, and his bathroom counter is most likely filled with male-targeted grooming products, including moisturizers (and perhaps even a little makeup). He may work on his physique at a fitness club (not a gym) and his appearance probably gets him lots of attention—and he's delighted by every stare. (Trubo 2003)

Since men are differently situated in the world, different groups have developed different standards of beauty. Peter Hennen did participant observation with a group of men in a gay subculture that valorizes a larger, hirsute body, like his own. In this excerpt from an article on his research, Hennen, a sociologist, describes the Bear culture as physically resisting the AIDS epidemic, culturally resisting stereotypical effeminacy, and sexually resisting a focus on the phallus.

Bear Bodies, Bear Masculinity

Peter Hennen
The Ohio State University at Newark

Just what is a Bear? Responses to this question reveal a variety of answers but almost all reference the Bear body in an attempt either to describe what the typical Bear looks like or to refute the idea that Bears can be defined exclusively by their bodies. As Travis, one of my interview participants, put it, "You know, physical attributes such as stockiness, height, weight, how much facial fur you have, things along those lines. But other people see it as being 90 percent attitude, 10 percent looks." What constitutes Bear attitude? Responses I encountered ranged from "natural, down-to-earth, easy going, likes to have fun" (Larry), "closer to the heterosexual community in their tastes" (Brian), "a sense of independence" (Burt), and finally "an easiness with the body" and "the masculinity thing" (Grant). "The masculinity thing" within Bear culture is complex and inextricably tied to the workings of hegemonic masculinity outside of it. "I think some of what is really appealing to me about the Bear group is that if you saw these guys on the street, they could just as easily be rednecks as gay guys," says Franklin. This suggests that the Bear image not only is conventionally gendered but includes a specifically classed presentation of self.

Bear culture was born of resistance. According to historian and founding figure Les Wright, in the early 1980s men frequenting leather bars in San Francisco and other cities began placing a small teddy bear in their shirt or hip pocket as a way of "refuting the clone colored-hanky code," whereby gay leathermen place different colored hankies in their back pockets to signal their interest in a variety of sex practices. Not willing to be objectified and reduced to an interest in one specific sexual activity, these men sported teddy bears to emphasize their interest in "cuddling" (1997a, 21). According to Wright, this was a way of saying, "I'm a human being. I give and receive affection" (1990, 54).

Bears reject the self-conscious, exaggerated masculinity of the gay leatherman in favor of a more "authentic" masculinity. This look includes (but is not limited to) jeans, baseball caps, T-shirts, flannel shirts, and beards. To the uninitiated, Bears seem above all to be striving for "regular-guy" status. "The Bear look is all-natural, rural, even woodsy," noted Silverstein and Picano; "full beards are common, as are bushy moustaches.... They're just regular guys—only they're gay" (1992, 128–30). But are Bears "just regular guys"? Feminist scholars Kelly and Kane (2001, 342) saw subversive potential in this community: "Is there perhaps something radically subversive of orthodox masculinity at work here, despite all the butch trappings? Might not bears represent the sort of 'marginalized men' that Susan Bordo describes as 'bearers of the shadow of the phallus, who have been the alchemical agents disturbing the (deceptively) stable elements' of orthodox masculinity in a newly percolating social psyche?"

With the Bears' emphasis on camaraderie instead of competition, the rejection of "body fascism" (as evidenced by the acceptance of heavier and older men), and by popularizing cuddling and "the Bear hug," one finds ample evidence that this is not the type of masculinity that predominates in other gay cultures. As Wright remarked, "Competition with other gay men for sex partners and the depersonalizing effects of a steady stream of sexually-consumed bodies is balanced by the humanizing effort to…establish contact with the person inside of each of those bodies" (1997b, 10). But at the same time, one finds signs of a recuperative current, a rejection of the insights of feminism, even outright hostility. As Lucie-Smith noted, "There is a challenge to aggressive feminism, which not only seeks female equality, but often tries to subject men to the tastes and standards imposed by women. To be a 'Bear' is to assert a homosexual masculinism which rejects this" (1991, 8).

Thus, in staking their claim to gay masculinity, Bears challenge hegemonic assumptions about male sexuality by introducing what feminists have identified as an "ethic of care" (Gilligan 1982) into an objectified sexual culture perceived as alienating. On the other hand, insofar as their rejection of effeminacy signals a broader devaluation of the feminine, Bear masculinity recuperates gendered hierarchies central to the logic of hegemonic masculinity. Furthermore, the pastoral fantasy encoded in Bear semiotics can be linked with earlier movements aimed at revitalizing an "essential" masculinity under assault from the feminizing effects of civilization by retreating to the wilderness, if only symbolically. How then, from a feminist perspective, is one to adjudicate these simultaneously resistant and recuperative features of Bear culture? In this research, I draw on ethnographic and historical evidence as I attempt to make sense of these conflicting currents, with a special emphasis on the way that Bear masculinity is embodied and the effect this has on Bear sexual culture.…

In addition to its appeal as a hedge against effeminacy and its eroticization of the heavier body, there are at least two factors contributing to the emergence of the Bear phenomenon during the 1980s. One was, unquestionably, the AIDS pandemic and the effect of AIDS-related wasting syndrome on the erotic imagination of gay men. In an era when thinness could be linked with disease and death, the fleshier body was reinterpreted as an indicator of health, vigor, strength, and virility. The second contributing factor was the Bear movement's ability to co-opt an existing subculture that had been operating on an informal basis for decades prior to the Bears' arrival on the scene. In 1976, a national network of "chubbies" (big men) and "chasers" (men who were sexually attracted to them) emerged as a new national organization called Girth and Mirth. A dozen years later, as the Bears became a recognizable subculture within the gay community, an uneasy relationship developed between the two groups. Interestingly, in many cities. Girth and Mirth chapters went into decline just as Bear organizations were cropping up (Suresha 2002). One reason for the out-migration from Girth and Mirth may be the more appealing imagery employed by the Bears. The iconic figure of the bear was enormously successful in linking the bigger body with nature, the wilderness, and more conventional notions of masculinity.…

Do Bears make gender trouble (Butler 1990)? What does it mean when Silverstein and Picano observe of Bears, "They're just regular guys—only they're gay" (1992, 128)? Clearly, there is a move toward normalization here, as well as an identification with heterosexual men, a move that may ironically turn out to be profoundly disruptive of hegemonic masculinity. When Franklin remarks, "Some of what is really appealing to me about the Bear group is that if you saw these guys on the street, they could just as easily be rednecks as gay guys," he speaks for many men who identify as Bears. Herein lies the possibility of subversion, as Bears have been largely successful in divorcing effeminacy from same-sex desire and creating a culture that looks like a bunch of "regular guys." The subversive implications, however, have everything to do with reorganizing sexuality and very little to do with challenging gendered assumptions. Most of these men would like nothing more than to have their masculinity accepted as normative, something that is largely accomplished within the group but remains problematic outside of it.

How is it that Bears come to understand their particular brand of masculinity as natural? It seems clear that this is accomplished quite deliberately, through the appropriation of back-to-nature masculinity narratives that are sustained inter-subjectively, as group members reinforce these meanings and associations through their day-to-day interactions. Thus, Bear culture seems currently disposed toward renaturalizing rather than denaturalizing gender relations. It seems far more likely, then, that increasing acceptance of Bear masculinity will encourage greater invest-ment in a heteronormative sexual culture, less experimentation with new pleasures, less dispersal of pleasure across the body, and a renewed appreciation for insertive intercourse as "doing what comes naturally." In this case, the perceived naturalness of the Bear body may be extended to naturalized understandings of sex practices that are increasingly compliant with norms of hegemonic masculinity.

References

Butler, J. 1990. *Gender trouble*. London: Routledge.

Gilligan, C. 1982. *In a different voice*. Cambridge, MA: Harvard University Press.

Kelly, E. A., and K. Kane. 2001. In Goldilocks's footsteps: Exploring the discursive con-
    struction of gay masculinity in Bear magazines. In *The Bear book II*, edited by
    L. K. Wright. New York: Harrington Park Press.

Lucie-Smith, E. 1991. The cult of the Bear. In *The Bear cult*. Swaffam, UK: GMP.

Silverstein, C., and F. Picano. 1992. *The new joy of gay sex*. New York: Harper Perennial.

Suresha, R. J. 2002. *Bears on Bears*. Los Angeles: Alyson Books.

Wright, L. K. 1990. The sociology of the urban Bear. *Drummer* 140: 53–55.

——. 1997a. A concise history of self-identifying Bears. In *The Bear book*, edited by
    L. K. Wright. New York: Harrington Park Press.

——. 1997b. Introduction: Theoretical Bears. In *The Bear book*, edited by L. K. Wright.
    New York: Harrington Park Press.

DON JUAN: THE IMPORTANCE OF SEXUAL PERFORMANCE

Casanova was an eighteenth-century man who fathered children in every city he lived in. Don Juan, the hero of Mozart's opera *Don Giovanni*, slept with 3,000 women of every size, shape, hair color, nationality, and rank. They both are much admired icons of male sexuality in Western culture, which is said to be phallocentric, focused on men and their sexual performance. The visual representation of sexual performance is the heroic phallus. Phallus, which literally means penis, also refers to imagery and symbolism that celebrates male generative power, often to the exclusion or denigration of female generative power.

The phallus is a model for both ancient and contemporary architectural structures. From the Mayan phallic structures of Chichén Itzá in Mexico, stone phallic symbols recovered at Zimbabwean ruins, the Washington Monument in the District of Columbia, the Eiffel Tower in Paris, and most recently, the Swiss Re Building in London, phallic structures have been erected to celebrate masculine accomplishment and male power. The destruction of the 110-story Twin Towers in New York City on September 11, 2001, was widely considered a castration of American power.

The preoccupation with the phallus is not only manifested in buildings. Linguist Deborah Cameron (1992) conducted a study of American college students to explore words and phrases that refer to the penis. She compiled a list of more than 140 terms, which she divided into categories, such as:

- Titles of authority: "Kimosabe, his Excellency, your Majesty, the chief, the commissioner, the mayor, the judge" (370)
- Personal authority: "scepter, rod of lordship, Excalibur, hammer of the gods" (370)
- Tool: "screwdriver, drill, jackhammer, chisel, lawnmower, hedgetrimmer, and fuzzbuster" (371)
- Weapon: "squirt gun, love pistol, passion rifle, lightsaber" (372)

Cameron concludes that the ways the penis is signified through language reinforces the underlying ideology that "the phallus must act, dominate, avenge itself on the female body. It is a symbol of authority to which we all must bow down. Its animal desires are uncontrollable; it has a life of its own" (1992, 373). Any reference to the vulnerable penis is notably absent.

Although men often boast about their penises, the grandiose vernacular and self-congratulatory talk indicates that the confidence men feel in their sexual performances may be somewhat exaggerated. When Lisa Jean Moore was working on a national sex information line throughout the 1990s, the most common question from male callers was, "What is the normal penis size?" Trained to provide anonymous, non-judgmental, and accurate information to callers, she would respond that most penises when erect were between five to seven inches. The relief in their voices then was evident—they were now secure in the validation that they (and their penises) were "okay." Anecdotal and research evidence from physician-patient interactions concurs that men and boys have a lot of questions about how large their penises should be (Lee 1996). The personal and cultural anxiety about penises has been elaborated upon by philosopher Susan Bordo:

> Most of our metaphors for the penis, as you will recall, actually turn it into some species of dildo: stiff torpedoes, wands, and rods that never get soft, always perform. These metaphors, I suggested, may be a defense against fears of being too soft, physically and emotionally. But at the same time as these metaphors "defend" men as they joke with each other in bars—or more hatefully—act as a misogynist salve for past or imaginary humiliations, they also set men up for failure. For men don't really have torpedoes or rods or heroic avengers between their legs. They have penises. And penises, like the rest of the human body and unlike dildoes, feel things. (1999, 64)

What has socialized men to be so concerned with presenting a certain image of their penises? We argue that this focus on sexual performance as a proof of masculinity is something that is learned by boys and reinforced in men in Western cultures through multiple sources. From pornography to sexology research, the erotic image and the human sexual response cycle are defined as almost exclusively phallocentric. The sexual act is penetration (vaginal, oral, or anal) and the goal is male orgasm and ejaculation. Anything less is tantamount to an embarrassing failure; repeated experiences end up with a diagnosis of "erectile dysfunction"—impotence (Tiefer 1994). Recent innovations in pharmaceuticals, as well as a long history of penis-improvement gadgets, also construct male sexuality in this limited way. (We are bombarded with constant spam email messages selling penile enhancement!) As psychologist Barry Bass observes, we have created a sexual-performance perfection industry where "good sex changes the basic nature of a sexual encounter from one of intimacy and pleasure to one of achievement and performance. In addition, these often unattainable standards of performance are guaranteed to make most of us feel like failures" (2001, 337).

This vulnerability goes a long way to explaining the enormous popularity of Viagra and similar medications, and their use by men whose only medical indication is fear of sexual failure (Kirby 2004, Loe 2004, Tuller 2004). In order to create less shame about the threat to masculinity due to impotence, drug companies select dominant males to be spokesmen for their products, for example, Bob Dole and Mike Ditka. Despite their soft-focus imagery, advertisements for Viagra, Cialis, Levitra, and similar pharmaceuticals are not selling the sensuality and emotions of sexual relationships but a way to achieve otherwise unattainable standards of the perfectly functioning penis and the always successful sexual performance.

MASCULINITY AND THE VULNERABLE PENIS

Research suggests that in general, men's health-seeking practices are lower than women's, because admission of illness is un-masculine. One report said that "many men suggested that the 'macho' image is adversely affected if illness means that they have to seek help or become dependent on others" (Chapple and Ziebland 2002, 836). It could be hypothesized that if illness were to strike a particularly vulnerable part of a man's body, he might be even less inclined to seek health care. Indeed, there have been numerous campaigns from public health organizations and community-based groups to encourage men (and their partners) to get screened for sexually transmitted diseases and prostate cancer. Icons of masculinity such as Joe Torre, coach of the New York Yankees, and Rudy Giuliani, former mayor of New York City, implore men to get screened for prostate cancer. Mass media campaigns invoke "experts" to dispel the prevailing wisdom that prostate cancer is a threat to masculinity (Nancarrow Clarke 1999, 67). Another male cancer, of the testes, is the most common cancer in men aged 15 to 34, and it is on the rise (Gurevich et al. 2004).

Prostate cancer is the most common cancer in America, even more common than breast cancer; men are 35 percent more likely to be diagnosed with prostate cancer than a woman to be diagnosed with breast cancer. The prostate is walnut-sized gland located between the bladder and the penis and positioned in front of the rectum. Urine and semen must pass through the prostate before leaving the body. The Prostate Cancer Foundation Web site (www.prostatecancerfoundation. org) and the American Cancer Society (www.cancer.org) include the following statistics for 2009:

- 80 percent of all prostate cancers are in men over 65
- 1 in 6 men will be diagnosed with prostate cancer at some point in their life
- African American men are 65 percent more likely to develop prostate cancer than Caucasian men, and when African American men do get prostate cancer, it is more likely to be a severe form of the disease
- Prostate cancer is most prevalent in North America and northwestern Europe, with a lower incidence in Asia, Central America, and South America
- Diet is suspected to be a major factor in these racial differences

Screening for prostate cancer is performed by a blood test and a digital rectal examination. Treatments for prostate cancer include prostatectomy (surgical removal of the prostate gland), chemotherapy, and radiation. Some potential side effects of prostate cancer and its treatment are incontinence, impotence, and loss of libido. These side effects, as well as the fears of anal penetration during a rectal examination, discourage men from being screened for prostate cancer. Ironically, interviews from Britain and Australia have found that men's perceived ideas about confronting impotence through prostate treatments are often different than their real-life experiences (Chapple and Ziebland 2002, Oliffe 2005). According to one study:

> The results … suggest that while the ability to have an erection may be an important part of male identity, men whose treatment only affects their sexual function were able to reframe this as "a small price to pay." … The greatest sense of loss is

described by men who have had hormone treatments that are described as affecting their interest in sex as well as their physical function. (Chapple and Ziebland 2002, 837)

Another view is expressed by Richard Wassersug, who was chemically castrated as a result of treatment for advanced prostate cancer. A professor in the department of Anatomy and Neurobiology at Dalhousie University, in Halifax, Canada, Dr. Wassersug has come out as a "eunuch"—an "emale." His body is no longer masculine—he has breasts and shrunken genitals, but he has a beard and says that he only looks different without clothes. His personality, though, has also changed, for the better, in his view—he is more emotional and empathic and sensually responsive to both men and women. In gender terms, he says, "Being free of hormonal compulsion, a modern eunuch can elect whatever gender orientation he wishes. If men are from Mars and women from Venus, then eunuchs can tour the whole solar system!" (2003).

Masculinity is also at play in how men understand their bodies as vulnerable entities. In a qualitative study of men's most humiliating experiences, the rankings were, from the most to the least: not maintaining an erection during sex, losing a testicle to cancer, being teased about penis size, having a rectal exam, being diagnosed as sterile, being left by an intimate partner, and being seen naked by male friends (Morman 2000). When confronted with digital rectal examinations (DREs) that screen for cancer, heterosexual men experience a challenge to their masculine sexual identity. As illustrated in this excerpt, based on a research study that interviewed 64 men about their experiences of DREs, there are racial differences in how men talk about the discomfort with the exam and its relationship to the threat of homosexuality.

How African-American and White Men Experience Cancer Screening Exams Involving the Rectum

◆◆◆

Julie A. Winterich, Sara A. Quandt, Joseph G. Grzywacz, Peter E. Clark, David P. Miller, Joshua Acuña, and Thomas A. Arcury
Wake Forest University

After skin cancer, prostate cancer is the most common and colorectal the third most common cancer among men in the United States (American Cancer Society, 2007; 2008). Health disparities persist for both cancers with higher incidence and mortality rates among African-American men compared to white men (ChengWu, Chen, Steele et al., 2001; Clegg, Li, Hankey, Chu, & Edwards, 2002; Grossfeld, Latini, Downs, Lubeck, Mehta, & Carroll, 2002). Because these cancers are more likely to be cured when detected early, the American Cancer Society recommends annual screening for all men beginning at age 50 or before, depending on risk factors (2007)....

Methods

The data for this paper were from in-depth interviews with 64 men, aged 40–64, from diverse socio-economic backgrounds. This study is part of a larger project on African-American and white men's beliefs, knowledge, and screening for prostate and colorectal cancer. The larger study consisted of two in-depth interviews for each man for a total of 128 interviews. During the first interview, general topics on beliefs about health, illness, cancer, and general cancer screening tests were discussed. The first meeting allowed the interviewer to develop rapport for the second interview, which covered potentially sensitive topics on men's beliefs, knowledge, and screening practices for prostate and colorectal cancer. In this paper, we focus on data collected from the second interview....

Findings

Overall, the most common sentiment among those men who disliked digital rectal exams (DREs) and colonoscopies was that the exams were "embarrassing" or "invasive." For DREs, some men could not explain in detail *why* it was unpleasant. In response to follow-up probes, men either repeated that they disliked it or said that part of their body was "personal." For example, one African-American man with low educational attainment (#43) said his doctor "violated" him and that "men don't like for people going up in…the rectum." When the interviewer asked him why, he replied: "I don't know! I'm a man, and I just don't feel, I don't feel comfortable like that!" Similarly, a white man with low educational attainment (#1) who has not had the DRE said he would prefer a colonoscopy because he "doesn't like the idea" of what is done with the DRE because it is "just part of the body guys feel uncomfortable about."

These views were shared by men across racial and educational groups. For example, a white man with high educational attainment (#27) said: "It's very undignified, that's what (laughs), I don't have anything else to add. (Tell me why it's undignified?) Well, that's the most personal part of a man besides his penis, it's just, I guess, you'd never want anyone to see that part of you (laughs)." An African-American man with high educational attainment (#2) said: "Well, not something I'd volunteer for if I could help it, it would be uncomfortable. (Why would you be uncomfortable?) Just, I'm not particular about having somebody's finger up my butt basically."

Men assumed that the rectum was inherently a private part of the body that no man would want another person to see or to penetrate. In the same way, the most common reason given by those men who associated colonoscopies with their masculinity was that they or other men did not like anything "going through the rectum" because it was "a problem for a lot of men…ain't no easy test where you got to do that" (#64, African-American man, low educational attainment) or that the "invasive nature of it" was the hardest part (#34, white man, high educational attainment). Some said their "biggest fear" was "someone placing something in my rectum, that's how most men are" (#8, African-American man, medium educational attainment) or that "something's up in your rectum would be kind of a compromised position for me" (#7, white man, medium educational attainment). A few men explained that men do not want to have a colonoscopy because "of that kind of macho stuff" (#61, white man, medium educational attainment).

Discrepant Views of High Educational Attainment Men: DREs

Although all men discussed their dislike of penetration, many of those with high educational attainment reported discrepant beliefs about the DRE. In the discussion of their own perspectives, they focused on the usefulness of the exam: "it's a good measure" (#18, white man); "you see the reason for it" (#15, white man); "practical and useful" (#49, African-American man), and "I figure early detection is a lot more important than the inconvenience of a test that's not painful" (#58, African-American man).

In contrast, when these men explained why other men dislike DREs, they projected reactions onto other men that the DRE is an affront to masculinity. In these accounts, they suggested that they dislike the exams themselves: "usually when you hear people talk about it, they begin to cringe…over the thought of…the invasive technique" (#18, white man); "they don't like it, it's not a manly thing (#15, white man); "they feel like it's pretty intimate and it's an invasion" (#49, African-American man); and "they feel that it is…demeaning (laughs), and that it, I guess, insults their manhood" (#58, African-American man).

Association of DREs with Gay Sex

…Several men explained that they dislike the DRE because they are not "gay" while only one man, a white with low educational attainment, associated a colonoscopy with homosexuality. The following quote suggests why men generally experience the DRE as more problematic than colonoscopies: "The finger test got a serious stigma with it.…the camera is not a human contact and the finger is human contact. And in that part of the body area, you know, it's just a, a stigma with it" (#34, African-American, low educational attainment).

Other respondents elaborated why they or other men associate DREs with gay sexual behavior. Some men may fear the DRE because they may become stimulated during the exam. Those men may have a difficult time if they have an uncontrollable, and unwanted, physical response during the exam. For example, a white man with medium educational attainment (#24) said that some men fear: "Somebody's gonna consider them gay….I had a friend that had one that, and he got an erection, and it embarrassed him to death in front of the doctor when...he got hard."

A white man with medium educational attainment (#7) provided additional insight about why men sexualize DREs, namely childhood heterosexual socialization and a lack of experience with health-care exams:

> I think probably a lot of them feel the same way I do about it, it's not very comfortable, kind of embarrassing...(And why do you think they feel that way?)...I just think it's the way that men are probably brought up, and, you know, raised up as to...be exposed to another man like that in that kind of setting.

An account from an African-American man with medium educational attainment (#10) pointed to the media as a further reason that men may associate DREs with gay sex in general, and with violence in particular:

> I think it has something to do with, I was watching Family Guy the other day, the other night on television, and he went to the doctor and had one, and he started having all these illusions about being raped by the doctor (laughs) and, becoming submissive or something like that. And I think that men have a hard time with that. (And why do you think that is?) I guess it has something to do with, I don't know, maybe it has a homosexual connotation to it I think.

Some African-American men were distinctly adamant that they dislike acts associated with gay sex. An African-American with high educational attainment (#55) said that because of his job in the sports field, he and his friends are aware of what "our bodies need to do," so they get regular screenings. If he was not in this line of work, however, he would have a difficult time; he imagined what his response would be: "Let me get this straight, you're going to take your finger and you're going to put it where to check on what? I don't think so, you know, homey don't play that. We ain't swinging that way." Also, an African-American with high educational attainment (#14) stressed his role in intercourse as he explained why he hates the DRE, which he said is: "an insult to my manhood....(And the reason that you don't like the finger test is because of the invasiveness?) Invasiveness, and maybe just call me homophobic. I don't play that. I'm the screwer, not the screwee."

Consequences

One consequence of the emotional experience of the DRE is that some men may avoid or delay the exam, as a white man with medium educational attainment (#17) explained. He has not had a DRE in ten years because he is "waiting for a different way to test rather than going through the rectum." A second consequence of the emotional impact of the DRE is that some men do not talk with other men about the exam because they fear teasing. When they do talk about it, they either joke or complain about it to minimize the toll for their masculinity. For example, an African-American with low educational attainment (#34) said: "It wouldn't be anything that I would tell my friends about," because they would tease him: "I bet you enjoyed that." He said that the "fear of being teased...(about) gay stuff" is why he wouldn't tell other guys about it. A white man with medium educational attainment (#25) talked about his friend who complained: "'Man, I hate it, I dreaded that part about that, getting that done'... because of the embarrassment of it."

A final consequence is the potential harm to doctors as an African-American man with high educational attainment (#14) explained when he discussed the psychological toll of the DRE. He said that if he is not in the right "mental state," his doctor might get hurt:

> I hate it. It's one of the most dangerous tests a doctor can give me. For him. (For him?) Yeah. Because it depends upon my mental state how I am going to respond to that test. Hopefully my mental state is analytical, scientific, and within control. I don't want it to be in my normal reaction of protection. Because I may be old but even old rattlesnakes can kill you (laughs).

...Past research on racial disparities in prostate and colorectal cancer finds that barriers to screening include beliefs that DREs are embarrassing (eg., Allen et al. 2007) and that colonoscopies are offensive (eg., Greiner, Born, Nollen, & Ahluwalia 2005); this study draws on masculinity and health theory to investigate why. Most men in this study, regardless of race or socioeconomic status, disliked the DRE with a range of views from "it's uncomfortable" to "I'm not gay." In contrast, most men believed the colonoscopy is a "good" test because it is "scientific." Some disliked colonoscopies, however, and the reason those men who experienced these exams as an affront to their masculinity was similar to that of most men who disliked DREs: they disliked penetration into their rectums. This finding provides insight into why past research finds some men dislike colorectal screenings due to their offensive nature (Beeker, Kraft, Southwell, & Jorgensen 2000). In the present study, men who generally asserted that exams involving the rectum were "invasive" associated their rectums as part of their masculinity that requires protection.

Those who explained why they disliked DREs in particular emphasized that they experienced it as a gay sexual act. Some men objected to penetration by a finger more than a medical instrument because of an aversion to gay sex. The data suggest that in the context of a rectal exam, many men support a dominant construction of masculinity by denouncing a masculinity they perceive as inferior— that is, being "gay." Indeed, a key way that hegemonic masculinity is maintained is by marginalizing those with less power, especially non-heterosexual men (Connell 1995; Kimmel 1994). The consequences of this marginalization of an inferior masculinity were not just men who objected to DREs, but included some men who avoided the exam altogether, "dreaded" their physicals, did not talk about the exam for fear of teasing by friends, and in one case even felt violent toward his doctor.

Men who disliked DREs overlooked the purpose of the exam for their health as they essentialized that part of their body as inherently off limits. This negotiation of masculinity and health could result in a health paradox (Courtenay 2000).

When men prioritize their masculinity by resisting an exam involving the rectum, they could risk their health by allowing undetected cancer to grow. Furthermore, when men refuse to talk about the importance of the exam with other men, they could put other men's health at risk by not sharing important health information.

As with all qualitative data, we found exceptions (Esterberg 2002). Three men, all African-American and one from each education group, said that DREs and colonoscopies are "good tests" and they did not discuss any negative views about either exam. Yet, only three men presented this view, which is striking in a sample of 64 men. Most men found exams that involve the rectum to be problematic, especially DREs.

We found presentations of masculinity unique to two groups: those with high educational attainment and African-American men. First, men with high educational attainment presented conflicting definitions of masculinity as they provided different answers about how they and other men experience DREs and colonoscopies. The interview itself was likely a presentation of masculinity in the social interaction between the interviewer and the respondent (O'Brien, Hunt, & Hart 2005). Compared to those with less education, men with more education and similar cultural capital (Bourdieu 1973) likely viewed the meeting with the interviewers, both of whom were college educated, as a conversation between equals. These men may have been conscious about presenting a knowledgeable self when asked direct questions about their own beliefs, in contrast to their views that the exams are an affront to masculinity when they discussed other men's fears. Their accounts suggested that although they are part of an educated group who usually complies with preventive health-care practices generally (Calnan & Rutter 1986), they view exams involving the rectum as negative. This finding suggests that health-care providers need to improve the administration of DREs and colonoscopies for all men, regardless of their educational level, to reduce men's negative associations with the exams.

Second, although most men in this study dislike penetration, African-American men were distinctly adamant about their aversion. Their lengthy explanations why they object to homosexual acts provide insight into one of the reasons why racial disparities persist with DRE rates. Past research finds that African-Americans generally disapprove of homosexuality and are specifically more likely to condemn gay family members and friends than whites (Lewis 2003). Religion and education do not explain African-Americans' seemingly greater dislike of homosexuality; both of those explanations affect whites' disapproval more than African-Americans' (Lewis 2003, 75). More research is needed to understand African-Americans' attitudes and beliefs about homosexuality (Lewis 2003), yet geographic region is important to consider in African-American men's constructions of masculinity in relationship to the health care system (Lichtenstein 2004). Being African-American in the Southeast, a politically conservative region with a strong history of racial discord generally, and within the health-care system specifically, may result in some African-American men strongly asserting their heterosexuality as a way to compensate for their marginalization in the hierarchy of masculinities (Connell 1987). In other words, African-American men who reacted to the DRE by insisting that they "don't swing that way" could be resisting a health-care exam that they perceive further marginalizes them. Therefore, intervention efforts to increase informed decision-making about screening among African-American men need to take place in settings that African-American men trust (Allen et al. 2007).

References

Allen JD, Kennedy M, Wilson-Glover A, Gilligan TD. 2007. African-American men's perceptions about prostate cancer: Implications for designing educational interventions. *Social Science & Medicine*. 64: 2189–220.

American Cancer Society. Prostate Cancer. 2007. [Retrieved December 10, 2007]. From http:/www.cancer.org/docroot/CRI/content.

American Cancer Society. What are the Key Statistics for Colorectal Cancer? 2008. [Retrieved March 30, 2008]. From http:/www.cancer.org/docroot/CRI/content.

Beecker C, Kraft JM, Southwell BG, Jorgensen CM. 2000. Colorectal cancer screening in older men and women: Qualitative research findings and implications for intervention. *Journal of Community Health*. 25(3) : 263–278.

Bourdieu P. Cultural reproduction and social reproduction. 1973. In: Brown R, editor. *Knowledge, Education and Social Change*. London: Tavistock.

Calnan M, Rutter DR. 1986. Preventive health practices and their relationships with socio-demographic characteristics. *Health Education Research*. 1: 247–253.

ChengWu X, Chen VW, Steele B, Ruiz B, Fulton J, Liu L, Carozza SE, Greenlee R. 2001. Subsite-specific incidence rate and stage of disease in colorectal cancer by race, gender and age group in the United States, 1992–1997, *Cancer*. 92 (10): 2547–2554.

Clegg LX, Li FP, Hankey BF, Chu K, Edwards BK. 2002. Cancer survival among U.S. whites and minorities: A SEER (surveillance, epidemiology and end results) program population-based study. *Archives of Internal Medicine*. 162: 1985–1993.

Connell RW. 1987. *Gender and power*. Stanford, CA: Stanford University Press.

Connell RW. 1995. *Masculinities*. Cambridge: Polity Press.

Courtenay WH. 2000. Constructions of masculinity and their influence on men's well-being: A theory of gender and health. *Social Science & Medicine*. 50: 1385–1401.

Esterberg KG. 2002. *Qualitative Methods in Social Research*. Boston: McGraw Hill.

Greiner KA, Born W, Nollen N, Ahluwalia JS. 2005. Knowledge and perceptions of colorectal cancer screening among urban African Americans. *Journal of General Internal Medicine*. 20: 977–983.

Grossfeld GD, Latini DM, Downs T, Lubeck DP, Mehta SS, Carroll PR. 2002. Is ethnicity an independent predictor of prostate cancer recurrence after radical prostatectomy? *The Journal of Urology*. 168: 2510–2515.

Kimmel MS. 1994. "Masculinity as homophobia: Fear, shame and silence in the construction of gender identity." In: Brod, Harry, Kaufman M., editors. *Theorizing masculinities*. Thousand Oaks, CA: Sage: 119–141.

Lewis GB. 2003. African-American-white difference in attitudes toward homosexuality and gay rights. *Public Opinion Quarterly*. 67: 59–78.

Lichtenstein B. 2004. Caught at the clinic: African American men, stigma, and STI treatment in the deep south. *Gender & Society*. 18 (3): 369–388.

O'Brien R, Hunt K, Hart G. 2005. "It's caveman stuff, but that is to a certain extent how guys still operate": Men's accounts of masculinity and help seeking. *Social Science & Medicine*. 61: 503–516.

THE MALE CIRCUMCISION CONTROVERSY

It is possible that the vulnerability and anxiety some men feel about their penises is related to their earliest childhood experiences, even their experiences in infancy. When the baby's tiny body has not even been gendered by the bombardment of unattainable media images of the perfect male form, many babies are implicated in the ongoing and unfolding debates about male circumcision.

In some Western societies, circumcision (removal of the foreskin) of newborns in hospitals for non-religious reasons became routine in the twentieth century. Due to changes in belief systems, trends in biomedical research, and social movements raising awareness about circumcision, male circumcision rates have varied throughout the past 50 years. The most recent data reveals the overall circumcision rate for newborn males prior to release from the hospital was 56 percent in 2005 in the United States (Circumcision Reference Library 2009). However, a representative nation-wide survey of adult males in the United States found the overall rate of 79 percent, with rates varying by race and ethnicity: 88 percent in non-Hispanic Whites, 73 percent in Blacks, 42 percent in Mexican-Americans, and 50 percent in others (Xu et al. 2007). Non-ritual circumcision is uncommon in Asia, South and Central America, and most of Europe—with the global rate approximately 34 percent globally (World Health Organization 2008).

A review of the benefits by the American Academy of Pediatrics found that the rate of urinary tract infections in the first year of life is 7 to 14 of 1,000 uncircumcised male infants and 1 to 2 of 1,000 circumcised male infants; however, the absolute risk of an uncircumcised male infant developing a urinary tract infection in the first year of life is less than 1 percent (AAP 1999). Neonatal circumcision offers some protection from cancer of the penis in later life; here, the overall risk is even lower—9 to 10 cases per year per 1 million men. In contrast, the risks of the circumcision itself (accidental injury, hemorrhaging, and infection) were 1 out of 476 in one study (Christakis et al. 2000). In 1999, the AAP concluded that the incidence of urinary tract infection and penile cancer in the United States is too low to warrant routine circumcision of male infants and now recommends that parents be informed of the potential benefits and risks of circumcision and that it is a strictly elective procedure.

A different picture of the benefits of circumcision occurs in sub-Saharan Africa, where circumcision has been shown to be highly effective in protecting men from the risk of HIV infection through heterosexual transmission (Lemle 2005; O'Farrell and Egger 2000; Weiss et al. 2000). There seem to be several reasons for this protection. One is that the foreskin is vulnerable to lesions, tears, and ulceration, which increase the likelihood of transmission of the AIDS virus and other sexually transmitted diseases. Second, the foreskin contains a high density of cells that may be the primary target for HIV infection (Szabo and Short 2000). This positive effect of circumcision has been touted as a rationale for public health officials in the United States to consider promoting routine circumcision for all baby boys. This proposed policy shift has led to controversy as reported in newspapers —"Members of Intact America, a group that opposes newborn circumcision, have rented mobile billboards that will drive around Atlanta (where the Centers for Disease Control are located) with their message that 'circumcising babies doesn't prevent HIV'" (Rabin 2009).

A volatile issue in the circumcision debate is whether removal of the foreskin diminishes sexual sensation. In the nineteenth century, circumcision (and clitorectomy in women) were recommended as deterrents to masturbation, which has led activists to argue that removal of the foreskin must deaden sexual feeling (Zoske 1998). However, data from 1,410 American men aged 18 to 59 who participated in the 1992 National Health and Social Life Survey found that self-identified circumcised men had a slightly lesser risk of experiencing sexual dysfunction, such as inability to have orgasms, especially when older (Laumann et al. 1997). The survey also found that circumcised men engaged in more varied sexual practices and masturbated more, but the variation across ethnic groups suggested that differences were due to social factors, which correlate with likelihood of being circumcised. It is unlikely that there will ever be objective data on the differences in sexual pleasure given and received by men with and without foreskins, since these evaluations are so subjective. As Karen Ericksen Paige predicted a generation ago:

> Men have debated the sexual sensitivity question for centuries. Circumcised men think that they have the more sensitive penises; uncircumcised men think that the constant exposure of the naked glans to clothes and the elements toughens it. Some men think that having a foreskin delays orgasm, giving a man more control; others think just the opposite. This discussion is never going to be settled. Sexual sensitivity appears to be in the mind of a man, not in his foreskin. (1978, 46)

Given the preoccupation with the penis, the widespread ritual practice of circumcision in male newborns or at puberty seems puzzling. For ritual circumcision, it is precisely the preciousness of the penis that underlies the rite. Male circumcision ceremonies indicate a father's loyalty to his lineage elders—"visible public evidence that the head of a family unit of their lineage is willing to trust others with his and his family's most valuable political asset, his son's penis" (Erickson-Paige and Paige 1981, 147).

CRITICAL SUMMARY

Although this chapter started with a description of idealized and homogeneous male bodies, we saw that alternative male bodies could also be valorized. Black male "cool" swaggering is one variation, a variation that is appropriated by high status White males as a means to amplify their masculinity, as the successful marketing of hip hop or "gangsta" merchandise to suburban youth demonstrates. Another type of male body is that of a metrosexual—heterosexual men whose use of cosmetics and attention to clothes borders on the "queer eye." Bears are one subset of gay men whose body types are large, hairy, and cuddly, and whose clothes style is down-market and working-class. Clearly, desirable male bodies are differentiated by the norms of the subcultures in which men claim membership. However, despite subcultures that celebrate diverse male body expressions, all men are still monitored by the larger patriarchal, heteronormative, and economically and racially stratified social structure of Western societies. Hegemonic men's values condition men and boys to use their bodies to express social power—be it through height, muscle, or phallus.

The proud penis and rampant sexuality celebrated in the Don Juan imagery is celebrated somewhat differently in male circumcision rituals, but then recurs in anti-circumcision, pro-sexuality rhetoric. The medical screenings through DREs reveals a deep anxiety about bodily integrity, which is intimately entangled with masculinity. The challenges of prostate cancer and male contraception call for a different vocabulary—an emphasis on relational, instead of penetrative, sexuality. The prediction is that in the twenty-first century, hegemonic masculinity may be more fluid and heterogeneous—leaving open the possibility of transgressing the rigid categories of dichotomous embodied genders. The ground for optimism, Raewyn Connell says, is the diversity of masculinities itself: "As this diversity becomes better known, men and boys can more easily see a range of possibilities for their own lives, and both men and women are less likely to think of gender inequality as unchangeable" (2005, 1817).

REFERENCES AND RECOMMENDED READINGS

Bass, Barry. 2001. "The Sexual Performance Perfection Industry and the Medicalization of Male Sexuality." *Family Journal: Counseling and Therapy for Couples and Families* 9: 337–340.

Beasley, Christine. 2008. "Rethinking Hegemonic Masculinity in a Globalizing World." *Men and Masculinities* 11: 86–103.

Bourdieu, Pierre. 2001. *Masculine Domination*. Stanford, CA: Stanford University Press.

Bordo, Susan R. 2000. *The Male Body: A New Look at Men in Public and Private*. New York: Farrar Straus Giroux.

Byrd, Rudolph, and Beverly Guy-Sheftall (eds.). 2001. *Traps: African American Men on Gender and Sexuality*. Bloomington: Indiana University Press.

Cameron, Deborah. 1992. "Naming of Parts: Gender, Culture and Terms for the Penis among American College Students." *American Speech* 67: 367–382.

Collins, M. A., and L. A. Zebrowitz. 1995. "The Contributions of Appearance to Occupational Outcomes in Civilian and Military Settings." *Journal of Applied Social Psychology* 25: 129–163.

Connell, Raewyn. 1995. *Masculinities*. Berkeley: University of California Press.

———. 2005. "Change Among the Gatekeepers: Men, Masculinities, and Gender Equality in the Global Arena." *Signs* 30: 1801–1825.

Connell, Raewyn, and James W. Messerschmidt. 2005. "Hegemonic Masculinity: Rethinking the Concept." *Gender & Society* 19: 829–859.

Duggan, Scott, and Donald McCreary. 2004. "Body Image, Eating Disorders and the Drive for Muscularity in Gay and Heterosexual Men." *Journal of Homosexuality* 47: 45–58.

Eng, David L. 2001. *Racial Castration: Managing Masculinity in Asian America*. Durham, NC: Duke University Press.

Friedman, David M. 2003. *A Mind of Its Own: A Cultural History of the Penis*. New York: Penguin USA.

Ghoussoub, Mai, and Emma Sinclair-Webb (eds.). 2006. *Imagined Masculinities: Male Identity and Culture in the Modern Middle East*. London: Saqi Books.

Gutmann, Matthew C. 1996. *The Meanings of Macho: Being a Man in Mexico City*. Berkeley: University of California Press.

Hall, Alex, Jenny Hockey, and Victoria Robinson. 2007. "Occupational Cultures and the Embodiment of Masculinity: Hairdressing, Estate Agency and Firefighting." *Gender, Work and Organization* 14: 534–551.

Hatoum, Ida Jodette, and Deborah Belle. 2004. "Mags and Abs: Media Consumption and Bodily Concerns in Men." *Sex Roles*. 51: 397– 407.

Health & Medicine Week. 2005. www.NewsRx.com & NewsRx.net, 21 February.

Hennen, Peter. 2008. *Faeries, Bears, and Leathermen: Men in Community Queering the Masculine*. Chicago: University of Chicago Press.

Howson, Richard. 2005. *Challenging Hegemonic Masculinity*. New York: Routledge.

Immergut, Matthew. 2010. "Manscaping: The Tangle of Nature, Culture and Male Body Hair," in *The Body Reader: Essential Social and Cultural Readings*, edited by Lisa Jean Moore and Mary Kosut. New York: New York University Press.

Jensen, Robert. 2008. "Masculine, Feminine or Human?" *Slepton Magazine*, 2 June. http://www.slepton.com/slepton/viewcontent.pl?id=1845.

Kam, Louie. 2003. *Asian Masculinities: The Meaning and Practice of Manhood in China and Japan*. London: Routledge.

Kimmel, Michael S. 1996. *Manhood in America: A Cultural History*. New York: Free Press.

———. 2005. *The Gender of Desire: Essays on Male Sexuality*. Albany, NY: SUNY Press.

———. 2008. *Guyland: The Perilous World Where Boys Become Men*. New York: HarperCollins.

Kirby, David. 2004. "Party Favors: Pill Popping As Insurance." *New York Times,* 21 June, F1, 11.

Lee, P. A. 1996. "Survey Report: Concept of Penis Size." *Journal of Sex and Marital Therapy* 22: 131–135.

Loe, Meika. 2004. *The Rise of Viagra: How the Little Blue Pill Changed Sex in America.* New York: New York University Press.

Luciano, Lynne. 2001. *Looking Good: Male Body Image in Modern America.* New York: Hill and Wang.

Majors, Richard, and Janet Mancini Billson. 1992. *Cool Pose: The Dilemmas of Black Manhood in America.* New York: Lexington Books.

McCabe, Marita, and Lina Ricciardelli. 2004. "Body Image Dissatisfaction Among Males Across the Lifespan: A Review of Past Literature." *Journal of Psychosomatic Research* 56: 675–685.

McLaren, Angus. 2007. *Impotence: A Cultural History.* Chicago: University of Chicago Press.

Moore, Lisa Jean. 2007. *Sperm Counts: Overcome by Man's Most Precious Fluid.* New York: New York University Press.

Mueller, Ulrich, and Allan Mazur. 1996. "Facial Dominance of West Point Cadets as a Predictor of Later Military Rank." *Social Forces* 74: 823–850.

Nardi Peter M., ed. 1999. *Gay Masculinities.* Thousand Oaks, CA: Sage.

Oudshoorn, Nelly. 2003. *The Male Pill: A Biography of a Technology in the Making.* Durham, NC: Duke University Press.

Ouzgane, Lahoucine, ed. 2006. *Islamic Masculinities.* London: Zed Books.

Pope, Harrison G. Jr., Katharine A. Phillips, and Roberto Olivardia. 2000. *The Adonis Complex: The Secret Crisis of Male Body Obsession.* New York: Free Press.

Ridgeway, Rebekah, and Tracy Tylka. 2005. "College Men's Perceptions of Ideal Body Composition and Shape. *Psychology of Men and Masculinity.*" 6: 209–222.

Riska, Elianne. 2004. *Masculinity and Men's Health: Coronary Heart Disease in Medical and Public Discourse.* Lanham: Rowman & Littlefield.

Rosenfeld, Dana, and Christopher Faircloth (eds.). 2006. *Medicalized Masculinities.* Philadelphia, PA: Temple University Press.

Sabo, Donald F., Terry A. Kupers, and Willie London (eds.). 2001. *Prison Masculinities.* Philadelphia, PA: Temple University Press.

Seidler, Vic. 2005. *Transforming Masculinities: Men, Cultures, Bodies, Power, Sex and Love.* New York: Routledge.

Slavishak, Ed. 2010. "'Made by the Work': A Century of Laboring Bodies in the United States," in *The Body Reader: Essential Social and Cultural Readings,* edited by Lisa Jean Moore and Mary Kosut. New York: New York University Press.

Srivastava, Sanjay (ed.). 2004. *Sexual Sites, Seminal Attitudes: Sexualities, Masculinities and Culture in South Asia.* Thousand Oaks, CA: Sage.

Tarrant, Shira (ed.). 2007. *Men Speak Out: Views on Gender, Sex, and Power.* New York: Routledge.

Tiefer, Leonore. 1994. "The Medicalization of Impotence: Normalizing Phallocentrism." *Gender & Society* 8: 363–377.

Trubo, Richard. 2003. "Metrosexuals: It's a Guy Thing!" WebMD 28 July. www.webmd.com.

Tuller, David. 2004. "Racing for Sales, Drugmakers Cast Erectile Dysfunction in Youthful Terms." *New York Times,* Men & Health, 21 June, F1.

Wassersug, Richard. 2003. "I Am a Eunuch." *OUT Magazine,* September. http://www. eunuch.org/Alpha/C/ea_195222castrati.htm.

Watson, Jonathan. 2000. *Male Bodies: Health, Culture and Identity.* Buckingham, UK: Open University Press.

Yelland, Christine, and Marika Tiggemann. 2003. "Muscularity and the Gay Ideal: Body Dissatisfaction and Disordered Eating in Homosexual Men." *Eating Behaviors* 4: 107–116.

Circumcision

AAP (American Academy of Pediatrics) Task Force on Circumcision. 1999. "Circumcision Policy Statement." *Pediatrics* 103: 686–693.

Benatar, Michael, and David Benatar. 2003. "Between Prophylaxis and Child Abuse: The Ethics of Neonatal Male Circumcision." *American Journal of Bioethics* 3: 35–48.

Christakis, Dimitri A., Eric Harvey, Danielle M. Zerr, et al. 2000. "A Trade–Off Analysis of Routine Newborn Circumcision." *Journal of the Ambulatory Pediatric Association* (Supplement) 105: 246–249.

Circumcision Reference Library. 2009. United States Circumcision Incidence. http://www.cirp.org/library/statistics/USA/.

Ericksen Paige, Karen. 1978. "The Ritual of Circumcision." *Human Nature,* May, 40–48.

Ericksen Paige, Karen, and Jeffrey M. Paige. 1981. *The Politics of Reproductive Ritual.* Berkeley: University of California Press.

Laumann, Edward O., Christopher M. Masi, and Ezra W. Zuckerman. 1997. "Circumcision in the United States." *Journal of the American Medical Association* 277: 1052–1057.

Lemle, Marina. 2005. "Circumcised Men Less Likely to Get HIV, Says Study." *Science Development Network,* 29 July.

O'Farrell, N. and M. Egger. 2000. "Circumcision in Men and the Prevention of HIV Infection: A Meta-analysis Revisited." *International Journal of Sexually Transmitted Diseases and AIDS* 11: 137–142.

Rabin, Roni Caryn. 2009. "Officials Weigh Circumcision to Fight HIV Risk." *The New York Times,* 24 August. http://www.nytimes.com/2009/08/24/health/policy/24circumcision.html.

———. 2009. "The Latest Fight Over the Foreskin." *The New York Times,* 29 August. http://www.nytimes.com/2009/08/30/weekinreview/30rabin.html.

Szabo, R., and R.V. Short. 2000. "How Does Male Circumcision Protect Against HIV Infection?" *British Medical Journal* 320: 1592–1594.

Weiss, H.A., M.A. Quigley, and R.J. Hayes. 2000. "Male Circumcision and Risk of HIV Infection in Sub-Saharan Africa: A Systematic Review and Meta-Analysis." *AIDS* 14 (Oct 20): 2361–2367.

World Health Organization. 2008. *Male Circumcision: Global Trends and Determinants of Prevalence, Safety and Acceptability.* World Health Organization.

Xu, F., Markowitz L.E, M.R. Sternberg, S.O. Aral. 2007. "Prevalence of Circumcision and Herpes Simplex Virus Type 2 Infection in Men in the United States: The National Health and Nutrition Examination Survey (NHANES), 1999–2004." *Sexually Transmitted Diseases* 34: 479–484.

Zoske, Joseph. 1998. "Male Circumcision: A Gender Perspective." *Journal of Men's Studies* 6: 189–208.

Prostate and Testicular Cancer

Chapple, Alison, and Sue Ziebland. 2002. "Prostate Cancer: Embodied Experience and Perceptions of Masculinity." *Sociology of Health and Illness* 24: 820–841.

Gray, Ross. 2003. *Prostate Tales: Men's Experiences with Prostate Cancer.* Harriman, TN: Men's Studies Press.

Gurevich, Maria, Scott Bishop, Jo Bower, Monika Malka, and Joyce Nyhof-Young. 2004. "(Dis) Embodying Gender and Sexuality in Testicular Cancer." *Social Science and Medicine* 58: 1597–1607.

Morman, M.T. 2000. "The Influence of Fears Appeals, Message Design, and Masculinity on Men's Motivation to Perform the Testicular Self-Exam." *Journal of Applied Communication Research* 28: 91–116.

Nancarrow Clarke, Juanne. 1999. "Prostate Cancer's Hegemonic Masculinity in Select Print Mass Media Depictions (1974–1995)." *Health Communication* 11: 59–74.

Oliffe, John. 2005. "Constructions of Masculinity Following Prostatectomy-induced Impotence." *Social Science and Medicine* 60: 2249–2259.

CHAPTER 5

Aligning Bodies, Identities, and Expressions

Transgender Bodies

Key concepts
cis-gender, cis-sexual, female-to-male (FTM), male-to-female (MTF), transgender people, transgressing and gender queerness

In the last two chapters, we discussed some of the ways that gendered norms and expectations pressure all of us to create gender-appropriate bodies, and most of us work hard to comply most of the time. Western societies do not have third genders or sexes, as some other societies do (Herdt 1994). We expect people to be "women" or "men," "female" or "male," not "other." We organize society on a two-gender system that most people believe is based on a clear-cut two-sex biology with a clear path to the "appropriate" or socially acceptable gendered body. The way we interact with others of the same or different gender reflects the "natural attitude," which assumes that there are two and only two sexes, that everyone is naturally one sex or the other no matter how they dress or act and will be that sex from birth to death, and that you can't really change your "natural" sex (Kessler and Mckenna 1978, 113–114). Those who believe that sex differences are biological believe that most gendered behavior emerges from this biology. The gendered social order and the many processes that go into the production of gender differences are not seen as powerful forces that shape bodies, identities, and behavior. In actuality, not only is biological sex not the ultimate determinant of gendered bodies and behavior, but some people construct gendered bodies that do not fit the sex declared at their birth.

Birth sex, the pronouncement of a newborn's (or fetus's) biological sex by birth attendants or sonograms is the foundation of the subsequent gender socialization of individuals. That is, those who are assigned male at birth are called boys and are supposed to feel, behave, and look masculine. The same process is supposed to turn female babies into feminine girls. But throughout our lives, many of us resist the gendered expectations of our original sex categorization at birth by varying our gendered expressions. For instance, a woman might wear a man's suit; a girl might play on the boys' football team. Quite often, these actions, or transgressions from the normative, are open to social commentary or ridicule to remind the person of the breach of gendered expectations. In October 2009, a female Mississippi high school senior, Ceara Sturgis, was barred from appearing in the yearbook because she wore a tuxedo in her senior photo (Adams 2009). A National Honors Society student and an out lesbian, Ceara was attempting to wear clothing that made her feel comfortable. This act of dressing was so transgressive to her community's gender norms that she was rendered invisible.

Breaching gendered expectations through our embodied activities is something many of us do to varying degrees without questioning the veracity of our birth sex. The term for those who live in the sex assigned at birth is *cis-sexual;* their social status is *cis-gender.*[1] There are people though who do question the truth of their birth sex and who wish to live in a way that more truthfully represents who they are. What do we do about people who feel that they are boys when their birth certificate says female, or girls when their birth certificate says male?

Political theorist Paisley Currah suggests that since the early 1990s, the term "transgender" has become most commonly used to describe people in the United States whose gender identity or gender expression does not conform to social expectations for their birth sex (Currah 2006). Historian Susan Stryker defines transgender people as those

> ...who move away from the gender they were assigned at birth, people who cross over (trans-) the boundaries constructed by their culture to define and contain that gender. Some people move away from their birth-assigned gender because they feel strongly that they properly belong to another gender in which it would be better for them to live; others want to strike out toward some new location, some space not yet clearly defined or concretely occupied; still others simply feel the need to get away from the conventional expectations bound up with gender that were initially put upon them. (2008, 1)

Transgender is a complicated concept because it refers to both people whose gender identity doesn't conform to the expectations of their birth sex, and it also refers to practices of non-conforming gender expression. Prior to the 1990s, the term transsexual was more commonly used, and sometimes the terms are used interchangeably. Transsexual is also used, most often, to describe a transgender person who uses medical methods, hormones or surgery, to transform their bodies.

MTFs, or transwomen, are individuals who were assigned male at birth but live their lives as women. FTMs, or transmen, are individuals who were assigned female at birth but live their lives as men. For transgender people, the pressure to make their bodies congruent with their chosen gender is reinforced in myriad small and constant ways. Some may take hormones to bring about some physical changes. Some do only "top surgery" and leave their genitalia intact. Many legally change their gender status to their chosen gender, and most change their appearance and the way they dress, talk, and act. They may also change their first names to be more culturally appropriate to their chosen gender.

Like all of us, transgender people want to be accepted as full-fledged members of their gender community. Forms that require individuals to place themselves in M or F boxes make indicating gender compulsory; the information that is required is exclusively binary and presumably permanent. To change this identity legally means changing one's birth certificate in societies that have that documentation. Birth certificates are "breeder documents" because they are the basis of all other identity documentation, such as passports. One's legal identity, as testified to by one's birth certificate, establishes whose child you are, where you were born, how old you are, and your sex. A transgender person must jump through many bureaucratic hoops in order to have identity documents that match their gender expression and identity. In some jurisdictions, you cannot change your birth certificate at all, and in other jurisdictions, genital surgery is required to change this certification (Currah and Moore 2009).

RECONSTRUCTING BODIES

There are various surgical and hormonal methods transsexual people use to construct bodies that will fit the norms for their chosen gender. Sometimes, what is changed are genitalia and usually secondary sex characteristics that result from hormonal input at puberty. Together, these are often called "sex changes" and the process "sex reassignment." There is not a one shot, or a one-size-fits-all surgical procedure for transsexual people. As anthropologist Eric Plemons (2010) has written:

> If we were to believe the childhood lesson that what makes boys boys and what makes girls girls are penises and vaginas respectively, it would follow that changing sex was primarily a genital affair. In fact, medical interventions meant to change sex involve hormonal as well as surgical interventions. Further, the category "sex reassignment surgery" describes a whole host of procedures that include operations on the genitalia but are not limited to them. Though any of these operations may be performed for a number of conditions, these operations (including genital restructuring) are only considered "sex reassignment" when they are performed on a person who has been diagnosed as transsexual. In addition to genital and chest reconstructions, male-to-female transsexuals may have operations to raise the pitch of their voice or to shave down a prominent Adam's apple, to reconstruct their hair patterns, or to soften their jaw line or brow. Female-to-male transsexuals may choose to have operations to produce a more square jaw line or prominent brow, or may have implants that approximate more defined musculature, such as pectoral or calf implants.

Despite the multiple ways individuals may modify their bodies, "many people transition using only hormones and/or non-genital surgeries (such as double mastectomies for transgender men, breast implants for transgender women). Others transition and live full-time in their new genders without any body modification at all" (Currah and Moore 2009, 125). Still others modify their bodies outside of the parameters of the binary gender system posited by medical professionals (Spade 2003), by circumventing the medical industrial complex or not ascribing to the medicalized narrative that is required to receive care.

The public tends to be extremely curious about the details of transgender body transformations. In the following excerpt, Julia Serano, a male-to-female transgender, examines the sensationalism surrounding the physical transitions of transsexual people and their sex reassignment surgeries. In this piece, Serano illustrates through media analysis and personal reflection on her own transition how the cultural obsession with surgical details confirms how obsessed we are with preserving assumptions and stereotypes about sex and gender.

Before and After:
Class and Body Transformation

Julia Serano
Independent scholar and artist

Transsexual lives are full of obstacles—childhood isolation, denial, depression, coming out, and managing our gender difference in a less than hospitable world. We have to navigate the legal limbo that surrounds what "sex" appears on our driver's licenses and passports, which restrooms we can safely use, and who we are allowed to marry. Many of us face workplace discrimination, police harassment, and the constant threat of violence. Yet the media focuses very little on any of this. Instead, TV shows and documentaries about transsexuals tend to focus rather exclusively on one particular aspect of our lives: our physical transitions.

Such transition-focused programs always seem to follow the same format, which includes rigorous discussions of all of the medical procedures involved (hormones, surgeries, electrolysis, etc.) and plenty of the requisite before-and-after shots. Before I transitioned, I found these programs predictable and formulaic, but I also found them helpful to a certain extent. As someone who had often thought about changing my sex, they gave me a certain understanding of what I might be able to expect if I were to pursue such a path myself. But of course, I was a demographic anomaly. Clearly these shows were being made by and for people who did not identify with the trans person in the program and who were not contemplating sex reassignment themselves. Back then, I never really questioned why a non-trans audience might be so interested in the minutiae of the transitioning process and trans-related medical procedures.

Now, after five years of living as an out transsexual, I have come to realize that these documentaries and TV programs reveal an even deeper underlying compulsion on the part of many cis-sexual people, one that goes way beyond nat-ural curiosity, to dwell almost exclusively on the physical aspects of the transition process when contemplating transsexuality. Like most transsexuals, I have scores of anecdotes that highlight this tendency: During the question and answer session at a literary event, after reading a piece about the murder of trans woman Gwen Araujo, I was asked by an audience member if I had any electrolysis done on my face; after I did a workshop for college students on binary gender norms and the way we project our ideals about gender onto other people, a young woman asked me several questions about whether or not I'd had a "sex change operation"; after creating switchhitter.net, my coming-out-as-trans Web site, I received an angry email from a stranger complaining that I did not put any before-and-after pictures up on the site, as if the 3,700-word question and answer section and the 4,500-word mini-autobiography describing my experiences being trans wasn't sufficient for that person to fully grasp my transsexuality—he needed to see the changes firsthand.

Of course, it's not just strangers who ask to see before-and-after shots of me. When friends, colleagues, or acquaintances find out that I am trans, it is not uncommon for them to ask if I have any "before" pictures they can see, as if I just so happen to keep a boy photo of myself handy, you know, just in case. I usually respond by telling them that before I transitioned I looked exactly like I do now, except that I was a boy. They never seem particularly satisfied with that answer.

The thing that strikes me the most about the desire to see before-and-after pictures, or to hear all of the gory details about sex reassignment procedures, is how bold people often are about it. After all, these people have to know that I felt uncomfortable as male, that it was a difficult and often miserable part of my life. So why on earth would they ask to see pictures of me from that time period? From my perspective, it is as thoughtless as if I had told someone that I was suffering from depression a few years ago and for them to have responded, "Oh, do you have any pictures of yourself from back then?" And really, is there anything more disrespectful and inappropriate than asking someone (in public, no less!) whether they have had any medical procedures performed on their genitals? So what drives these otherwise well-meaning people to want to know about the physical aspects of my transition so badly that they are willing to disregard common courtesy and discretion?

Well, I wasn't quite sure myself until about two years ago, during the height of the reality TV plastic surgery craze, when shows like *Extreme Makeover, The Swan,* and *I Want a Famous Face* filled the airwaves. These shows seemed to be catering to a very similar audience desire: to witness a dramatic physical transformation process replete with before-and-after photos of the subject. Also around that time, gastric bypass surgery began receiving a lot of media attention, and there were numerous programs dedicated to following people who were described as being "morbidly obese" through their surgery and recovery, ending of course with the mandatory before-and-after shots punctuating just how much weight the subjects had lost. On Discovery Health Channel, there is even a series that's called *Plastic*

Surgery: Before & After, which often combines conventional plastic surgeries and gastric bypasses in the same episode.

What really impressed me about these shows was how similar they are in format to many of the transsexual documentaries I have seen: They feature subjects who are unhappy with their bodies in some way, sympathetic and able doctors who describe the forthcoming procedures in great detail, hospital shots on the day of surgery and immediately afterward, a final scene after full recovery where the subject talks about how happy they are with the results, and side-by-side before-and-after photos that demonstrate the remarkable transformation in its entirety. Sometimes these shows are even set to slightly disturbing music that, when combined with the narrator's dramatic voice-over, impresses upon the viewer that they are watching something that is simultaneously wondrous and taboo. The only significant difference between many transsexual documentaries and these plastic surgery shows is that the former require a little more background and explanation as to why the subject wants to change their sex in the first place (presumably, the desire to become thinner or more conventionally attractive needs no explanation).

So why do plastic surgeries, gastric bypasses, and sex reassignment procedures receive such similar treatment in these programs? It is not simply because they all portray cutting-edge medical procedures. After all, there are plenty of shows that feature various medical techniques and surgeries, but they are generally far more serious and less sensationalistic in tone. Nor can it be said that the rarity of these procedures leads to the public's fascination with them. While sex reassignment is still fairly rare, 9.2 million cosmetic plastic surgery procedures and an estimated 140,000 gastric bypass surgeries were performed in 2004.[1] It also can't simply be that these shows depict transformations of some kind. After all, one occasionally sees behind-the-scenes programs about Hollywood makeup artists and costume designers who can drastically change an actor's appearance, yet they arc never given the sensationalistic spin that these other types of transformations receive. There are also plenty of programs that feature nonsurgical makeovers (for example, *Queer Eye for the Straight Guy* and *What Not to Wear*), but they tend to have a more laid-back and informative feel, seducing the audience with their you-can-do-this-yourself attitude, in contrast to plastic surgery and sex reassignment shows, which have a far more cold and voyeuristic feel to them. And while a woman who changes her hair color and style, or a man who shaves off his beard, undergoes a significant transformation, one that often leaves them looking like a completely different person, the audience is not encouraged to gawk over their before-and-after pictures in the same way they do with the subjects of plastic surgery and sex reassignment programs.

I would argue that the major reason that plastic surgeries, gastric bypasses, and sex reassignments are all given similar sensationalistic treatments is because the subjects cross what is normally considered an impenetrable class boundary: from unattractive to beautiful, from fat to thin, and in the case of transsexuals, from male to female, or from female to male.

Of course, attractiveness as a class issue permeates much of what we see on TV—it determines who gets to be the protagonist or love interest and who ends up being the nerdy next-door neighbor or comic relief. And while TV advertisements may encourage us to buy various beauty products that are supposed to make us look incrementally more attractive, or dieting and exercising programs that are supposed to help us lose that extra ten, twenty, even forty pounds, it is commonly accepted that we each have certain physical limits that we are unable to overcome, limits that generally determine our social status regarding attractiveness. In fact, the large amount of effort that many of us put into attaining the relatively small improvements in our appearance that are achievable by exercising, dieting, and purchasing beauty products is a testament, to how much we are judged (and how we judge others) based on conventional standards of beauty and size. So when somebody does cross those supposedly impassable boundaries, essentially changing their social class from not-so-attractive to stunning, or from "morbidly obese" to thin, it can change our thinking about beauty and attraction.

As a transsexual, I find myself dealing with this same phenomenon all the time, only with gender. Whether people realize it or not, most of us value, treat, and relate to women and men very differently, although not necessarily in a conscious or malicious way. Rather, like our attitudes about beauty and attraction, these prejudices are practically invisible to us, as they are woven into our social fabric. So when I tell someone that I used to be male, they are often dumbfounded at first, as if they have difficulty reconciling that someone who seems so naturally female to them could have once been something they consider to be so completely different. The fact that a single individual can be both female and male, or ugly and beautiful, at different points in their life challenges the commonly held belief that these classes are mutually exclusive and naturally distinct from one another.

Coming face-to-face with an individual who has crossed class barriers of gender or attractiveness can help us recognize the extent to which our own biases, assumptions, and stereotypes create those class systems in the first place. But rather than question our own value judgments or notice the ways that we treat people differently based on their size, beauty, or gender, most of us reflexively react to these situations in a way that reinforces class boundaries: We focus on the presumed "artificiality" of the transformation the subject has undergone. Playing up the "artificial" aspects of the transformation process gives one the impression that the class barrier itself is "natural," one that could not have been crossed if it were not for modern medical technology. Of course, it is true that plastic surgeries and sex reassignments are "artificial," but then again so are the exercise bikes we work out on, the antiwrinkle moisturizers we smear on our faces, the dyes we use to color our hair, the clothes we buy to complement our figures, and the TV shows, movies, magazines, and billboards that bombard us with "ideal" images of gender, size, and beauty that set the standards that we try to live up to in the first place. The class systems based on attractiveness and gender are extraordinarily "artificial"— yet only those practices that seem to subvert those classes (rather than reaffirm them) are ever characterized as such.

These programs' concentration on trans people who undergo multiple medical procedures, or who take lessons to help them "pass" as their identified sex, tends to make invisible the many trans men and women who "pass" rather easily after hormone replacement therapy alone, or who choose not to undergo all of the procedures commonly associated with transsexuality. Focusing primarily on those trans people who undergo the most procedures during their transitions not only shows a more dramatic change—one that reinforces the idea that sex reassignment is "artificial"—but also fosters the audience's assumption that trans people are merely mimicking or impersonating the other sex rather than expressing their natural gender identity or subconscious sex.

Perhaps no element in these sex reassignment and plastic surgery shows helps confirm the audience's assumptions about gender and attractiveness more than the before-and-after photos. These pictures are designed to overemphasize stereotypes. In the programs that feature plastic surgery and gastric bypass surgery, the subject is almost always wearing frumpy clothes and frowning in the "before" picture, and dressed smart and smiling in the "after" picture, adding to the perception that they have become more attractive. In the transsexual documentaries, "before" photos of trans women almost always depict them in the most masculine of ways: playing sports as a young boy, with facial hair and wearing a wedding tuxedo or military uniform as a young man. Similarly, "before" shots of trans men often include pictures of them wearing birthday dresses as a child, or high school yearbook photos of them with long hair. The purpose for choosing these more stereotypically female and male images over other potential "before" pictures (for instance, ones where the subject looks more gender-variant or gender-neutral) is to emphasize the "naturalness" of the trans person's assigned sex, thereby exaggerating the "artificiality" of their identified sex.

In real life, before-and-after photos don't always depict such clear-cut gender differences. One time, a friend who has only known me as a woman visited our apartment and saw wedding photos of me and my wife, Dani, for the first time. Despite the fact that I am physically male and wearing a tuxedo in the pictures (as we were married before I physically transitioned), I do not look very masculine; instead, I look like the small, long-haired, androgynous boy that I used to be. My friend seemed a little let down by the photos. She muttered, "It's weird, because it looks just like you in the pictures, except that you're a guy." Similarly, whenever old friends meet up with me for the first time since my transition, they almost invariably comment on how strange it is that I seem like the exact same person to them, except that now I am female. It's as if our compulsion to place women and men into different categories of our brain, to see them as "opposite" sexes, is so intense that we have trouble imagining that it is possible for a person to change their sex without somehow becoming an entirely different person.

These days, whenever people ask me lots of questions about my previous male life and the medical procedures that helped facilitate my transition to female, I realize that they are making a desperate and concerted effort to preserve their own assumptions and stereotypes about gender, rather than opening their minds up to the possibility that women and men do not represent mutually exclusive categories. When they request to see my "before" photos or ask me what my former name was, it is because they are trying to visualize me as male in order to anchor my existence in my assigned sex. And when they focus on my physical transition, it is so they can imagine my femaleness as a product of medical science rather than something that is authentic, that comes from inside me.

I know that many in the trans community believe that these TV shows and documentaries following transsexuals through the transition process serve a purpose, offering us a bit of visibility and the rare chance to be depicted on TV as something other than a joke. But in actuality, they accomplish little more than reducing us to our physical transitions and our anatomically "altered" bodies. In other words, these programs objectify us. And while it has become somewhat customary for trans people to allow the media to use our "before" pictures whenever we appear on TV, this only enables the cissexual public to continue privileging our assigned sex over our subconscious sex and gender identity. If we truly want to be taken seriously in our identified sex, then we must not only refuse to indulge cissexual people's compulsion to pigeonhole us in our assigned sex, but call them out on the way that they continuously objectify our bodies while refusing to take our minds, our persons, and our identities seriously.

Note

1. American Society of Plastic Surgeons, "9.2 Million Cosmetic Plastic Surgery Procedures in 2004—Up 5% Growth Paces U.S. Economy Despite Reality TV Fad," press release, March 16, 2005; Nancy Hellmich, "Gastric Bypass Surgery Seeing Big Increase," *USA Today,* December 19, 2005.

TRANSITIONING AND
WORKPLACE DISCRIMINATION

The consequences of changing gender can be unexpected. In some contexts, FTMs may gain economic advantages and men's privileges, but to many who are feminists, their new enhanced status is a bittersweet prize, since it is at the expense of women. In the United States, Black FTMs find they have acquired an intimidating persona—a Black man. Asian FTMs find just the opposite—if they are short and slender, they are denigrated as men, as are gay FTMs. The privileges of manhood and whiteness are reserved for White heterosexual FTMs. Transitioning at work might lead to individual changes in status and power, but a vast majority of transgender people who transition openly face tremendous workplace discrimination (Broadus 2006, Winerip 2009).

Sociologist Kristen Schilt has examined the ways that FTMs experience workplace changes in authority, respect, and recognition after they become men. As she reports in the following excerpt, one transgender man who continued to work at the same job was told by a client that he was so glad "Susan" was fired, because she was incompetent, while he was so good at the work. Of course, he and "Susan" were the same worker. Some in Schilt's study were openly transgender; others did not reveal their transgender status—they are "stealth."

Just One of the Guys

◆◆◆

Kristen Schilt
University of Chicago

Illustrating the authority gap that exists between men and women workers (Elliott and Smith 2004; Padavic and Reskin 2002), several of my interviewees reported receiving more respect for their thoughts and opinions post-transition. For example, Henry, who is stealth in a professional workplace, says of his experiences, "I'm right a lot more now.... Even with folks I am out to [as a transsexual], there is a sense that I know what I am talking about." Roger, who openly transitioned in a retail environment in the 1980s, discussed customers' assumptions that as a man, he knew more than his boss, who was a woman: "People would come in and they would go straight to me. They would pass her and go straight to me because obviously, as a male, I knew [sarcasm]. And so we would play mind games with them.... They would come up and ask me a question, and then I would go over to her and ask her the same question, she would tell me the answer, and I would go back to the customer and tell the customer the answer." Revealing how entrenched these stereotypes about masculinity and authority are, Roger added that none of the customers ever recognized the sarcasm behind his actions. Demonstrating how white men's opinions are seen to carry more authority, Trevor discusses how, post-transition, his ideas are now taken more seriously in group situations—often to the detriment of his women coworkers: "In a professional workshop or a conference kind of setting, a woman would make a comment or an observation and be overlooked and be dissed essentially. I would raise my hand and make the same point in a way that I am trying to reinforce her and it would be like [directed at me], 'That's an excellent point!' I saw this shit in undergrad. So it is not like this was a surprise to me. But it was disconcerting to have happen to me." These last two quotes exemplify the outsider-within experience: Both men are aware of having more authority simply because of being men, an authority that happens at the expense of women coworkers.

Looking at the issue of authority in the women's professions, Paul, who openly transitioned in the field of secondary education, reports a sense of having increased authority as one of the few men in his work environment:

> I did notice [at] some of the meetings I'm required to attend, like school district or parent involvement [meetings], you have lots of women there. And now I feel like there are [many times], mysteriously enough, when I'm picked [to speak].... I think, well, why me, when nobody else has to go to the microphone and talk about their stuff? That I did notice and that [had] never happened before. I mean there was this meeting...a little while ago about domestic violence where I appeared to be the only male person between these 30, 40 women and, of course, then everybody wants to hear from me.

Rather than being alienated by his gender tokenism, as women often are in predominantly male workplaces (Byrd 1999), he is asked to express his opinions and is valued for being the "male" voice at the meetings, a common situation for men in "women's professions" (Williams 1995). The lack of interest paid to him as a woman in the same job demonstrates how women in predominantly female workspaces can encourage their coworkers who are men to take more authority and space in these careers, a situation that can lead to the promotion of men in women's professions (Williams 1995).

Transmen also report a positive change in the evaluation of their abilities and competencies after transition. Thomas, an attorney, relates an episode in which an attorney who worked for an associated law firm commended his boss for firing Susan, here a pseudonym for his female name, because she was incompetent— adding that the "new guy" [i.e., Thomas] was "just delightful." The attorney did not realize that Susan and "the new guy" were the same person with the same abilities, education, and experience. This anecdote is a glaring example of how men are evaluated as more competent than women even when they do the same job in careers that are stereotyped requiring "masculine" skills such as rationality (Pierce 1995; Valian 1999). Stephen, who is stealth in a predominantly male customer service job, reports, "For some reason just because [the men I work with] assume I have a dick, [they assume] I am going to get the job done right, where, you know, they have to second guess that when you're a woman. They look at [women] like well, you can't handle this because you know, you don't have the same mentality that we [men] do, so there's this sense of panic...and if you are a guy, it's just like, oh, you can handle it." Keith, who openly transitioned in a male dominated blue-collar job, reports no longer having to "cuddle after sex," meaning that he has been able to drop the emotional labor of niceness women often have to employ when giving orders at work. Showing how perceptions of behavior can change with transition, Trevor reports, "I think my ideas are taken more seriously [as a man]. I had good leadership skills leaving college and um...I think that those work well for me now.... Because I'm male, they work better for me. I was 'assertive' before. Now I'm 'take charge.'" Again, while his behavior has not changed, his shift in gender attribution translates into a different kind of evaluation. As a man, being assertive is consistent with gendered expectations for men, meaning his same leadership skills have more worth in the workplace because of his transition. His experience under-scores how women who take on leadership roles are evaluated negatively, particu-larly if their leadership style is perceived as assertive, while men are rewarded for being aggressive leaders (Butler and Geis 1990; Valian 1999).[1]

This change in authority is noticeable only because FTMs often have expe-rienced the reverse: being thought, on the basis of gender alone, to be less com-petent workers who receive less authority from employers and coworkers. This sense of a shift in authority and perceived competence was particularly marked for FTMs who had worked in blue-collar occupations as women. These transmen report that the stereotype of women's incompetence often translated into difficulty in finding and maintaining employment. For example, Crispin, who had worked as a female construction worker, reports being written up by supervisors for every small infraction, a practice Yoder and Aniakudo (1997, 330) refer to as "pencil whipping." Crispin recounts, "One time I had a field supervisor confront me about simple things, like not dotting i's and using the wrong color ink...Anything he could do, he was just constantly on me....I ended up just leaving." Paul, who was a female truck driver, recounts, "Like they would tell [me], 'Well we never had a female driver. I don't know if this works out.' Blatantly telling you this. And then [I had] to go, 'Well let's see. Let's give it a chance, give it a try. I'll do this three days for free and you see and if it's not working out, well then that's fine and if it works out, maybe you want to reconsider [not hiring me].'" To prove her competency, she ended up working for free, hoping that she would eventually be hired....

Thus, respondents described situations of being ignored, passed over, pur-posefully put in harm's way, and assumed to be incompetent when they were working as women. However, these same individuals, as men, find themselves with more authority and with their ideas, abilities, and attributes evaluated more positively in the workforce.

Respect and Recognition

Related to authority and competency is the issue of how much reward workers get for their workplace contributions. According to the transmen I interviewed, an increase in recognition for hard work was one of the positive changes associated with working as a man. Looking at these stories of gaining reward and respect, Preston, who transitioned openly and remained at his blue-collar job, reports that as a female crew supervisor, she was frequently short staffed and unable to access necessary resources yet expected to still carry out the job competently. However, after his transition, he suddenly found himself receiving all the support and mate-rials he required:

> I was not asked to do anything different [after transition]. But the work I did do was made easier for me. [Before transition] there [were] periods of time when I would be told, "Well, I don't have anyone to send over there with you." We were one or

two people short of a crew or the trucks weren't available. Or they would send me people who weren't trained. And it got to the point where it was like, why do I have to fight about this? If you don't want your freight, you don't get your freight. And, I swear it was like from one day to the next of me transitioning [to male], I need this, this is what I want and [snaps his fingers]. I have not had to fight about anything.

He adds about his experience, "The last three [performance] reviews that I have had have been the absolute highest that I have ever had. New management team. Me not doing anything different than I ever had. I even went part-time." This comment shows that even though he openly transitioned and remained in the same job, he ultimately finds himself rewarded for doing less work and having to fight less for getting what he needs to effectively do his job. In addition, as a man, he received more positive reviews for his work, demonstrating how men and women can be evaluated differently when doing the same work.

As with authority and competence, this sense of gaining recognition for hard work was particularly noticeable for transmen who had worked as women in blue-collar occupations in which they were the gender minority. This finding is not unexpected, as women are also more likely to be judged negatively when they are in the minority in the workplace, as their statistical minority status seems to suggest that women are unsuited for the job (Valian 1999)....

Talking about gender discrimination he faced as a female construction worker, Crispin reports,

> I worked really hard....I had to find myself not sitting ever and taking breaks or lunches because I felt like I had to work more to show my worth. And though I did do that and I produced typically more than three males put together—and that is really a statistic—what it would come down to a lot of times was, "You're single. You don't have a family." That is what they told me. "I've got guys here who have families."...And even though my production quality [was high], and the customer was extremely happy with my work...I was passed over lots of times. They said it was because I was single and I didn't have a family and they felt bad because they didn't want Joe Blow to lose his job because he had three kids at home. And because I was intelligent and my qualities were very vast, they said, "You can just go get a job anywhere." Which wasn't always the case. A lot of people were—it was still a boy's world and some people were just like, uh-uh, there aren't going to be any women on my job site. And it would be months...before I would find gainful employment again.

While she reports eventually winning over many men who did not want women on the worksite, being female excluded her from workplace social interactions, such as camping trips, designed to strengthen male bonding.

These quotes illustrate the hardships that women working in blue-collar jobs often face at work: being passed over for hiring and promotions in favor of less productive male coworkers, having their hard work go unrecognized, and not being completely accepted.[2] Having this experience of being women in an occupation or industry composed mostly of men can create, then, a heightened appreciation of gaining reward and recognition for job performance as men.

Another form of reward that some transmen report receiving post-transition is a type of bodily respect in the form of being freed from unwanted sexual advances or inquiries about sexuality. As Brian recounts about his experience of working as a waitress, that customer service involved "having my boobs grabbed, being called 'honey' and 'babe.'" He noted that as a man, he no longer has to worry about these types of experiences. Jason reported being constantly harassed by men bosses for sexual favors in the past. He added, "When I transitioned...it was like a relief! [laughs]...I swear to God! I am not saying I was beautiful or sexy but I was always attracting something." He felt that becoming a man meant more personal space and less sexual harassment. Finally, Stephen and Henry reported being "obvious dykes," here meaning visibly masculine women, and added that in blue-collar jobs, they encountered sexualized comments, as well as invasive personal questions about sexuality, from men uncomfortable with their gender presentation, experiences they no longer face post-transition. Transitioning for stealth FTMs can bring with it physical autonomy and respect, as men workers, in general, encounter less touching, groping, and sexualized comments at work than women. Open FTMs, however, are not as able to access this type of privilege, as coworkers often ask invasive questions about their genitals and sexual practices.

Economic Gains

As the last two sections have shown, FTMs can find themselves gaining in authority, respect, and reward in the workplace post-transition. Several FTMs who are stealth also reported a sense that transition had brought with it economic opportunities that would not have been available to them as women, particularly as masculine women.

Carl, who owns his own company, asserts that he could not have followed the same career trajectory if he had not transitioned:

> I have this company that I built, and I have people following me; they trust me, they believe in me, they respect me. There is no way I could have done that as a woman. And I will tell you that as just a fact. That when it comes to business and work, higher levels of management, it is different being a man. I have been on both sides [as a man and a woman], younger obviously, but I will tell you, man, I could have never done what I did [as a female]. You can take the same personality and it wouldn't have happened. I would have never made it.

While he acknowledges that women can be and are business entrepreneurs, he has a sense that his business partners would not have taken his business venture idea seriously if he were a woman or that he might not have had access to the type of social networks that made his business venture possible. Henry feels that he would not have reached the same level in his professional job if he were a woman because he had a non-normative gender appearance:

> If I was a gender normative woman, probably. But no, as an obvious dyke, I don't think so...which is weird to say but I think it's true. It is interesting because

I am really aware of having this job that I would not have had if I hadn't transitioned. And [gender expression] was always an issue for me. I wanted to go to law school but I couldn't do it. I couldn't wear the skirts and things females have to wear to practice law. I wouldn't dress in that drag. And so it was very clear that there was a limit to where I was going to go professionally because I was not willing to dress that part. Now I can dress the part and it's not an issue. It's not putting on drag; it's not an issue. I don't love putting on a tie, but I can do it. So this world is open to me that would not have been before just because of clothes. But very little has changed in some ways. I look very different but I still have all the same skills and all the same general thought processes. That is intense for me to consider.

As this response shows, Henry is aware that as an "obvious dyke," meaning here a masculine-appearing woman, he would have the same skills and education level he currently has, but those skills would be devalued due to his non-normative appearance. Thus, he avoided professional careers that would require a traditionally feminine appearance. As a man, however, he is able to wear clothes similar to those he wore as an "obvious dyke," but they are now considered gender appropriate. Thus, through transitioning, he gains the right to wear men's clothes, which helps him in accessing a professional job. . . .

In my sample, the transmen who openly transitioned faced a different situation in terms of economic gains. While there is an "urban legend" that FTMs immediately are awarded some kind of "male privilege" post-transition (Dozier 2005), I did not find that in my interviews. Reflecting this common belief, however, Trevor and Jake both recount that women colleagues told them, when learning of their transition plans, that they would probably be promoted because they were becoming white men. While both men discounted these comments, both were promoted relatively soon after their transitions. Rather than seeing this as evidence of male privilege, both respondents felt that their promotions were related to their job performance, which, to make clear, is not a point I am questioning. Yet these promotions show that while these two men are not benefiting undeservedly from transition, they also are not disadvantaged.[3] Thus, among the men I interviewed, it is common for both stealth and open FTMs to find their abilities and skills more valued post-transition, showing that human capital can be valued differently depending on the gender of the employee.

Barriers to Workplace Gender Advantages

Having examined the accounts of transmen who feel that they received increased authority, reward, and recognition from becoming men at work, I will now discuss some of the limitations to accessing workplace gender advantages. About one-third of my sample felt that they did not receive any gender advantage from transition. FTMs who had only recently begun transition or who had transitioned without using hormones ("no ho") all reported seeing little change in their workplace treatment. This group of respondents felt that they were still seen as women by most of their coworkers, evidenced by continual slippage into feminine pronouns, and thus were not treated in accordance with other men in the workplace. Other transmen in this group felt they lacked authority because they were young or looked extremely young after transition. This youthful appearance often is an effect of the beginning stages of transition. FTMs usually begin to pass as men before they start taking testosterone. Successful passing is done via appearance cues, such as hairstyles, clothes, and mannerisms. However, without facial hair or visible stubble, FTMs often are taken to be young boys, a mistake that intensifies with the onset of hormone therapy and the development of peach fuzz that marks the beginning of facial hair growth. Reflecting on how this youthful appearance, which can last several years depending on the effects of hormone therapy, affected his work experience immediately after transition, Thomas reports, "I went from looking 30 to looking 13. People thought I was a new lawyer so I would get treated like I didn't know what was going on." Other FTMs recount being asked if they were interns, or if they were visiting a parent at their workplace, all comments that underscore a lack of authority. This lack of authority associated with looking youthful, however, is a time-bounded effect, as most FTMs on hormones eventually "age into" their male appearance, suggesting that many of these transmen may have the ability to access some gender advantages at some point in their careers.

Body structure was another characteristic some FTMs felt limited their access to increased authority and prestige at work. While testosterone creates an appearance indistinguishable from bio men for many transmen, it does not increase height. Being more than 6 feet tall is part of the cultural construction for successful, hegemonic masculinity. However, several men I interviewed were between 5' 1" and 5' 5", something they felt put them at a disadvantage in relation to other men in their workplaces. Winston, who managed a professional work staff who knew him only as a man, felt that his authority was harder to establish at work because he was short. Being smaller than all of his male employees meant that he was always being looked down on, even when giving orders. Kelly, who worked in special education, felt his height affected the jobs he was assigned: "Some of the boys, especially if they are really aggressive, they do much better with males that are bigger than they are. So I work with the little kids because I am short. I don't get as good of results if I work with [older kids]; a lot of times they are taller than I am." Being a short man, he felt it was harder to establish authority with older boys. These experiences demonstrate the importance of bringing the body back into discussions of masculinity and gender advantage, as being short can constrain men's benefits from the "patriarchal dividend" (Connell 1995).

In addition to height, race/ethnicity can negatively affect FTMs' workplace experiences post-transition. My data suggest that the experiences of FTMs of color is markedly different than that of their white counterparts, as they are becoming not just men but Black men, Latino men, or Asian men, categories that carry their own stereotypes. Christopher felt that he was denied any gender advantage at work not only because he was shorter than all of his men colleagues but also because he was viewed as passive, a stereotype of Asian men (Espiritu 1997). "To the wide world of America, I look like a passive Asian guy. That is what they think when they see me. Oh Asian? Oh passive.... People have this impression that Asian guys aren't macho and therefore they aren't really male. Or they are not as male as [a white guy]." Keith articulated how his social interactions changed with his change in gender attribution in this way: "I went from being an obnoxious Black woman to a scary Black man." He felt that he has to be careful expressing anger and frustration at work (and outside of work) because now that he is a Black man, his anger is viewed as more threatening by whites. Reflecting stereotypes that conflate African Americans with criminals, he also notes that in his law enforcement classes, he was continually asked to play the suspect in training exercises. Aaron, one of the only racial minorities at his workplace, also felt that looking like a Black man negatively affected his workplace interactions. He told stories about supervisors repeatedly telling him he was threatening. When he expressed frustration during a staff meeting about a new policy, he was written up for rolling his eyes in an "aggressive" manner. The choice of words such as "threatening" and "aggressive," words often used to describe Black men (Ferguson 2000), suggests that racial identity and stereotypes about Black men were playing a role in his workplace treatment. Examining how race/ethnicity and appearance intersect with gender, then, illustrates that masculinity is not a fixed construct that automatically generated privilege (Connell 1995), but that white, tall men often see greater returns from the patriarchal dividend than short men, young men and men of color.

Notes

1. This change in how behavior is evaluated can also be negative. Some transmen felt that assertive communication styles they actively fostered to empower themselves as lesbians and feminists had to be unlearned after transition. Because they were suddenly given more space to speak as men, they felt they had to censor themselves or they would be seen as "bossy white men" who talked over women and people of color. These findings are similar to those reported by Dozier (2005).
2. It is important to note that not all FTMs who worked blue-collar jobs as women had this type of experience. One respondent felt that he was able to fit in, as a butch, as "just one of the guys." However, he also did not feel he had an outsider-within perspective because of this experience.
3. Open transitions are not without problems, however. Crispin, a construction worker, found his contract mysteriously not renewed after his announcement. However, he acknowledged that he had many problems with his employers prior to his announcement and had also recently filed a discrimination suit. Aaron, who announced his transition at a small, medical site, left after a few months as he felt that his employer was trying to force him out. He found another job in which he was out as a transman. Crispin unsuccessfully attempted to find work in construction as an out transman. He was later hired, stealth, at a construction job.

References

Butler, D., and F. L. Geis. 1990. Nonverbal affect responses to male and female leaders: Implications for leadership evaluation. *Journal of Personality and Social Psychology* 58: 48–59.

Byrd, Barbara. 1999. Women in carpentry apprenticeship: A case study. *Labor Studies Journal* 24 (3): 3–22.

Connell, Raewyn. 1995. *Masculinities.* Berkeley: University of California Press.

Dozier, Raine. 2005. Beards, breasts, and bodies: Doing sex in a gendered world. *Gender & Society* 19: 297–316.

Elliott, James R., and Ryan A. Smith. 2004. Race, gender, and workplace power. *American Sociological Review* 69: 365–386.

Espiritu, Yen. 1997. *Asian American women and men.* Thousand Oaks, CA: Sage.

Padavic, Irene, and Barbara Reskin. 2002. *Women and men at work.* 2d ed. Thousand Oaks, CA: Pine Forge Press.

Pierce, Jennifer. 1995. *Gender trials: Emotional lives in contemporary law firms.* Berkeley: University of California Press.

Valian, Virginia. 1999. *Why so slow? The advancement of women.* Cambridge, MA: MIT Press.

Williams, Christine. 1995. *Still a man's world: Men who do "women's" work.* Berkeley: University of California Press.

Yoder, Janice, and Patricia Aniakudo. 1997. Outsider within the firehouse: Subordination and difference in the social interactions of African American women firefighters. *Gender & Society* 11: 324–341.

DISENTANGLING GENDER FROM SEX

Those whose bodies are most congruent with the established categories still have to learn to use them in socially appropriate ways. Sex-designated public bathrooms are a common form of category control. Bathrooms are a major hassle for many transgender people and even other gender non-conforming people. The social policing of bathrooms has led to many individuals having to account for themselves, often in humiliating detail. Like bathroom traffic, much of social life and ritual is based on bodily gendered expectations. Individuals are encouraged, through positive and negative social sanctions, to behave in gender-congruent ways. "Pregnant man" sounds like a complete contradiction. When actually confronted with one, interactions are destabilized, as Paisley Currah's excerpt illustrates.

Expectant Bodies: The Pregnant Man

◆◆◆

Paisley Currah

Brooklyn College, City University of New York

In April 2008, news about an Oregon man's impending parenthood spawned a media tsunami across the United States and even internationally. "Man Is Six Months Pregnant," reported CBS news. "The Pregnant Man Speaks Out," announced *People* magazine as it hyped the first published show-all pictures. "Pregnant Man Is Feeling Swell," punned the *New York Post*. ABC news highlighted his television debut in its story "'It's My Right to Have Kid,' Pregnant Man Tells Oprah." "She's Pregnant, but She's a Man," headlined the *Sydney Morning Herald*. "Pregnant, yes—but not a man," huffed an editorialist in the *International Herald Tribune*.

The riveting "pregnant man" lead drew readers and viewers further into the story. It was usually in the second paragraph that audiences were provided with an explanation. The pregnant man was Thomas Beatie, a transgender man who had had "top" surgery and been on hormone therapy but had stopped taking testosterone in anticipation of getting pregnant. A quick and unscientific survey of the blogosphere indicates that the news was met with disbelief, curiosity, revulsion, annoyance, indifference, and, less often, celebration. Some bloggers felt that "she" was still a woman; others thought transitioning should mean Beatie had forfeited his right to give birth; still others (usually women) expressed annoyance at all the attention the first "pregnant man" was getting. A small proportion seemed to have no problem getting their mind around the idea.

The story originally came to light at the end of March, when Beatie published a first-person account in the *Advocate*, a *Time*–like weekly magazine marketed to the U.S. gay community. In that essay, Beatie describes the travails he and his wife went through as they tried to find medical professionals who would work with them. Some refused to treat Beatie because of their religious beliefs; one physician told Beatie he would have to shave his beard; a third consulted with his hospital's ethics board and then turned him away (Beatie 2008).

For trans people in the United States, much of Beatie's narrative resonated with their own experience. While it is rare, but not unheard of in trans communities, for people who have transitioned to give birth, his larger story of discrimination in the health care industry is depressingly familiar. T. Benjamin Singer has studied the inability of many medical professionals to provide appropriate care to people whose bodies somehow exceed conventional expectations. He examines the "terror" engendered by the unknown through a frame he labels the "transgender sublime," which he describes as the "conceptual limit to a service-provider's ability to recognize the legibility and meanings of trans identities and bodies" (2006, 616). The "common sense" of gender says that birth sex, gender identity, and the secondary sex characteristics that later develop will all be in alignment.

But the histories, spatial arrangements, and physical terrains of trans people's bodies can confound conventional expectations. Some bodies are modified through hormones, various types of gender reassignment surgeries, or both, to produce bodies culturally commensurate with gender identities. In those cases, the perceived incongruence comes only from knowing the *history* of that individual's body. Other bodies, however, have unexpected configurations in their particular *geographies*—for example, breasts with penises for some, male chests with vaginas in others—that produce a dissonance. (This dissonance, to be clear, belongs not to the trans body but to those gazers who have conventional gender expectations.) The more easily read and specific physical terrains of bodies, such as the presence or absence of facial hair, baldness, or patterns of musculature, can add a third layer of potential contradiction. (Ironically, these configurations of geography and terrain often are determined by one's lack of access to medical care. Medicaid and almost all private insurance plans specifically exclude hormones and gender reassignment surgeries for trans people. From personal choice or because of the great expense, the vast majority of transgender men and most transgender women forego genital surgery [Pooja and Arkles 2007]. Hormones, whether attained through prescriptions or bought on the street, are cheaper.)

The stupefied resistance to bodies that confound gender expectations isn't limited to ob-gyn offices or maternity wards. The presence of someone whose gender identity or gender expression is not traditionally associated with the sex assigned to them at birth can bring people to very brink of cognition, and beyond it, in any setting customarily segregated by gender: bathrooms and locker rooms, homeless shelters, and correctional facilities, among others.

Judging (unscientifically, again) from informal conversations I've had with acquaintances, that a man can get pregnant may be the central, and for many the only, fact that most people in the United States now know about transgender issues. But among trans people, Beatie's story was of interest primarily because it generated so much scrutiny in the mainstream media.

It's not just in gender-segregated physical locations like locker rooms or maternity wards where the sex binary is policed. State processes of sex classification also rely on the idea that the body must cohere in predictable ways with gender identity. For example, in 2005–2006, advocates attempted to get New York City to amend its rules for sex classification on birth certificates. They argued that requiring transgender people to have genital surgery before changing their sex on their birth certificate was unfair and did not reflect the current state of transgender health care (Currah and Moore 2009). The public response to the proposal is summed up by this comment: "How might it be possible for someone with male genitals to now be listed as being female? Is everyone expected to be blind? I can understand if one had a sex change but simply dressing in the clothing of the opposite sex does not qualify a person of that sex" (New York City Board of Health and Mental Hygiene 2006). The effort failed. In New York City, to have the "M" on their birth certificate replaced with an "F," transgender women must prove they have had a vaginoplasty; to have an "M" on the birth certificate, transgender men must prove they have had a phalloplasty, although less than 3 percent of trans men have had one, according to one study (Newfield, Hart, Dibble, and Kohler 2006).

In the past three decades, feminist theory and activism has had great success in dislodging the notion that gender is the same as sex. Many of the social imperatives that used to be explained through the biologistic prism of sex difference are now framed as gender norms. For example, even conservatives have accepted the gradual expansion of sex discrimination laws to include discrimination based on gender stereotyping. As Justice Antonin Scalia points out, "The word 'gender' has acquired the new and useful connotation of cultural or attitudinal characteristics (as opposed to physical characteristics) distinctive to the sexes" (*J.E.B. v. Alabama* 1994).

Despite the inroads made in divorcing sex from gender *norms* and gender *expression*, however, we haven't yet succeeded in disentangling gender identity from sex. In much of the legislation, case law, and administrative rules that discipline the identities of transgender people, it's still the sexed characteristics of bodies that matter. And notions of sex are still governed by logics demanding coherence. Bodies that disrupt those expectations aren't always welcome.

References

Beatie, Thomas. 2008. "Labor of Love." *Advocate*, March 26, 2008. http://www.advocate.com/exclusive_detail_ektid52947.asp.

Currah, Paisley, and Lisa Jean Moore. 2008. "'We Won't Know Who You Are': Contesting Sex Designations on New York City Birth Certificates." *Hypatia: Journal of Feminist Philosophy* 24: 113–135.

Dahir, Mubarak. 1999. "Whose Movement Is It?" *Advocate*, 26 May, 50–55.

Employment Non-Discrimination Act of 2007. 2007. U.S. Congress. House. HR 2015 and HR 3685. 110th Cong., 1st session.

Gehi, Pooja S., and Gabriel Arkles. 2007. "Unraveling Injustice: Race and Class Impact of Medicaid Exclusions of Transition-Related Health Care for Transgender People." *Sexuality Research and Social Policy: Journal of NSRC* 4 (4): 7–35. J.E.B. v. Alabama Ex Rel. T.B. 1994. 511 U.S. 127.

National Center for Transgender Equality and the Transgender Law and Policy Institute. 2003. "Transgender Leaders Laud Unified Voice of GLBT Community in Federal Legislative Efforts." News release, June 17. http://www.transgenderlaw.org/release.htm.

Newfield, Emily, Stacey Hart, Suzanne Dibble, and Lori Kohler. 2006. "Female-to-Male Transgender Quality of Life." *Quality of Life Research* 15(9): 1447–57.

New York City Board of Health and Mental Hygiene. 2006. "Resolution Comments-NYC Birth Certificate for Transgender People."

Singer, T. Benjamin. 2006. "From the Medical Gaze to *Sublime Mutations*: The Ethics of (Re)Viewing Non-normative Body Images." In *The Transgender Studies Reader*, ed. Susan Stryker and Stephen Whittle. New York: Routledge.

CRITICAL SUMMARY

Multiple genders, sexes, and sexualities show that the conventional categories are not universal or essential, nor are the social processes that produce dominance and subordination. Border crossers and those living on borders have opened a social dialogue over the power of categories, and their resistances, refusals, and transgressions have encouraged political activism.

The goals and political uses of community and identity have not been uniform. Those whose bodies don't conform to norms—hefty, tall women and short, slender men—don't want to change their bodies or their gender; they want gender norms to expand. Some MTFs and FTMs modify their bodies surgically and hormonally and walk, talk, dress, and gesture convincingly in order to embody femininity or masculinity. Like most of us, they support rather than challenge the gendered social order. Other transgender people have mixed gender presentations, or want to live openly as "transgender."

What would happen if a third category—"transgender"—was added to the familiar two? Rather than weakening the power of categories to control heterogeneous and diverse lives, the establishment of another category starts the cycle of boundary definition and border disputes all over again. New categories also enter the political arena with demands for social recognition and distribution of rewards and privileges. Older identity-based political groups of gays, lesbians, transgender, and intersexed people argue that the new groups undercut their claims of discrimination and siphon off economic resources.

As this chapter demonstrates, all gendered bodies to varying degrees must engage with the larger gendered social order. Transgender people are often forced to account for themselves in deeply private ways or in humiliating detail. This act of accounting for oneself demonstrates the depths of social expectations of our gendered bodies and how our culture reproduces gender binaries. By learning about the experiences of transgender people, we can better understand the ways *all* gendered bodies are produced at the intersections of the material and the symbolic, the flesh and the self.

NOTE

1. The terms come from the Latin prefix *cis*, meaning "on the same side." Contrasted to *trans, cis* refers to the alignment of gender identity with assigned gender.

REFERENCES AND RECOMMENDED READINGS

Adams, Ross. 2009. "Senior Yearbook Photo Causes Controversy." WJTV.COM. http://www2.wjtv.com/jtv/news/local/article/senior_yearbook_photo_causes_controversy/43650/.

Ames, Jonathan (ed.). 2005. *Sexual Metamorphosis: An Anthology of Transsexual Memoirs.* New York: Vintage.

Bernstein, Fred A. 2004. "On Campus, Rethinking Biology 101." *New York Times*, Sunday Styles, 7 March. http://www.nytimes.com/2004/03/07/style/on-campus-rethinking-biology-101.html?sec=health.

Bettcher, Talia, and Ann Garry. 2009. "Transgender Studies and Feminism: Theory, Politics and Gendered Realities." Special Issue of *Hypatia*. 24 (3).

Bornstein, Kate. 1994. *Gender Outlaw: On Men, Women and the Rest of Us*. New York: Routledge.

Broadus, Kylar. 2006. "The Evolution of Employment Discrimination Protections for Transgender People," in *Transgender Rights*, edited by Paisley Currah, Richard Juang, and Shannon Price Minter. Minneapolis: University of Minnesota Press.

Brown, Patricia Leigh. 2005. "A Quest for a Restroom That's Neither Men's Room Nor Women's Room." *New York Times*, 4 March, A14.

Butler, Judith. 2001. "Doing Justice to Someone: Sex Reassignment and Allegories of Transsexuality." *GLQ: A Journal of Lesbian and Gay Studies* 7: 621–636.

Califia, Pat. 1997. *Sex Changes: The Politics of Transgenderism*. San Francisco CA: Cleis Press.

Connell, Raewyn. 2009. "Accountable Conduct: 'Doing Gender' in Transsexual and Political Retrospect. *Gender & Society* 23: 104–111.

Cromwell, Jason. 1999. *Transmen and FTMs: Identities, Bodies, Genders, and Sexualities*. Chicago: University of Chicago Press.

Currah, Paisley. 2006. "Gender Pluralisms Under the Transgender Umbrella," in *Transgender Rights*, edited by Paisley Currah, Richard M. Juang, and Shannon Price Minter. Minneapolis: University of Minnesota Press.

Currah, Paisley. 2009. "The Transgender Rights Imaginary," in *Feminist and Queer Legal Theory: Intimate Encounters, Uncomfortable Conversations*, edited by Martha Albertson Fineman, Jack E. Jackson, and Adam P. Romero. Surrey, UK: Ashgate Press.

Currah, Paisley, and Lisa Jean Moore. 2009. "'We Won't Know Who You Are': Contesting Sex Designations on New York City Birth Certificates." *Hypatia: Journal of Feminist Philosophy* 24: 113–135.

Denny, Dallas (ed.). 1997. *Current Concepts in Transgender Identity*. New York: Garland Publishing.

Devor, Holly [Aaron Devor]. 1989. *Gender Blending: Confronting the Limits of Duality*. Bloomington: Indiana University Press.

———. 1997. *FTM: Female-to-Male Transsexuals in Society*. Bloomington: Indiana University Press.

Dozier, Raine. 2005. "Beards, Breasts, and Bodies: Doing Sex in a Gendered World." *Gender & Society* 19: 297–316.

Ekins, Richard, and Dave King. 2006. *The Transgender Phenomenon*. London: Sage.

Epstein, Julia, and Kristina Straub (eds.). 1991. *Body Guards: The Cultural Politics of Gender Ambiguity*. New York: Routledge.

Feinberg, Leslie. 1996. *Transgender Warriors: Making History from Joan of Arc to Dennis Rodham*. Boston: Beacon Press.

Gamson, Joshua G. 1995. "Must Identity Movements Self-Destruct? A Queer Dilemma." *Social Problems* 42: 390–407.

———. 1997. "Messages of Exclusion: Gender, Movements and Symbolic Boundaries." *Gender & Society* 11: 178–199.

———. 1998. *Freaks Talk Back: Tabloid Talk Shows and Sexual Nonconformity*. Chicago: University of Chicago Press.

Girshick, Lori B. 2008. *Transgender Voices: Beyond Women and Men*. Lebanon, NH: University Press of New England.

Halberstam, Judith. 1998. *Female Masculinity*. Durham, NC: Duke University Press.

Hale, C. Jacob. 1998. "Consuming the Living, Dis(re)membering the Dead in the Butch/ FTM Borderlands." *Journal of Gay and Lesbian Studies* 4: 311–348.

Hausman, Bernice L. 1995. *Changing Sex: Transsexualism, Technology, and the Idea of Gender*. Durham, NC: Duke University Press.

Herdt, Gilbert (ed.). 1994. *Third Sex, Third Gender: Beyond Sexual Dimorphism in Culture and History*. New York: Zone Books.

Heyes, Cressida J. 2003. "Feminist Solidarity after Queer Theory: The Case of Transgender." *Signs* 28: 1093–1120.

Hines, Sally. 2005. " 'I am a Feminist but…': Transgender Men and Women and Feminism," in *Different Wavelengths: Studies of the Contemporary Women's Movement*, edited by Jo Reger. New York: Routledge.

Hines, Sally. 2007. "(Trans)Forming Gender: Social Change and Transgender Citizenship." *Sexualities*. 7: 345–362.

Jacobs, Sue-Ellen, Wesley Thomas, and Sabine Lang (eds.). 1997. *Two-Spirit People: Native American Gender Identity, Sexuality, and Spirituality*. Urbana: University of Illinois Press.

Kessler, Suzanne J., and Wendy McKenna. 1978. *Gender: An Ethnomethodological Approach*. Chicago: University of Chicago.

Lorber, Judith. 1999. "Crossing Borders and Erasing Boundaries: Paradoxes of Identity Politics." *Sociological Focus* 32: 355–369.

———. 2001. "It's the 21st Century—Do You Know What Gender You Are?" in *An International Feminist Challenge to Theory*, edited by Marcia Texler Segal and Vasilikie Demos, *Advances in Gender Research*, V.5, Greenwich, CT: JAI Press.

Mason-Schrock, Douglas. 1996. "Transsexuals' Narrative Construction of the True Self." *Social Psychology Quarterly* 59: 176–192.

Meyerowitz, Joanne. 2002. *How Sex Changed: A History of Transsexuality in the United States*. Cambridge, MA: Harvard University Press.

Middlebrook, Diane Wood. 1998. *Suits Me: The Double Life of Billy Tipton*. Boston: Houghton Mifflin.

Najmabadi, Afsaneh. 2005. *Women with Mustaches and Men without Beards: Gender and Sexual Anxieties of Iranian Modernity*. Berkeley, CA: University of California Press.

Namaste, Viviane. 2000. *Invisible Lives: The Erasure of Transsexual and Transgendered People*. Chicago: University of Chicago Press.

Pfeffer, Carla A. 2010. "Women's Work? Women Partners of Transgender Men Doing Housework and Emotion Work." *Journal of Marriage and Family* 72: 165-183.

Plemons, Eric. 2010. "Envisioning The Body in Relation: Finding Sex, Changing Sex," in *The Body Reader: Essential Social and Cultural Readings*, edited by Lisa Jean Moore and Mary Kosut. New York: New York University Press.

Prosser, Jay. 1998. *Second Skin: The Body Narratives of Transsexuality*. New York: Columbia University Press.

Raymond, J. G. 1979. *The Transsexual Empire: The Making of the She-male*. Boston: Beacon.

Roen, Katrina. 2002. " 'Either/Or' and "Both/Neither": Discursive Tensions in Transgender Politics." *Signs* 27: 501–522.

Rubin, Gayle S. 1992. "Of Catamites and Kings: Reflections on Butch, Gender, and Boundaries," in *The Persistent Desire: A Femme-Butch Reader*, edited by Joan Nestle. Boston: Allyson Publications.

Schilt, Kristen, and Laurel Westbrook. 2009. "Doing Gender, Doing Heteronormativity: 'Gender Normals,' Transgender People, and the Social Maintenance of Heterosexuality." *Gender & Society* 23: 440–464.

Schrock, Douglas, Lori Reid, and Emily M. Boyd. 2005. "Transessuals' Embodiment of Womanhood." *Gender & Society* 19: 317–335.

Scott-Dixon, Krista. 2006. *Trans/Feminisms: Transfeminist Voices Speak Out.* Toronto: Sumach Press.

Spade, Dean. 2003. "Resisting Medicine/Remodeling Gender." *Berkeley Women's Law Journal.* 18: 15–37.

Stone, Sandy. 1991. "The Empire Strikes Back: A Posttranssexual Manifesto," in *Body Guards: The Cultural Politics of Gender Ambiguity,* edited by Julia Epstein and Kristina Straub. New York: Routledge.

Stryker, Susan. 2008. *Transgender History.* Berkeley, CA: Seal Press.

Stryker, Susan, and Stephen Whittle. 2006. *The Transgender Studies Reader.* New York: Routledge.

Valentine, David. 2007. *Imagining Transgender: An Ethnography of Category.* Durham, NC: Duke University Press.

Vidal-Ortiz, Salvador. 2009. "The Figure of the Transwoman of Color Through the Lens of 'Doing Gender'." *Gender & Society.* 23: 99–103.

West, Candace, and Sarah Fenstermaker. 1995. "Doing Difference." *Gender & Society* 9: 8–37.

West, Candace, and Don Zimmerman. 1987. "Doing Gender." *Gender & Society* 1: 125–151.

Wickman, J. 2001. *Transgender Politics: The Construction and Deconstruction of Binary Gender in the Finnish Transgender Community.* Åbo, Finland: Åbo Akademi University Press.

Wilchins, Ricky Anne. 1997. *Read My Lips: Sexual Subversion and the End of Gender.* New York: Firebrand Books.

Winerip, Michael. 2009. "Anything He Can Do, She Can Do." *New York Times,* Sunday Styles, 15 November, 2.

CHAPTER 6

Sports

The Playing Grounds of Gender

Key concepts

gender verification, intersex, locker-room mentality, manhood sports formula,
media production of professional athletes, sex tests, sports and violence, Title IX

"Can you have sports without gender?" That seems like a stupid question, because humans have always devised games and competitions that pit people of similar size and strength against each other, and since males and females differ on those two aspects, of course they would divide by gender. Isn't the division then by physiology—musculature, endurance, and other physical abilities? And do human males and females so clearly divide on physical abilities? We behave as if they do, because when other criteria for competition are introduced—people in wheelchairs competing against each other, amputees competing against each other and even against able-bodied athletes, weight classes, age groups—they, too, are divided into two different gender categories. Girls and boys may play on the same teams when they are young, but not when they reach puberty. In professional sports, in major collegiate competitions, and in the Olympics, the rule is that women don't compete against men. The rationale, of course, is that it wouldn't be fair, because women would always lose. Would they? We'll never know, because they don't compete publicly against men.

In a well-known article that challenged the gendered division of bodies in sports, Mary Jo Kane, Director of the Tucker Center for Research on Girls & Women in Sport at the University of Minnesota, argued that we are prevented from seeing sports as a continuum by strict gender segregation. Through several interrelated practices, we become blinded to the extent of overlap between women's and men's sports performances and to the possibility that women could outperform men. Kane says,

> Although we should never underestimate the importance of male bonding as an exclusionary practice or of men's extreme desire to differentiate themselves from women, we have tended to ignore another reason why men resist integration so fiercely: They are deeply afraid that many women can outperform them, even in

those sports and physical skills/attributes that they have claimed as their own. What better way to deflect such fears than to create segregationist ideologies and practices that will ensure that these possibilities rarely (if ever) come to pass. (1995, 206)

Exactly how women and men are segregated in sports is easy to list: Many sports are gender-typed—few women in the United States play football, and few men are synchronized swimmers. Where women and men play the same popular sports, such as tennis, golf, and gymnastics, the rules and events are different. The women front-runners in marathons, who have beaten the times of a couple of hundred men, are compared only to the men front-runners, who run faster, although women are quickly catching up to them (McDonagh and Pappano 2008, 71–74).

Sports, especially public sports—professional, major collegiate, the Olympics— are divided by *gender*, not sex. Gender is a culturally constructed category whose markers are physical anatomy—visible genitalia, internal procreative organs, hormonal output, chromosomes—none of which are securely and permanently and in every case neatly demarcated into two and only two clearly distinguishable groups. Variations and transmutations in all of these physical markers have caused contentions over gender categorization in sports. The International Olympic Committee dropped gender verification tests for women in 2000. In 2004, it ruled that male-to-female and female-to-male transgender people could compete in their new gender, provided they had had "appropriate surgery," had completed hormone treatment two years before, and were legally recognized as members of their new gender.

The contested issue has now shifted to possible intersex effects. In 2009, when Caster Semenya, an 18-year-old South African woman, won the 800-meter race at the World Championships in Athletics in Berlin, her womanhood was challenged by one of her competitors, and a gender verification test was called for (Clarey and Kolata 2009). Semenya won with a time of 1 minute 55.45 seconds, the best in the world in 2009, beating the defending champion by 2.45 seconds. Her time was not the all-time fastest, yet none of the other champions had to prove they are women. Semenya was described in one news report as having "an unusually developed muscular frame and a deep voice" (Kessel 2009), hardly accurate criteria for gender verification. After extensive testing, Semenya was allowed to keep her medal, but the results of the tests were not made public (Longman 2009b).

The Olympics Committee, faced with the "muddled and vexing mess" of sex testing, was advised by experts to give up the attempt to clearly categorize athletes as male or female:

> The Endocrine Society, the organization whose members treat people with such disorders, says sports federations should not even try to use medical tests to rule on who is a woman. Instead, it says, the criterion should be: Was the athlete raised as a male or a female? Someone who was raised as a female and considers herself female, the organization says, should be allowed to compete as a female.

> Sports is inherently unfair, regardless of sex ambiguities, says Dr. Eric Vilain, an invited participant at the Olympic committee meeting and the director of the U.C.L.A. Center for Gender-Based Biology. Elite athletes have inborn advantages

over the rest of the population. That is why they can train and be the best in the world. "Nobody says there should be a level playing field," Vilain said. "On the contrary. If you are gifted, you should do the sport." And while it might seem desirable to find some way of dealing with women whose sex is ambiguous, Dr. Vilain and other endocrinologists say it is best to abandon that quest. "It's just impossible," Vilain said. "We are going to have to accept that at the fringes, there are no perfect categorizations." (Kolata 2010a, D2) The Olympic Committee's decision was to recommend treatment in cases of sex ambiguity and testing on a case-by-case basis for eligibility to compete (Kolata 2010b).

Trying to develop "simple rules for complex gender realities" presents a major challenge to gender segregation, wrote Alice Dreger (2009), professor of clinical medical humanities and bioethics at Northwestern University. Genes don't tell you how a body functions physically. Measuring testosterone levels might give an indication of muscle mass, but testosterone levels aren't criteria for gender division. Men with low testosterone levels don't compete with women who have similar levels; rather, the men are allowed to boost their levels. In the following excerpt, Dreger lays out the variation in biological sex, which challenges the belief that sex is clearly binary, with clearly distinguishable markers of female and male.

Where's the Rulebook for Sex Verification?

◆◆◆

Alice Dreger
Feinberg School of Medicine, Northwestern University

The only thing we know for sure about Caster Semenya, the world-champion runner from South Africa, is that she will live the rest of her life under a cloud of suspicion after track and field's governing body announced it was investigating her sex. Why? Because the track organization, the I.A.A.F., has not sorted out the rules for sex typing and is relying on unstated, shifting standards.

To be fair, the biology of sex is a lot more complicated than the average fan believes. Many think you can simply look at a person's "sex chromosomes." If the person has XY chromosomes, you declare him a man. If XX, she's a woman. Right?

Wrong. A little biology: On the Y chromosome, a gene called SRY usually makes a fetus grow as a male. It turns out, though, that SRY can show up on an X, turning an XX fetus essentially male. And if the SRY gene does not work on the Y, the fetus develops essentially female.

Even an XY fetus with a functioning SRY can essentially develop female. In the case of Androgen Insensitivity Syndrome, the ability of cells to "hear" the masculinizing hormones known as androgens is lacking. That means the genitals and the rest of the external body look female-typical, except that these women lack body hair (which depends on androgen-sensitivity). Women with complete Androgen Insensitivity Syndrome are less "masculinized" in their muscles and brains than the average woman, because the average woman makes and "hears" some androgens. Want to tell women with Androgen Insensitivity Syndrome they have to compete as men, just because they have a Y chromosome? That makes no sense.

So, some say, just look at genitals. Forget the genes—pull down the jeans! The I.A.A.F. asks drug testers to do this. But because male and female genitals start from the same stuff, a person can have something between a penis and a clitoris, and still legitimately be thought of as a man or a woman. Moreover, a person can look male-typical on the outside but be female-typical on the inside, or vice versa.

A few years ago, I got a call from Matthew, a 19-year-old who was born looking obviously male, was raised a boy, and had a girlfriend and a male-typical life. Then he found out, by way of some medical problems, that he had ovaries and a uterus. Matthew had an extreme form of Congenital Adrenal Hyperplasia. His adrenal glands made so many androgens, even though he had XX chromosomes and ovaries, that his body developed to look male-typical. In fact, his body is mostly male-typical, including his muscle development and his self-identity.

O.K., you say, if chromosomes and genitals do not work, how about hormones? We might assume that it is hormones that really matter in terms of whether someone has an athletic advantage. Well, women and men make the same hormones, just in different quantities, on average. The average man has more androgens than the average woman. But to state the obvious, the average female athlete is not the average woman. In some sports, she is likely to have naturally high levels of androgens. That is probably part of why she has succeeded athletically. By the way, that is also why she is often flat-chested, boyish looking and may have a bigger-than-average clitoris. High levels of androgens can do all that. Sure, in certain sports, a woman with naturally high levels of androgens has an advantage. But is it an unfair advantage? I don't think so. Some men naturally have higher levels of androgens than other men. Is that unfair?

Consider an analogy: Men on average are taller than women. But do we stop women from competing if a male-typical height gives them an advantage over shorter women? Can we imagine a Michele Phelps or a Patricia Ewing being told, "You're too tall to compete as a woman?" So why would we want to tell some women, "You naturally have too high a level of androgens to compete as a woman?" There seems to be nothing wrong with this kind of natural advantage.

So where do we draw the line between men and women in athletics? I don't know. The fact is, sex is messy. This is demonstrated in the I.A.A.F.'s process for determining whether Semenya is in fact a woman. The organization has called upon a geneticist, an endocrinologist, a gynecologist, a psychologist and so forth. Sex is so messy that in the end, these doctors are not going to be able to run a test that will answer the question. Science can and will inform their decision, but they are going to have to decide which of the dozens of characteristics of sex matter to them. Their decision will be like the consensus regarding how many points are awarded for a touchdown and a field goal—it will be a sporting decision, not a natural one, about how we choose to play the game of sex.

These officials should—finally—come up with a clear set of rules for sex typing, one open to scientific review, one that will allow athletes like Semenya, in the privacy of their doctors' offices, to find out, before publicly competing, whether they will be allowed to win in the crazy sport of sex. I bet that's a sport no one ever told Semenya she would have to play.

Reprinted from Alice Dreger, "Where's the Rulebook for Sex Verification?" *New York Times*, August 22, 2009, D1, 3. Copyright © 2009 The New York Times Company. Reprinted by permission.

Given the variety of sex physiologies, as well as overlapping U-shaped curves of height and body mass for women and men, how do sports so successfully maintain gender segregation? It is by excluding those defined as women from men's terrain. In Western societies, gender-segregated sports, especially sports organized by schools, colleges, the Olympics, and professionally, are primarily men's sports. These sports produce gendered bodies and, in the process, masculinity and masculine cultural values. Girls and women athletes are a minor part of the picture. Heterosexuality is assumed, and is reinforced by a streak of homophobia (Anderson 2005, Roberts 2007).

LEARNING GENDER THROUGH SPORTS

Sports and gender are mutually reinforcing. Gendering creates an illusion that men's and women's athletic bodies are the result of natural physiologic differences, although it is quite evident that sports, among other social processes, shape children's and adults' bodies. The ways the resulting gendered bodies are used in sports feeds the gendering back into the culture, deepening the belief that female and male bodies are completely different, masking the extent to which they are *made* so very different from an early age, particularly through sports (Messner 2002, 2009).

Many gendered body characteristics we think of as inborn are the result of social practices. The phenomena of boys' boisterousness and girls' physical awkwardness in Western societies are examples. When little boys run around noisily, we say, "Boys will be boys," meaning that their physical assertiveness has to be in the Y chromosome, because it is manifest so early and so commonly in boys. Boys the world over, however, are not boldly physical—just those who are encouraged to use their bodies freely, cover space, take risks, and play outdoors at all kinds of games and sports. Conversely, what do we mean when we say, "She throws like a girl"? We usually mean that she throws like a female child, a carrier of XX chromosomes. After all, she is only 4 or 5 years old, so how could she have learned to be so awkward? In fact, as Iris Marion Young notes, she throws like a person who has already been taught to restrict her movements, to protect her body, and to use her body in ways that are approved of as feminine:

> Not only is there a typical style of throwing like a girl, but there is a more or less typical style of running like a girl, climbing like a girl, swinging like a girl, hitting like a girl. They have in common first that the whole body is not put into fluid and directed motion, but rather...the motion is concentrated in one body part; and...tends not to reach, extend, lean, stretch, and follow through in the direction of her intention. (Young 1990, 146)

The girl who experiences her body in such a limited way at an early age is a product of her culture and time. As she learns to restrict her moves, she simultaneously closes opportunities to develop the fluid, whole-bodied, unconstrained moves that are associated with outstanding achievement in sports. As social practices change and girls are encouraged to use their bodies the way boys do, they become formidable competitors—but they still are kept in their gendered place.

Children's body gendering starts very early. Children's play is organized in gendered ways, especially when it takes place in groups. Boys and girls are first separated by gender; then, these groups are gender-marked as girls' and boys' teams and expected to behave in gendered ways. Even the parents are gender segregated: fathers act as coaches, mothers as behind-the-scenes supportive "team moms" (Messner and Bozada-Deas 2009). For children, sports are important sites of developing self-esteem. They also offer talented athletes from poor families the possibility of upward mobility through college scholarships. Until recently, boys were encouraged to join sports teams as sites for the development of competitive masculinity; girls were trained through physical education to maintain their femininity. Over the past 30 years, through the strides of feminism and its advocacy of gender equity, girls and women have their own sports teams, but there is still uneasiness over how they should act as women, with the "threat" of lesbianism always lurking dangerously in the background (Ezzell 2009, Griffin 1998).

For boys and young men, vicarious participation in sports, as audience and as amateur players, validates their masculinity, but it also encourages aggression and violence.

SPORTS AND VIOLENCE

It is interesting to consider how many war or battle metaphors there are in sports. First, there is the internal battle to conquer physical limits and fight through pain. Part of the masculine embodiment in sports is to suffer pain as a rite of passage to legitimate manhood. Often, the pain is flaunted as a physical distinction of male bodies being different from and inherently superior to female bodies. To motivate their male teams, coaches will use female descriptors to humiliate or degrade—yelling at a soccer team during a dribbling drill, "You look like a bunch of girls!" and to a boxer in the ring, "You hit like a lady!" Alternatively, pejorative homosexual references are made about opponents—"Look at those fags." These degradations are an attempt to motivate boys and men to use their bodies more aggressively. Second, competition becomes an external battle, where individuals and teams are exhorted to "kill" their opponents. Third, sporting events often inspire violence among spectators in the form of hooliganism and riots. In the United States after major football and basketball victories, there is a rise in looting, arson, and assault. In Britain, a study of racist, xenophobic, and drunk British football fans showed the connection between sports fanaticism and mob violence (Buford 1993).

Vicarious participation in sports as fans is a way that men who have limited access to resources in educational and corporate institutions can express their masculinity. Another way is to engage in a one-on-one sport where training can be found locally. Boxing, a relatively inexpensive sport, has traditionally induced participation by men from minority ethnic backgrounds (Woodward 2006). Through this training, a young man enters a ritual-filled world and a community of men whose masculinity rides on being able to control and use violence to knock out a competitor.

As part of an ethnographic study of an economically depressed African-American neighborhood in Chicago, Loïc Wacquant, a White graduate student at the University of Chicago, signed up for boxing training at a gym a few blocks from his apartment. He stayed on for three-and-a-half years and turned his experience of the education of a boxer into a book, *Body and Soul*, from which the following excerpt is taken. Wacquant argues that not only the body is trained, but also the mind and emotions.

Controlled Violence: The Manly Sport

◆◆◆

Loïc Wacquant
University of California, Berkeley

... Sparring is not only a physical exercise; it is also the means and support of a particularly intense form of "emotion work."[1] Because "few lapses of self-control are punished as immediately and severely as loss of temper during a boxing bout,"[2] it is vital that one dominate at all times the impulses of one's affect. In the squared circle, one must be capable of managing one's emotions and know, according to the circumstances, how to contain or repress them or, on the contrary, how to stir and swell them; how to muzzle certain feelings (of anger, restiveness, frustration) so as to resist the blows, provocation, and verbal abuse dished out by one's opponent, as well as the "rough tactics" he may resort to (hitting below the belt or with his elbows, head-butting, rubbing his gloves into your eyes or over a facial cut in order to open it further, etc.); and how to call forth and amplify others (of aggressiveness or "controlled fury," for instance) at will while not letting them get out of hand.[3] In gloving up at the gym, boxers learn to become "businesslike" in the ring, to channel their mental and affective energies toward "getting the job done" in the most effective and least painful manner.

A boxer must exercise not only a constant inner surveillance over his feelings but also continual "expressive control" over their external "signaling"[4] so as not to let his opponent know if and when punches hurt him, and which one. Legendary trainer-manager Cus D'Amato, the "discoverer" of Mike Tyson, sums up the matter thus: "The fighter has mastered his emotions to the extent that he can conceal and control them. Fear is an asset to a fighter. It makes him move faster, be quicker and more alert. Heroes and cowards feel exactly the same fear. Heroes react to it differently."[5] This difference has nothing innate about it; it is an acquired ability, collectively produced by prolonged submission of the body to the discipline of sparring. Butch explains:

> **BUTCH:** You have to stay in control, because yer emotions will burn up all yer oxygen, so you have to stay calm and relaxed though you know this guy's tryin' to knock yer head off. You have to stay calm and relaxed. So you have to deal with the situation.

> **LOUIE:** Was it hard learning to control emotions, like to not get mad or frustrated if a guy is slippery and you can't hit him with clean shots?

> **BUTCH:** It was hard for me. It took me years-an'-years-an'-years to git that and juuus' when I was gittin' it under control real goo', then thin's, hum, started movin' for me. It works, well, I guess when it was time, it worked itself into place.

> **LOUIE:** Is that something that DeeDee taught you?

> **BUTCH:** He kept tellin' me to stay calm, relax. Jus' breathe, take it easy—but [his pace picks up] I foun' it har' to stay calm and relax when this guy's tryin' to kill ya over in the next corner, but eventually it sunk in and I understood what he was sayin'.

...Finally, the strictly physical aspect of sparring should not be neglected on account of being self-evident: one must not forget that "[b]oxing is more about getting hit than it is about hitting"; it is "primarily about being, and not giving, hurt."[6] The idiolect of boxing is replete with terms referring to the ability to take a punch and glorifying the capacity to endure pain. Now, beyond one's congenital endowment such as an "iron chin" or the mysterious and revered quality called "heart" (which also holds a central place in the masculine street culture of the ghetto), there is only one way to harden yourself to pain and to get your body used to taking blows, and that is to get hit regularly. For, contrary to a widespread popular notion, boxers have no personal predilection for pain and hardly enjoy getting pummeled. A young Italian-American welterweight from the Windy City Gym who recently turned pro gets indignant when I mention the lay stereotype of the "sadomasochistic" fighter.[7] "*Nah, we're human man! We're human,* you know, we're jus' like anybody else, our feelings are jus' as much as your feelin's, we—you can't put us outside, you know, (vehemently) *we're no different than you:* we're in the same world, we're the same world, the same flesh, same blood, same everything." What boxers have done is to elevate their threshold of tolerance for pain by submitting to it in graduated and regular fashion....

To learn how to box is to imperceptibly modify one's bodily schema, one's relation to one's body and to the uses one usually puts it to, so as to internalize a set of dispositions that are inseparably mental and physical and that, in the long run, turn the body into a virtual punching machine, but *an intelligent and creative machine capable of self-regulation* while innovating within a fixed and relatively restricted panoply of moves as an instantaneous function of the actions of the opponent in time. The mutual imbrication of corporeal dispositions and mental dispositions reaches such a degree that even will power, morale, determination, concentration, and the control of one's emotions change into so many reflexes inscribed within the organism. In the accomplished boxer, the mental becomes part of the physical and vice versa; body and mind function in total symbiosis. This is what is expressed in the scornful comments that DeeDee makes to boxers who argue that they are not "mentally ready" for a fight. After Curtis's loss in his first nationally televised fight in Atlantic City, the old trainer is fuming: "He don't lose 'cos he's not 'mentally ready.' That don' mean nuthin', mentally ready. If you're a fighter, you're ready. I was just tellin' Butch mentally ready, tha's bullshit! If you're a fighter, you get up in d'ring an' [hissing for emphasis] you *fight* there's no bein' mentally ready or not ready. It's not mental, ain't nuthin' mental bout it. If you're not a fighter, you don't get up in there, you don't fight. If you're a fighter, you're ready and you fight—tha's all. All d'rest is just *bullshit for the birds*." [Fieldnotes, 17 April 1989]

Notes

1. On the notion of "emotion work," see Arlie Hochschild, "Emotion Work, Feeling Rules, and Social Structure," *American Journal of Sociology* 85, 3 (November 1979): 551–575.
2. Konrad Lorenz, *On Aggression* (New York: Harcourt, Brace and World, 1966), 281.
3. One could show that this "sentimental education" is not limited to the sole pugilist: it encompasses all the specialized agents of the pugilistic field (trainers, managers, referees, judges, promoters, etc.) and even extends to spectators.
4. Erving Goffman, *Presentation of Self in Everyday Life* (Harmondsworth, England: Penguin, 1959), 59–60.
5. Cited by Stephen Brunt, *Mean Business* (Markham, Can: Penguin Books, 1987), 55.
6. Joyce Carol Oates, *On Boxing* (Garden City, N.Y.: Doubleday, 1987), 25 and 60.
7. This stereotype can be found in numerous scholarly works, such as Allen Gutman's historical thesis on the evolution of sports, *From Ritual to Record: The Nature of Modern Sports* (New York: Columbia University Press, 1989: see 160), as well as non-scholarly works, such as the encyclopedia of academic and journalistic cliches about prizefighting compiled from newspaper and sports magazine articles by André Rauch, *Boxe violence du XXe siècle* (Paris: Aubier, 1992). I detail other problems with Rauch's tome in the French edition of this book, *Corps et âme* (Marseilles: Agone, 2d expanded ed. 2002), 276–277.

PROFESSIONAL ATHLETES AND THE MEDIA

Gendering in sports is bolstered by the way athletes are depicted on television and described in newspapers. According to Michael Messner, there is a televised manhood sports formula that virtually trains a young male audience to the locker-room mentality that will govern their cultural lives—a version of masculinity "grounded in bravery, risk taking, violence, bodily strength, and heterosexuality" (2002, 126). The telecasts, announcers' commentaries, and commercials glorify violence, denigrate men who don't seem to be masculine enough, and show women as sexy prizes for the truly masculine, winning guys. The connection between audience, athletes, and corporations is tightly woven:

> The televised sports manhood formula is a master narrative that is produced at the nexus of the institutions of sport, mass media, and corporations that hope to sell products and services to boys and men. As such, this formula appears well suited to discipline boys' and men's bodies, minds, and consumption choices....The perpetuation of these commercial interests appears to be predicated on boys and men accepting—indeed, glorifying and celebrating—a set of bodily and relational practices that resist and oppose a view of women as fully human and place boys' and men's long-term health prospects in jeopardy. (Messner 2002, 126)

The masculine glorification in sports leads to steroid use, recurrent injuries, and concussions in boys playing high school sports (Berler 2009, Kreager 2007, Schwarz 2007). Girls push themselves, too, taking steroids, compulsively dieting, and incurring injuries, in the winner-takes-all model of sports (Sokolove 2008).

The media, team owners, ticket buyers, and home-viewing audience make professional men's sports a major money-making industry in Western societies, and it is men athletes' bodies that are bought and sold and brutally exploited. The history of steroid use to build bodies in Major League Baseball in the United States tarnished that sport, at least for a while (Sokolove 2004). The National Football League is finally acknowledging the prevalence of early dementia from head trauma in retired professional football players (McGrath 2007, Schwarz 2009), but it is unlikely to change the game. As sports commentator William C. Rhoden said, "The good news is that today's N.F.L. players are more aware of the dangers of concussions and brain damage than their predecessors were. The sobering news is that the athletes have gotten bigger, faster and stronger, and they embrace the essence of the game: inflicting and absorbing punishment" (2009, 7).

These injuries are the other side of the glorification of men's bodies that takes place during major sports events, such as Super Bowl Sunday. In 2008, one billion fans watched throughout the world (Eitzen 2009, 5). The players' salaries and income from endorsements are huge, but it is the owners and managers who are making most of the money. In 2006, Anthony Prior, retired NFL player and author of *The Slave Side of Sunday,* said that African-American professional football players were no better than slaves, because they were bought and sold by White owners. Two-thirds of the players in the league were African-American, but 94 percent of general managers and all the owners were White (Zirin 2006). Black coaches are discriminated against as well, with few being hired, even those with more experi-ence than White coaches (Sanchez 2007). Stanley Eitzen, sports sociologist, says that sports are corrupted by money:

> As the level of sport becomes more sophisticated, sport shifts from play to work and from pleasurable participation to pageantry meant to please fans, owners, alumni, and other powerful people. Today, sport has become a spectacle ruled by money. (2009, 5–6)

The masculine center of sports marginalizes women's sports and its audience through invisibility, trivialization, and sexualization. Media owners can claim there is no audience, so why feature women athletes, but there is no audience because women athletes are not seen as *athletes.* Young women identify with them but young men don't, and young men, and their adult counterparts, are the target audience. Michael Messner and his associates (1993), comparing the coverage of the men's and women's NCAA and U.S. Open events, found that women basketball and tennis players were always gender-marked as "women," while men athletes were just athletes. The researchers concluded:

> Men appeared to succeed through talent, enterprise, hard work and risk tak-ing. Women also appeared to succeed through talent, enterprise, hard work and intelligence. But commonly cited along with these attributes were emotion, luck, togetherness and family. Women were also more likely to be framed as failures due to some combination of nervousness, lack of confidence, lack of being "comfort-able," lack of aggression, and lack of stamina. Men were far less often framed as failures—men appeared to miss shots and lose matches not so much because of their own individual shortcomings but because of the power, strength and intelligence of their (male) opponents....Men were framed as active agents in control of their des-tinies, women as reactive objects. (Messner, Duncan, and Jensen 1993, 130)

A retrospective study of televised reports of women's sports in the Los Angeles area from 1989 to 2004 found that women were less frequently trivialized or humor-ously sexualized than in the past, but the extent of coverage had declined (Duncan, Messner, and Willms 2005). In 2004, women's sports received only 6.3 percent of the airtime; in 1999, it had received 8.7 percent.

Despite the media biases, women athletes have become increasingly recog-nized for their contributions to sports. As role models, they have transformed the cultural milieu about girls and women as legitimate and competitive athletes. Mia Hamm's longtime NCAA soccer coach Anson Dorrance notes, "She laid to rest the insult, 'You play like a girl'" (Longman 2004).

The increasing popularity and visibility of women's sports in their own countries has led women athletes from the United States, Canada, Europe, and Australia to form global organizations to encourage the participation in sports of girls from all over the world (Hargreaves 1999). A parallel development has been the establishment of professional women's sports associations, such as the Women's Tennis Association, the Women's National Basketball Association, and the Ladies' Professional Golf Association. These organizations encourage women student and professional athletes to excel in the gender-segregated world of sports, but their financial resources and media exposure tend to be vulnerable.

Women who have challenged men at their own game have done so to show that women are as good athletes as men are, but they have not usually challenged sports' gender segregation. A young woman golfer, Michelle Wie, did so in 2005. She played successfully against men and, in the process, upset both women and men professional golfers: men because she invaded their space, and women because she implied that the women's competitions were not good enough for her:

> "In simple terms, people say, 'Michelle just wants to play against men,'" said Jeff O'Brien, an expert on gender issues in sports at Northeastern University. "It's far more complicated than that." On one level, her enamored view of the P.G.A. plays into cultural biases in sports. "She is basically following the norm of culture," Mr. O'Brien said. "By the TV deals and the endorsement money, dunk highlights on ESPN and the salaries male athletes are paid, society is inherently saying what we value: men's sports." (Roberts, 2005)

Professional women athletes are paid much less than men, and their professional associations are short-lived (Fairchild 2009, Goldstein 2009, Jones 2006). Their potential audience is never developed, except during the Olympics, when they become a lucrative asset. The bottom line, then, is that as long as sports are gender-segregated, women's sports will be a poor runner up to the main event: men's sports.

TITLE IX AND GENDER EQUITY IN SPORTS

In 1972, in an effort to create gender equity in the distribution of federal educational resources, the United States Congress included Title IX as an amendment to the Civil Rights Act of 1964. Title IX created regulatory policies to foster gender parity of high school and college athletes in recruitment, facilities, scholarships, teams, and coaching. When Title IX is enforced, it creates positive change for girls' athletic opportunities. The change in the United States over the past 35 years was summed up in a report by the National Coalition for Women and Girls in Education (NCWE):

> Opportunities for girls and women in athletics have increased exponentially since the passage of Title IX. Before Title IX, only 294,015 girls participated in high school athletics; in 2006, that number was nearly 3 million, a 904% increase. At the college level, prior to Title IX, only 29,977 women participated in athletics compared with 166,728 in 2006, a 456% increase. (2008, 7)

Male students have not been short-changed by Title IX. Their athletic participation at both the high school and college level is almost twice that of female students, and at the high school level, opportunities for boys to engage in athletics are growing at a faster pace than for girls (NCWE 2008, 10). The importance of Title IX in redressing the gender imbalance in school sports is shown by significant evidence that girls' participation in organized athletics has the potential to increase academic achievement (Hanson and Kraus 1998), improve body image (Robinson and Ferraro 2004), and reduce sexual risk-taking (Miller et al. 2002).

In a more critical view of Title IX, Eileen McDonagh, a political science professor, and Laura Pappano, a journalist, argue that it reinforced gender segregation in sports (they use the term "sex segregation"):

> Title IX is celebrated for opening the door to organized athletics for women. Yet Title IX opened a sex-segregated door, a type of door the federal government would have prohibited if it were a matter of race. Title IX regulations, as clarified by Congress, explicitly permit separate teams for each sex when team selection is based on competitive skill or for contact sports. This means that when a school has a team for boys but no such team for girls, regulations require that "members of the excluded sex must be allowed to try out for the team *unless the sport is a contact sport.*" Contact sports, according to the regulations, included boxing, wrestling, rugby, ice hockey, football, basketball. . . . The rule merely acts as a warning to schools: create a girls-only team to match every boys-only team. . . . Unfortunately, this approach failed to consider abilities of individual girls and failed to address the real matter, which was sex discrimination. More profoundly, explicitly allowing sex segregation in contact sports had the far-reaching effect of sex segregating not only contact sports but virtually all sports (2008, 105–106)

In the following excerpt from their book, *Playing with the Boys: Why Separate is Not Equal in Sports,* McDonagh and Pappano say that gender segregation in sports, especially in schools, is the kind of discrimination that has been outlawed for race in the United States for half a century. Noting that there are few bona fide occupational qualifications (BFOQs) that justify racial ethnic or gender discrimination in the workplace, McDonagh and Pappano argue that there are no bona fide athletic qualifications (BFAQs) that justify gender segregation in sports; we just take it for granted that there are.

Playing with the Boys: Why Separate is Not Equal in Sports

◆◆◆

Eileen McDonagh
Northeastern University

Laura Pappano
Wellesley College

. . . [W]e have argued that sports are more than entertainment, that they represent a site which reflects, reinforces, and constructs the meaning of race, class, and sex differences in American society. Beyond that, athletics can also be used to challenge inequalities and injustices that are inconsistent with the egalitarian promise of American society. We often see sports used as a conservative tool to maintain social, economic, and political inequalities and injustices. But sports can just as well be a transformative tool for deconstructing social norms that perpetuate old hierarchies and stereotypes of racial, class, and gender groups, thus producing what some refer to as the paradox of sports.[1]

What is critical to the culture of a democratic society is not so much what sports are played as how they are played. Sports were once segregated by race, thereby reflecting racial inequalities, injustices, and tensions in American society. Such policies mirrored assumptions that African Americans were inferior to whites in general, a flawed belief then extended to sports. The racial segregation of sports competitions reflected and reinforced racial segregation as an operating principle in the American state. This, in turn, supported underlying assumptions about the racial inferiority of African Americans and the social impropriety of whites and blacks interacting, which included playing sports together....

While women have faced similar presumptions about their lack of fitness as athletes and the propriety of their inclusion in sports, they have been less successful than African Americans in using the athletic field as a tool for political gain. While the Anglo-American psyche was able to overcome myths of white athletic supremacy to appreciate and accept the black athlete, women have made no such strides. Women have beaten or outperformed men, but rather than yielding recognition of female power, such results have spurred suppression.

Baseball: Striking Out Babe Ruth

In 1931, 17-year-old pitcher Virne "Jackie" Mitchell became the second woman in history to sign a professional baseball contract when she was recruited to play for the all-male AA Chattanooga Lookouts by owner Joe Engel. On April 2, 1931, Mitchell pitched in an exhibition game against the Yankees, playing before a crowd of 4,000, including press. After Mitchell struck out both Babe Ruth and Lou Gehrig, she was pulled from the game. A few days later the baseball commissioner, Kennesaw Mountain Landis, voided Mitchell's contract, saying baseball was "too strenuous for a woman."[2] Judge Landis's reasoning appeared to embrace general concerns about female physical frailty, but it's hard not to read the greater worry. How does it look when a 17-year-old girl strikes out two future Hall of Fame hitters?...

Swimming

From the afternoon in 1918 when Sybil Bauer was noticed by a swim coach at the Illinois Athletic Club (which had just begun allowing females into the pool), it was clear she had exceptional athletic talent.[3] Bauer would have a brief (she died at age 23) but stunning swim career. By the time she died in 1927, she held 23 world records. During an October 1922 swim meet in Bermuda, Bauer broke three world records in the backstroke, including the men's world record in the 440-yard event. Bauer cut four seconds off the record previously held by Harold Krueger of Honolulu. The

New York Times buried the story on page 19, but the headline relayed the magnitude of the feat: "Woman Breaks Man's Record For First Time in Swim History."[4] She later beat even that record, bettering her time by another second to 6:23.

Bauer was such a dominant backstroke swimmer that she sought to compete with men at the 1924 Olympics. As a February 1924 editorial in *The Nation* noted, "No man in the annals of sport has finished the quarter-mile back-stroke swim within five seconds of Miss Sybil Bauer's time, and naturally Miss Bauer wants to enter the regular event in the Olympic games."[5] Bauer, described by the writer as "a woman who can outclass all the women in her field and all the men as well," simply wanted to compete at an appropriate level during an era when women's events were not taken seriously. After all, the writer noted, "women of today have had only a few years of participation in sport," and few pursued athletic competition with any rigor.[6]

A *New York Times* writer framed the matter on many minds: "Is it conceivable that a woman shall be allowed to compete against men?"[7] The answer would be no. The Olympic rules committee quickly turned down her request. Bauer would not be allowed to defend her record against male challengers.[8] The problem was evident: Bauer upset the gender order and news accounts said so, describing her request as "a modest invasion of men's rights"[9] and suggesting the problem with her competing against males was that keeping sexes separate had "ages of precedent behind it, and therefore is not to be sneezed at."[10] ...

How—or Why—Does Title IX Allow Men's Sports and Women's Sports?

If Title VII effectively banned the notion of male and female work, how do we have the American social, cultural, and business institution known as organized athletics practiced on a sex-segregated basis? Why do we have men's sports and women's sports? Many people make the obvious point about physical differences between males as a group and females as a group. But so what?

As Title VII regulations specify, statistical group differences cannot be used as employment criteria. What matters is the individual's strength and physical characteristics in relation to employment qualifications, not their sex. If a woman is strong enough to lift the weight required for a job, she is qualified to hold that job. End of discussion.

Why doesn't the same principle apply to sports? If a 17-year-old girl can strike out Babe Ruth, why can't she keep her minor league contract instead of being fired? If a woman wins a fencing match against a man, why can't she keep her title? If Donna Lopiano was, at 10 years old, the biggest and best Little League player in town, why exclude her from the team? If Michelle Wie or Annika Sorenstam are among the nation's top golfers, why should they need a sponsor's exemption or special invitation to play PGA events? Why do sports remain the most sex-segregated secular institution in American society, exceeding even the military? And why do people barely notice, much less fail to complain?

There are several ways to approach such questions. It is important to see that these issues are inseparable from cultural beliefs about masculinity and femininity, as well as a historic understanding of sex roles. But we must also consider the role of legislative logic, which not only influenced the structure of organized athletics but also aided the course of men's and women's sports as distinct entities excused from ordinary expectations of sex equity.

If the reason Title IX permits sex segregation in contact sports is to protect boys' masculinity from the injury of losing to or even competing with girls, even that would not be recognized as an acceptable BFOQ under Title VII. Thus what was (and still is) missing from Title IX is anything comparable to a BFOQ that would specify when and where sex segregation is legitimate in sports. That is, there is no bona fide athletic qualification (BFAQ) for sports, and if Congress wishes to permit sex segregation in sports, there must be.

Title IX was important, even critical. But it unfortunately reinforced—rather than challenged—the belief that women are inherently inferior to men. The law also failed to challenge cultural norms of propriety when it comes to direct physical contact between men and women in athletics. Yes, football is a contact sport, but why does that warrant excluding women from playing with the boys? Surely, at some levels and in some settings, females can play football as successfully as males. Doug Flutie was allowed to prove wrong those who would write off a quarterback generously listed at 5 foot 10 on the basis of height alone.

What we must do (which was never done when establishing Title IX as the law of the land) is look again at the foundation. We must consider what, if anything, would constitute a BFAQ for sex-segregated sports. Aside from any sex group differences we may link to athletic competition, we must remember that sports come down to a challenge between individuals, and the Equal Protection Clause of the Fourteenth Amendment requires [that the] government treat similarly situated individuals equally in spite of their race or sex, even if Title IX doesn't.

The policy objective here is to combine sameness and difference in sports programs for women. We seek sex-integrated sports policies that not only allow but also encourage females to "play with the boys." We advocate programs for girls that promote their involvement in traditionally male sports, much as there are programs for girls to promote their involvement in traditionally male educational subjects, such as math and science. Girls should be encouraged to play football if they are interested, instead of believing their only proper role is cheering on the sidelines. In fact, the vast majority of boys who play youth football lack the skills necessary for high school teams, making it particularly troubling that most girls feel they can't participate in what has become the most popular spectator sport in America. Why should girls feel that "they don't belong" in pads and helmets when their playing ability differs little from that of the boys who do suit up? The overarching goal of sameness feminism in this setting is to actively encourage and promote sex-integrated athletic programs wherever possible. On the other hand, there are virtues in difference feminism. Those women who, as the traditionally subordinated group in sports programs, wish to play only on same-sex teams or within same-sex sports arenas should be able to do so. But this should be voluntary (rather than coercive) sex segregation. Women who eschew math for literature in college, thereby affirming intellectual interests traditionally associated with women, may do so. The problem exists when educational policies coercively restrict women from taking math classes with boys, even if there are same-sex math classes for women. Women may self-segregate when they find themselves in traditionally male fields, but it must be their choice. More to the point, however, women should not merely be allowed to enroll in male-dominated math programs, they should be urged to do so. Likewise, females who want to play traditionally male sports ought not to be merely tolerated but actively encouraged.[11]

Notes

1. Douglass Hartmann, "What Can We Learn From Sport If We Take Sport Seriously as a Racial Force? Lessons from C.L.R. James's *Beyond a Boundary*," *Ethnic and Racial Studies,* May 2003, 462. For an elaboration of the paradox, namely, how sport can reinforce gender and racial hierarchies as well as challenge them, see Margaret Gatz, Michael A. Messner, and Sandra J. Ball-Rokeach, *Paradoxes of Youth and Sport* (Albany: State University of New York Press, 2002).
2. Ruth M. Sparhawk, Mary E. Leslie, Phyllis Y.Turbow, and Zina R. Rose. 1989. *American Women in Sport, 1887–1987: A 100-Year Chronology.* Metuchen, NJ: Scarecrow, 14.
3. *New York Times.* 1924. "Girl May Race Men Olympians," 9 March, XX2.
4. *New York Times.* 1922. "Woman Breaks Man's Record for First Time in Swim History," 9 October, 19.
5. *The Nation.* 1924. "Greeks, Girls, and 1944," 27 February, 222.
6. For a review of the history of discrimination against women in sports in the context of the development of Title IX and a doctrine of formal equality, see Jessica E. Jay, 1997, "Women's Participation in Sports: Four Feminist Perspectives," *Texas Journal of Women and the Law,* Fall, 1.
7. "Girl May Race Men Olympians."
8. Mark Dyreson. 1996. "Scripting the American Olympic Story-Telling Formula: The 1924 Paris Olympic Games and the American Media," *Olympic Perspectives,* October, 62.
9. "Greeks, Girls, and 1944," 222.
10. "Girl May Race Men Olympians."
11. For an insightful analysis from global perspectives of how power relations are embodied in sport and how women circumvent a wide array of barriers, see Jennifer Hargreaves, 2000, *Heroines of Sport: The Politics of Difference and Identity.* New York: Routledge.

THE CORPORATE LOCKER ROOM

Gender segregation in public sports spills over into the general culture, and sport's values of violence, aggression, and extreme competitiveness get transformed into a corporate locker-room mentality that permeates politics as well. Vicarious participation in sports demonstrates not just masculinity, but the traits that supposedly make for success—aggressive competitiveness and no-holds-barred individual or team effort. Winning is everything.

President Obama, who started playing basketball in high school as a way of validating his masculinity ([1995] 2004, 78–80), continues to play recreationally. During the primary campaign preceding his election, his basketball prowess was described as a definite asset, especially when compared to his rival's lack of sports engagement. One journalist wrote that Hillary Rodham Clinton's

> ...favorite fitness activity, according to her MySpace page, is speed walking. Her hobbies include crossword puzzles, Scrabble and gardening....Her chief rival for the Democratic presidential nomination, Barack Obama, meanwhile, has already shown a touch for channeling the varsity glamour of John F. Kennedy, who radiated vigor and charisma by playing touch football and skippering boats. Mr. Obama loves to play pickup basketball, a game that is the definition of cool for a lot of men. (Healy 2007)

Then, during the first year of his presidency, despite his appointment of many women to his cabinet and White House staff, President Obama was criticized on the front page of the *New York Times* for playing only with "the boys":

> He presides over a White House rife with fist-bumping young men who call each other "dude" and testosterone-brimming personalities like Rahm Emanuel, the often-profane chief of staff; Lawrence Summers, the brash economic adviser; and Robert Gibbs, the press secretary, who habitually speaks in sports metaphors.

> The technical foul over the all-male [basketball] game has become a nagging concern for a White House that has battled an impression dating to the presidential campaign that Mr. Obama's closest advisers form a boys' club and that he is too frequently in the company of only men—not just when playing sports, but also when making big decisions. (Leibovich 2009a, 1)

A day after this news report, it was reported that the President played golf with a woman aide, the first time in his presidency (Leibovitch 2009b). Obviously sports, even recreationally, capture the public imagination, as President Obama's games are worthy of national coverage.

Sports play a particularly important part in the culture of politics and corporations. It is the source of metaphors in everyday language; last night's game is the subject of water-cooler talk; the golf course is the place to entertain clients; tickets to the big games are the deal sweeteners. Not being able to talk the language, share the post-game analysis, play golf with the guys, and be a proper sports audience are all grounds for informal devaluation on the job. Michele Gregory, who was herself a basketball player and corporate employee, did a study of the locker-room mentality at British advertising agencies. According to Gregory,

> ...the locker room consists more specifically of both a place and a value associated with male power and identity, masculinities, competition, solidarity and adolescent

behavior. Furthermore, the locker room—metaphorical or otherwise—provides a safe space for men to discuss their ideas about their values, motivations, fears, desires, wives, girlfriends, mistresses, sexuality, career and family on a personal level.... The locker room helps men promote their own interests, as well as discover the activities, hobbies, forms of entertainment and values of the hegemonic masculine culture. (2009a, 326–327)

In the locker-room culture, women are sex objects—to be conquered or shown off as prizes to the winners. Misogyny and violence, as well as homophobia and fear of appearing soft or feminine, are rampant among athletes at the center of the sport world (Messner 2002). In the corporate world, the violence is verbal— language is earthy, sexual, and aggressive, transposing male physicality into words, even over the Internet (Gregory 2009b, Knorr Cetina and Bruegger 2002).

The ideological subtext of sports in Western culture is that physical strength is men's prerogative, and it justifies men's physical and sexual domination of women. Women's physical capabilities, especially in male-identified sports, challenge these assumptions. As Catharine MacKinnon says,

It's threatening to one's takeability, one's rapeability, one's femininity, to be strong and physically self-possessed. To be able to resist rape, not to communicate rape-ability with one's body, to hold one's body for uses and meanings other than that can transform what being a woman means. (MacKinnon 1987, 122)

CRITICAL SUMMARY

Is there a possibility of less gender segregation in sports—more mixed-gender teams? There might be less opposition to this idea if young boys and girls were grouped into teams by size or ability and learned to use their bodies together. As a long-term effect, we might see less glorification of violence as intrinsic to men's sports. Of course, if men's sports did not glorify a certain kind of masculinity, professional teams might lose their glamour, their endorsements and advertising revenues, and their audiences, and poor boys would have one less avenue to what they now dream of as a better life.

With gender segregation, what is the probability of truly equal rewards for women's sports—not just in prize money, but in prestige? It would mean alternating men's and women's finals as the capstone event in championship competitions, and valuing the way women play equally with men's prowess. As Jennifer Hargreaves said, "If endurance, skill, artistry, creativity and timing were accorded higher value, sports would have a very different meaning" (1994, 286). How do we create this very different meaning if the glory games are men's sports and the goal of many women athletes is to have women's teams of the same sports, even if they have to end up playing by adapted, supposedly more "feminine" rules? Then, by comparison, they end up lesser. To gain visibility, they don't show off their athleticism but their bodies—strong and sexy. In *Taking the Field,* Messner says, "As long as women quietly play adapted forms of sports in their separate and unequal ghettos or allow themselves to be marketed as media sex goddesses, the unmodified cultural definition of 'athlete' remains securely male" (2002, 140).

Even if women athletes got more respect and prestige, it is unlikely that hegemonic men's values of aggression, constant competition, and violence will disappear from men's sports. Nor will women athletes necessarily bring nurturance, empathy, and participatory playfulness to women's sports; they can be aggressive and violent, too (Longman 2009a). But some deliberate degendering practices might bring women's sports into the male-dominated center and might dampen the prevalence of vicious violence, misogyny, and homophobia. These practices start by focusing on gender, but the ultimate goal is to make gender irrelevant. Here are some suggestions:

Visibility. A daily woman's sports story in every newspaper and a woman's sports feature in every sports newscast, reported straightforwardly and respectfully, without coy feminization, voyeuristic sexualization, or emphasis on "human interest."

Balance. Refer to men's sports as *men's* sports, the way women's sports are always *women's* sports. Now, men's sports are just sports. As Messner says, "This asymmetrical gender marking tends to position women's sports and women athletes as secondary and derivative to men's sports" (2002, 193, fn. 4). In championship events, rotate the coveted last playoff between the women and the men.

Resources. Pay equal prize money. Have women coaches for men's teams, the way the men coaches have taken over women's teams. Create professional women's leagues that have secure financial investment, and attractive salaries.

Gender freedom. Encourage mixed teams and showcase matches where women and men play together. Discourage announcers from constant gendered comparisons. Encourage reporting that refers to them all as "athletes."

Degendering. Devise and promote games that put less emphasis on body shapes and more on skill. In competitions, match people of different levels of body functioning and abilities, regardless of gender.

These are small practices, yet some of them sound quite revolutionary, even impossible. But to make revolutionary changes, we need to think the impossible, so that one day, the impossible might become possible, and sports would no longer be the stereotypically gendered endeavor it is today.

REFERENCES AND RECOMMENDED READINGS

Aitchison, Cara Carmichael (ed.). 2006. *Sport and Gender Identities: Masculinities, Femininities and Sexualities.* New York: Routledge.

Anderson, Eric. 2005. *In the Game: Gay Athletes and the Cult of Masculinity.* Albany, NY: State University of New York Press.

Berler, Ron. 2009. "Arms-Control Breakdown." 7 August. http://www.nytimes.com/2009/08/09/magazine/09littleleague-t.html.

Buford, Bill. 1993. *Among the Thugs.* New York: Vintage.

Cahn, Susan K. 1994. *Coming on Strong: Gender and Sexuality in Twentieth-Century Women's Sport.* New York: Free Press.

Clarey, Christopher, and Gina Kolata. 2009. "Gold is Awarded, but Dispute over Runner's Sex Intensifies." *New York Times,* 21 August, B9, 11.

Dowling, Collette. 2000. *The Frailty Myth: Redefining the Physical Potential of Women and Girls.* New York: Random House.

Ezzell, Matthew B. 2009. "'Barbie Dolls' on the Pitch: Identity Work, Defensive Othering, and Inequality in Women's Rugby." *Social Problems* 56: 111–131.

Dreger, Alice. 2009. "Seeking Simple Rules in Complex Gender Realities." *New York Times,* 25 October, 8.

Duncan, Margaret Carlisle, and Michael Messner, with Nicole Willms. 2005. "Gender in Televised Sports: News and Highlights Shows, 1989–2004." Amateur Athletic Foundation of Los Angeles (AAF). http://www.aafla.org/9arr/ResearchReports/tv2004

Eitzen, D. Stanley. 2009. *Fair and Foul: Beyond the Myths and Paradoxes of Sport,* 4th edition. Lanham, MD: Rowman and Littlefield.

Fairchild, Elizabeth. 2009. "WNBA Salaries Fall Far Short of Their Male Counterparts." http://personalmoneystore.com/moneyblog/2009/04/09/wnba-salaries-fall-short-male-counterparts/.

Flintoff, Anne, and Sheila Scraton (eds.). 2001. *Gender and Sport: A Reader.* New York: Routledge.

Grasmuck, Sherri. 2005. *Protecting Home: Class, Race, and Masculinity in Boys' Baseball.* New Brunswick, NJ: Rutgers University Press.

Gregory, Michele R. 2009a. "Inside the Locker Room: Male Homosociability in the Advertising Industry." *Gender, Work and Organization* 16: 323–347.

———. 2009b. "'Talking Sports': Sports and the Construction of Hegemonic Masculinities at Work," in *Equality, Diversity and Inclusion at Work: A Research Companion,* edited by Mustafa F. Özbilgin. Cheltenham, UK: Edward Elgar.

Griffin, Pat. 1998. *Strong Women, Deep Closets.* Champaign, IL: Human Kinetics.

Goldstein, Nancy. 2009. "Women's Basketball, Latest Recession Victim." Salon.com 6 February. http://www.salon.com/mwt/broadsheet/feature/2009/02/06/wnba/print.html.

Hager Cohen, Leah. 2005. *Without Apology: Girls, Women, and the Desire to Fight.* New York: Random House.

Hanson, Sandra L., and Rebecca S. Kraus. 1998. "Women, Sports, and Science: Do Female Athletes Have an Advantage?" *Sociology of Education* 71: 93–110.

Hargreaves, Jennifer. 1994. *Sporting Females: Critical Issues in the History and Sociology of Women's Sports.* New York: Routledge.

———. 1999. "The 'Women's International Sports Movement:' Local-Global Strategies and Empowerment," *Women's Studies International Forum* 22: 461–471.

Healy, Patrick. 2007. "Hillary Clinton Searches for Her Inner Jock." *New York Times,* 10 June. http://www.nytimes.com/2007/06/10/weekinreview/10healy.html.

Heywood, Leslie. 1998. *Bodymakers: A Cultural Anatomy of Women's Bodybuilding.* New Brunswick, NJ: Rutgers University Press.

Heywood, Leslie, and Shari Dworkin. 2003. *Built to Win: The Female Athlete as Cultural Icon*. Minneapolis, MN: Univ of Minnesota.

Hogshead-Makar, Nancy, and Andrew Zimbalist (eds.). 2007. *Equal Play: Title IX and Social Change*. Philadelphia: Temple University Press.

Jones, Rachel. 2006. "Football's Women Huddle and Hustle for Their Sport." *WeNews*, 19 November. http://www.womensenews.org/story/athleticssports/061119/footballs-women-huddle-and-hustle-their-sport.

Kane, Mary Jo. 1995. "Resistance/Transformation of the Oppositional Binary: Exposing Sport as a Continuum." *Journal of Sport and Social Issues* 19: 191–218.

Kessel, Anna. 2009. "Gold Medal Athlete Caster Semenya Told to Prove She is a Woman." *Guardian*, 19 August. http://www.guardian.co.uk/sport/2009/aug/19/caster-semenya-gender-verification-test.

Klein, Alan. M. 1993. *Little Big Men: Bodybuilding Subculture and Gender Construction*. Albany: State University of New York Press.

Knorr Cetina, Karin, and Urs Bruegger. 2002. "Global Microstructure: The Virtual Societies of Financial Markets." *American Journal of Sociology* 107: 905–950.

Kolata, Gina. 2010a. "Gender Testing Hangs Before the Games as a Muddled and Vexing Mess." *New York Times*, 16 January, D2.

———. 2010b. "Panel Calls for Treatment in Cases of Sex Ambiguity." *New York Times*, 21 January, B23, 25.

Kreager, Derek A. 2007. "Unnecessary Roughness: School Sports, Peer Networks, and Male Adolescent Violence." *American Sociological Review* 72: 705–724.

Leibovich, Mark. 2009a. "Man's World at White House? No Harm, No Foul, Aides Say." *New York Times*, 25 October, 1, 18.

———. 2009b. "A First for President Obama: Female Aide Joins Round of Golf." *New York Times*, 25 October. http://thecaucus.blogs.nytimes.com/2009/10/25/a-first-for-president-obama-female-aide-joins-round-of-golf.

Levy, Ariel. 2009. "Either/Or: Sports, Sex, and the Case of Caster Semenya." *The New Yorker*, 30 November, 46–59.

Lindemann, Gesa. 1996. "The Body of Gender Difference." *European Journal of Women's Studies* 3: 341–361.

Longman, Jeré. 2004. "Mia Hamm, Soccer Star, to Retire Tonight." *New York Times*, 8 December. http://www.nytimes.com/2004/12/08/sports/soccer/08hamm.html.

———. 2009a. "For All the Wrong Reasons, Women's Soccer is Noticed." *New York Times* 11 November, B15, 19.

———. 2009b. "South African Runner's Sex-Verification Result Won't Be Public." *New York Times*, 20 November, B10, 15.

MacKinnon, Catharine A. 1987. *Feminism Unmodified*. Cambridge, MA: Harvard University Press.

Martin, Karin A., 1998. "Becoming a Gendered Body: Practices of Preschools." *American Sociological Review* 63: 494–511.

McDonagh, Eileen, and Laura Pappano. 2008. *Playing with the Boys: Why Separate Is Not Equal in Sports*. New York: Oxford University Press.

McGrath, Ben. 2007. "Walking Away: Tiki Barber, After the Game." *The New Yorker*, 29 January, 65–71.

McKay, Jim, Michael A. Messner, and Don Sabo (eds.). 2000. *Masculinities: Gender Relations in Sport*. Thousand Oaks, CA: Sage.

Messner, Michael A. 1992. *Power at Play: Sports and the Problem of Masculinity*. Boston: Beacon Press.

——. 2002. *Taking the Field: Women, Men and Sports*. Minneapolis: University of Minnesota Press.

——. 2007. *Out of Play: Critical Essays on Gender and Sport*. Albany: State University of New York Press.

——. 2009. *It's All for the Kids: Gender, Families, and Youth Sports*. Berkeley: University of California Press.

Messner, Michael A., and Suzel Bozada-Deas. 2009. "Separating the Men from the Moms: The Making of Adult Gender Segregation in Youth Sports." *Gender & Society* 23: 49–71.

Messner, Michael A., Margaret Carlisle Duncan, and Darnell Hunt. 2000. "The Televised Manhood Sports Formula." *Journal of Sport and Social Issues* 24: 380–394.

Messner, Michael A., Margaret Carlisle Duncan, and Kerry Jensen. 1993. "Separating the Men from the Girls: The Gendered Language of Televised Sports." *Gender & Society* 7: 121–137.

Messner, Michael A., and Donald F. Sabo (eds.). 1994. *Sex, Violence, and Power in Sports: Rethinking Masculinity*. Freedom, CA: Crossing Press.

Miller, Kathleen, Grace Barnes, Merrill Melnick, Donald Sabo, and Michael Farrell. 2002. "Gender and Racial/Ethnic Differences in Predicting Adolescent Sexual Risk: Athletic Participation versus Exercise." *Journal of Health and Social Behavior* 43: 436–450.

National Coalition for Women and Girls in Education. 2008. *Title IX at 35: Beyond the Headlines*. Washington, DC.

Obama, Barack. [1995] 2004. *Dreams from My Father*. New York: Random House.

Prior, Anthony E. 2006. *The Slave Side of Sunday*. Charleston, SC: BookSurge Publishing.

Rhoden, William C. 2009. "Paying a Heavy Price for Playing in the Moment." *New York Times,* Sports Sunday, 15 November, 7.

Roberts, Selena. 2005. "Where the Boys Are. There She Is." *New York Times* Week in Review, 17 July, 14.

——. 2007. "A Player Serves Notice to Homophobic Sports Culture." *New York Times,* 8 February. http://select.nytimes.com/2007/02/08/sports/ncaabasketball/08roberts.html.

Robinson, Kirsten, and Richard F. Ferraro. 2004. "The Relationship Between Types of Female Athletic Participation and Female Body Type." *Journal of Psychology* 138: 115–129.

Roth, Amanda, and Susan A. Basow. 2004. "Femininity, Sports, and Feminism: Developing a Theory of Physical Liberation." *Journal of Sport and Social Issues* 28: 245–265.

Sanchez, Jarad. 2007. "Beyond the Superbowl: Race and Pro-Football." *Colorlines,* January/February. http://www.colorlines.com/article.php?ID=190.

Schwarz, Alan. 2007. "High School Players Shrug Off Concussions, Raising Risks." *New York Times,* 15 September, A1, 10, 11.

——. 2009. "N.F.L. Acknowledges Long-Term Concussion Effects." *New York Times,* 21 December, D1, 6.

Sokolove, Michael, 2004. "The Lab Animal: In Pursuit of Doped Excellence." *New York Times Magazine,* 18 January, 28–33, 48, 54, 58.

——. 2008. *Warrior Girls: Protecting Our Daughters Against the Injury Epidemic in Women's Sports*. New York: Simon and Schuster.

Theberge, Nancy. 2000. *Higher Goals: Women's Ice Hockey and the Politics of Gender.* Albany: State University of New York Press.

Thorne, Barrie. 1993. *Gender Play: Girls and Boys at School.* New Brunswick, NJ: Rutgers University Press.

Verbrugge, Martha H. 1997. "Recreating the Body: Women's Physical Education and the Science of Sex Differences in America, 1900–1940." *Bulletin of the History of Medicine* 71: 273–304.

Wacquant, Loïc. 2004. *Body and Soul: Notebooks of an Apprentice Boxer.* New York: Oxford University Press.

Woodward, Kath. 2006. *Boxing, Masculinity and Identity: The 'I' of the Tiger.* New York: Routledge.

Young, Iris Marion. 1990. *Throwing Like a Girl and Other Essays in Feminist Philosophy and Social Theory.* Bloomington: Indiana University Press.

Zirin, Dave. 2006. "The Slave Side of Sunday." *The Nation,* 20 January. http://www.thenation.com/doc/20060206/zirin.

Intersexuality

Dreger, Alice Domurat. 1998. *Hermaphrodites and the Medical Invention of Sex.* Cambridge, MA: Harvard University Press.

—— (ed.). 1999. *Intersexuality in the Age of Ethics.* Hagerstown MD: University Publishing Group.

Hird, Myra J. 2000. "Gender's Nature: Intersexuals, Transsexuals, and the 'Sex'/'Gender' Binary." *Feminist Theory* 1: 347–364.

Kessler, Suzanne J. 1998. *Lessons from the Intersexed.* New Brunswick, NJ: Rutgers University Press.

Preves, Sharon E. 1998. "For the Sake of the Children: Destigmatizing Intersexuality." Special Issue on Intersex, *Journal of Clinical Ethics* 9(4): 411–20.

——. 2003. *Intersex and Identity: The Contested Self.* New Brunswick, NJ: Rutgers University Press.

Swarr, Amanda Lock, with Sally Gross and Liesl Theron. 2009. "South African Intersex Activism: Caster Semenya's Impact and Import." *Feminist Studies* 35: 657–662.

Zucker, Kenneth J. 1999. "Intersexuality and Gender Identity Differentiation." *Annual Review of Sex Research* 10: 1–69.

CHAPTER 7

You Don't Need Arms and Legs to Sing

Gender and Disability

Key concepts
continuum of physical functioning, gendering and disabling, social construction of disability, sitpoint, transcending the body

Throughout this book, we have focused on the ways that the body is socially and culturally constructed, showing how human bodies are given meanings beyond the biological. We have focused on how the body is gendered—made masculine or feminine—according to social norms. We have interwoven racial ethnic and social class effects in the gendering processes and argued that women's and men's bodies are not uniform, but vary by both physical characteristics and social patterning. Now we bring in another crucial way that bodies vary—on a continuum of physical functioning, and on the gendered social construction of the meaning of that continuum.

Consider the following newspaper accounts: A description of "Murderball," a documentary of paraplegic athletes playing wheelchair rugby, in which the players "perform remarkable feats of wheeling and spinning, executing artful feints and lobbing courtwide passes to one another" (McGrath 2005, B7). A description of a concert by Thomas Quasthoff, a bass-baritone who "will be introduced as a distinguished artist, a Grammy Award winner and popular recitalist who appears regularly with the major orchestras of the world;" nothing will be said about his "abnormally short legs and vestigial arms, a result of his mother's having taken thalidomide when she was pregnant"—he used to talk about it but now "considers it irrelevant" (Tommasini 2004, E1). A description of Matt Fraser, "a handsome, six-foot-tall English actor, singer and sometime drummer with pouty lips, a black belt in karate," who starred in "The Flid Show," a stage drama about "a British nightclub singer who was born with abnormally foreshadowed arms;" Fraser's "flipper arms" are also a result of his mother having taken thalidomide (Schillinger 2005, 8). Fraser has not only appeared as himself; he previously played a heroin dealer

167

in a British TV series, "Metrosexuality." All are described in ways that emphasize their masculinity and de-emphasize their disability.

It's not only successful men with paralyzed or missing limbs who are newsworthy. The obituaries of Diana Golden Brosnihan, who died of cancer at 38, called her life "remarkable" (Araton 2000, D1). A skier from the age of five, she developed bone cancer when she was 12 and resumed skiing six months after her right leg was amputated above the knee. Skiing on one leg with regular ski poles, she competed against two-legged skiers and won a gold medal in the giant slalom in the 1988 Winter Olympics, as well as 10 world and 19 U.S. championships from 1986 to 1990, skiing against others with disabilities (Litsky 2001). Golden Brosnihan didn't want to be admired because she had overcome a disability. "She wanted admiration for her technique, her skill, for how she had discarded disabled ski equipment for regular ski poles to produce faster times and fought successfully to compete in the same races with the nonhandicapped" (Araton 2001, D1). In recognition of her fight for equal status, her citation when she was inducted into the Women's Sports Foundation International Hall of Fame in 1997 read, "She persuaded the ski world to treat all athletes the same, regardless of ability or, in her case, disability" (Litsky 2001, D7). The emphasis on her athletic abilities effectively degenders her. Unlike masculinity, femininity would not be considered an asset for a disabled athlete.

Athletes and performers use their bodies in their work; people whose careers rely on their minds need to surmount their bodies. Stephen Hawking is a famous 63-year-old physicist who has had amyotrophic lateral sclerosis (ALS) since he was 21. An incurable, progressive neurological disease, ALS has confined Hawking's paralyzed body to a wheelchair and 24-hour nursing care. To enable him to speak and write, colleagues in Britain and the United States devised a computer program and voice synthesizer system that attaches to his wheelchair. He has written groundbreaking, best-selling books, such as *The History of Time*, teaches at Cambridge University in Great Britain, and gives scientific lectures and popular talks. He has been married twice, and has three children and one grandchild. His private life, like his extraordinary career, are testimonials to his masculinity.

WHAT IS A DISABILITY?

Given these accounts, we could well ask what a disability is. Each of us is likely, at some time in our lives, to become disabled—temporarily for an acute episode through illness or accident or permanently for all or the rest of our lives through congenital conditions, injuries, chronic illnesses, or the debilities of aging. The World Health Organization defines disability, physical and mental, in three ways: *impairment*, any loss or abnormality of psychological, physiological, or anatomical structure or function; *disability*, any functional restriction (resulting from an impairment) or lack of ability to perform an activity within the range considered normal for a human being; and *handicap*, the relationship between impaired and/or disabled people and their surroundings affecting their ability to participate normally in a given activity and putting them at a disadvantage.

It is difficult to obtain global estimates on disability, but during 2005–2006, the United Nations and World Health Organization worked on developing a way to measure the global prevalence of disability. One important finding of their research so far is that "at a global level, women live on average 3.9 years longer than men, but lose the equivalent of 1.9 extra years of good health to the non-fatal consequences of diseases and injuries. In other words, although women live longer, they spend a greater amount of time with disability" (Mathers et. al. 2001, 1689). They also spend a greater amount of time as caretakers of aging and disabled male partners and other family members.

Having a permanent disability may not be an identity or a role for the person concerned; instead, it may be hidden because it is stigmatizing. Conversely, when diminished body functioning is heroically compensated by athletic, creative, or intellectual feats, the stigma is converted to a charismatic aura. But even ordinary people who live ordinary lives in spite of disabilities are celebrated. In Trafalgar Square in London, from 2005 to 2007, there was a prominently displayed statue of woman who had been born with phocomelia:

> The statue, 11 feet 7 inches of snow-white Carrara marble, shows the naked, eight-and-a-half-month-pregnant figure of 40-year-old Alison Lapper, a single mother who was born with shortened legs and no arms. Ms. Lapper is a friend of the sculptor, Marc Quinn, who has said that Nelson's Column, the focal point of Trafalgar Square, is "the epitome of a phallic male moment" and that he thought "the square needed some femininity." (Lyall 2005, E1)

Ironically, Admiral Horatio Nelson, a famous British eighteenth century naval commander in the Napoleanic Wars, was also disabled—he lost an arm and was blinded in one eye during the battles he fought. His statue at the top of the column shows him with a pinned sleeve, but it is so high up that it is hard to see without binoculars.

The stories of public heroes don't often tell us about the caregivers and technologists that make it possible for them to thrive, if not to live. Just like the rest of us, people with lesser physical functioning are embedded in relationships, according to a feminist ethics of care (Tronto 1993). We are all, at one time or another, care receivers or caregivers, and sometimes are both simultaneously. According to Joan Tronto, a feminist philosopher:

> The care perspective requires that we think about the moral dimension of receiving care as well as that of giving care. It requires that we reflect upon the place of dependency, illness, insecurity, and death in human life. These have not been the central concerns of moral philosophy and political theory. Furthermore, exploring the personal provision of care makes clear how limited our individual capacities are and how much we depend upon others for guidance and direction. (2006, 431)

The ways that someone who is disabled thrives in a supportive social environment are described in the following excerpt about Diana DeVries. Like Alison

Lapper, DeVries was born with stumps for arms and legs, refused prostheses as a child, and lived a full life as a proud "Venus on wheels," going to college, getting married (several times), and pursuing a career as a social worker. (Venus de Milo is the famous Greek statue of a woman that has lost its arms.) The article is by Geyla Frank, who began writing about DeVries' life in 1976 as a graduate student in anthropology, when DeVries was 26. Frank participated in DeVries' life over the next 20 years and says that the resulting cultural biography is a description of "meaningful solutions to life's challenges" (2000, 2). The "arm" she refers to is a short stump.

Venus on Wheels

◆◆◆

Gelya Frank
University of Southern California

Much of Diane's childhood was dominated by surgeries and therapeutic regimens prescribed by physician-led rehabilitation teams. At the same time, Diane experienced a life fairly typical for a child raised in Long Beach, in a trim grid of single-family tract houses that was the prototypical American suburb. By the time Diane finished high school in 1968, she had effectively resisted being defined by the heavy impress of institutionalized medicine and had abandoned the artificial arms and cosmetic legs with which she had been supplied. Such antiauthoritarian attitudes and behaviors were becoming increasingly common among young adults with disabilities. Influenced by the gains of the women's and civil rights movements, a full-fledged movement for independent living and disability rights was emerging that was to have a profound effect on Diane's life and on American culture....

Two of Diane's developmental milestones stand out for her mother, Irene.[1] The first was Diane's discovery that she could pick up an object. She was in her wooden high chair, tied in so that she wouldn't "scoot out the bottom." Diane had some large round plastic pop-it beads in front of her when she discovered that she could pick one up and drop it. Diane laughed to see that she could move something like that by herself, and they called her father, Kenny, to show him. The family began to give Diane plastic dishes with a wooden spoon to stir and let her make mud pies. Pouring the contents of one bowl to another, hitting the bowl with her spoon, and splashing made Diane "really excited," to the point of falling asleep in her high chair. Irene thought Diane was about a year old when this occurred.[2]

Diane's mother also recalled Diane's first steps. Diane had learned to sit up by herself by age one or two. They used to prop her up on pillows, and she learned to right her own position. One day Irene and Kenny were sitting in the living room with Diane's Aunt Hazel and Uncle Burt when they noticed Diane walk across the room. She was concentrating very seriously, looking down, and moving with a rocking motion from side to side. She was two or three years old.

As a baby Diane hadn't moved her toys around very much. She had a teddy bear and pink stuffed cow that she snuggled against to sleep. Later she used her arm and cheek to cuddle dolls.[3] When her baby sister Debbie was on the floor, Diane would put her cheek against her. Irene surmised that touching things with her cheek "must have had a warmer feel." Diane's favorite toys were Little Red Riding Hood, a bride, and a soft squeaky toy bought by her father, "a red Indian with a feather." She loved to hit the feather with her arm to make it squeak.

These recollections capture Diane busily accomplishing some of the main work of childhood: the acquisition of competence in daily occupations.[4] She used the intact resources of her body to strive to do the things she saw others do....

Diane's memories of Camp Paivika, where she spent two weeks every year between the ages of eight and eighteen, were those of a perennially happy camper. High in the San Bernardino mountains, Paivika was the first resident camp in the United States built especially for children with physical disabilities.[5] It offered swimming, archery, horseback riding, arts and crafts, sing-alongs around the campfire—in short, all the activities that a child from the city or the suburbs could want at a sleep-away camp.

Diane began her first session at Paivika looking somewhat withdrawn. But by the second week she was folk dancing and square dancing on her wooden rocker legs. She became fast friends with the caretaker's daughter, who, it was noted by a counselor, was not disabled. Diane impressed her fellow campers and staff by "her amazing abilities," which included feeding herself and going on overnight trips.[6]

Four summers later, when Diane was eleven years old, she was praised by her counselor as "the most delightful camper in our cabin, and perhaps the whole camp."[7] Diane was described as agreeable, enthusiastic, and popular—if special, even among children with handicaps, because quadrilateral limb deficiencies were so rare.[8] Diane loved crafts, swimming, and horseback riding. She moved around the camp using her three-wheeled tripod and a crutch. Diane was always coming up with clever remarks and constructive suggestions for cabin activities (she originated the idea for her cabin's flag) and could be depended on for articles for the camp newspaper and ideas for skits. Her attitude toward her disability was self-accepting and compensatory: "She would talk freely about her disability and seemed to want to show everyone that she could do things as well as anyone. The first day, as I was carrying her, Diane remarked, 'You know, I'm not very heavy because I don't have arms and legs and stuff like that.' Carrying articles under her chin from the table after meals was a favorite task, and she could dust bed tops in the cabin very well."[9]

It turns out that Diane's orientation toward *doing* without arms and legs, which originated in her childhood, is common among children with congenital limb deficiencies. A study conducted in the early 1960s found that "contrary to expectations, congenitally malformed children of normal and superior intelligence develop an early and gratifying curiosity about their environment; they manage to explore outside reality almost as adequately as non-handicapped children."[10]

Diane entered the stormy years of her adolescence with a fair amount of experience and confidence with the opposite sex. At Camp Paivika she had had a series of "summer loves." ...

Too many women with disabilities struggling under conditions of inadequate financial and social support have been worn down by their fight. Discouraged by negative stereotypes, institutionalized discrimination, and lack of sustainable opportunities, some have considered suicide their best option. Despite her remarkable success in meeting the challenges posed by the dominant able-bodied culture, Diane DeVries too has sometimes felt that life's demands are too heavy to bear. At those times, she has talked about suicide. While she and Jim were in Bible school, however, Diane wrote: "I was created and formed by God the Father, to demonstrate His glory and His power in a person's life ... by living an abundant life, filled with purpose and direction."[11]

If God helps those who help themselves, then Diane's successes are due to her ability to manage a complex set of resources to maintain a stable lifestyle. When an essential element is missing or destabilized, I have seen Diane's adaptive system teeter and fold like a house of cards. Otherwise, Diane is pretty much like anyone else going about her daily occupations: pursuing her career as a social worker, browsing shops in her neighborhood, painting ceramic masks with acrylic colors, attending a birthday party in the park for her goddaughter, or serving as a volunteer in an agency for AIDS patients.

Diane's conviction that she can and should be able to make it in the community is a legacy from three sources in American culture. First, her family maintained an adaptable, "can-do" approach to Diane's early strivings with her disability. Second, institutions of rehabilitation had the unintended effect of sponsoring Diane's participation in a distinct peer culture of disability as she grew up in the 1950s and 1960s. Finally, since the early 1970s, she has been empowered by the burgeoning independent living and disability rights movements.

Notes

1. Interviews with Irene Fields, February 3, 1983, and March 10, 1983.
2. If this event happened while they lived in Pacific Beach, as Irene remembered it, Diane may have been age two or older. However, there is no reason to assume that Diane's development was delayed.
3. Diane usually describes her stumps as "arms," as did her mother in the interviews.
4. Occupations are defined in occupational science as "chunks of daily activity that can be named in the lexicon of the culture. Fishing, grooming, weaving, and dining are all occupations. When we come to understand these occupations within the framework of a human life, we can say 'People are shaped by what they have done, by their daily patterns of occupation.' ... Thus a person's history of occupation, to some extent, shapes what he or she will become in the future" (Zemke and Clark, *Occupational Science*, vii).
5. Camp Paivika was founded in 1944 at Tamarack Lodge in Big Bear by the Crippled Children's Society of Los Angeles County, then affiliated with the Easter Seals Society.

6. Phone report from Lila Beal, M.S.W., to Wilma Gurney, Child Amputee Prosthetics Project, July 30, 1958.

7. Judy Ferguson, A.C.H., Resident Camp Report, Crippled Children's Society of Los Angeles County, June 19–July 1, 1961. Diane's popularity in camp and at school shows the importance of context to attitudes toward children with amputations among their peers. In research by Centers and Centers ("Peer Group Attitudes toward the Amputee Child," 1963) among children five to twelve years old in regular school classes, rejecting attitudes were more frequently expressed toward children with amputations than toward children without amputations. Mean scores ranked the amputee children as least fun, least liked, and saddest. It should be noted, however, that scores for some individuals with amputations were in the same range as the non-amputees.

8. At least one other camper also had quadrilateral limb deficiencies and was a patient at CAPP during the years Diane attended Camp Paivika.

9. Ferguson, Resident Camp Report.

10. Gingras et al., "Congenital Anomalies of the Limbs," 1964. This study was undertaken by the Rehabilitation Institute of Montreal to gear itself up to treat the cases that occurred in 1962 as a result of the introduction of the sedative thalidomide, which had teratogenic effects. The sample provides a good comparison group for Diane historically and functionally: its members were described as having "more or less severe handicaps," although none had quadrilateral limb deficiencies. Of the forty-one subjects ten were contemporaries of Diane, age twelve to eighteen. The rest were a stratified sample spanning age fourteen months to nineteen years and over.

11. DeVries, "Autobiography."

References

Centers, Louise, and Richard Centers. 1963. "Peer Group Attitudes toward the Amputee Child." *Journal of Social Psychology* 61:27–132.

Devries, Diane. N.D. "The Autobiography of Diane Devries."

Gingras, G., M. Mongeau, P. Moreault, M. Dupuis, B. Hebert, and C. Corriveau. 1964. "Congenital Anomalies of the Limbs, part II: Psychological and Educational Aspects." *Canadian Medical Association Journal* 91: 115–19.

Hamilton, Marguerite. 1958. *Borrowed Angel*. Garden City, N.J.: Hanover House.

Zemke, Ruth, and Florence Clark, eds. 1996. *Occupational Science: The Evolving Discipline*. Philadelphia: F. A. Davis.

GENDERING AND DISABLING

How does gendering intersect with processes of disabling? Is the process of disabling different for women and men? Gendering separates women and men in their work and family roles, and thus affects the extent to which disabling modifies work opportunities, living arrangements, family life, and a person's sense of self differently for women and men. People with physical impairments certainly resist and reshape social expectations about what they can or cannot do, but the behavior of physicians, families, and professional and lay caretakers often reflects conventional ideas about what women and men can do when disabled. These beliefs about "normal" gendered behavior lead them to encourage or discourage surmounting or giving in to body limitations.

In a widely cited paper, Michelle Fine and Adrienne Asch (1985) argue that women with disabilities face "sexism without the pedestal." Compared to men of a similar level of physical functioning, women are less likely to find jobs that allow them to be economically independent. They are also less likely to have a lifetime partner if they are heterosexual, because they need the care and attention that women are expected to give to men. Given the expectations of women's nurturance, it would be logical that lesbians might be better able to find a life partner, but Asch and Fine caution that "comments made by many disabled lesbians indicate that within the community of lesbians the disabled woman is still in search of love. Disabled lesbians have described being dismissed, shunned, or relegated to the status of friend and confidante rather than lover, just as have heterosexual disabled women" (1988, 19). As for men's caretaking capabilities, the history of the AIDS epidemic, during which gay men cared for each other, and accounts of heterosexual men acting as caretakers for elderly parents and wives with Alzheimer's contradict gendered stereotypes (Bayley 1998, Kaye and Applegate 1990, Lipton 2004).

A woman with disabilities can run a household, take care of her children, and also work outside the home, yet gynecologists are more likely to suggest a hysterectomy than help with getting pregnant. Women with quite severe physical limitations have devised ways of caring for small children: "One mother who could not use her arms found that her two children both learned to scramble up her and hang around her neck" (Lonsdale 1990, 79). Carrie Killoran says of her own parenting, "People with disabilities are already accustomed to doing everything differently and more slowly, and caring for children is no different" (1994, 122). Nonetheless, because she is viewed as not being able to be the chief caretaker in a household, a woman with disabilities is often discouraged from having children. Interviews with 31 women aged 22 to 69, with a variety of disabilities and of different racial ethnic groups, well educated and highly productive, revealed "the common experience of having their reproductive needs undervalued. Many said their physicians treated them as asexual, thought they should not be having children, and assumed that they would not be having children and that they did not want menstrual periods. In many cases, the first recommendation offered was to have a hysterectomy" (Nosek et al. 1995, 512). Such treatment keeps women with disabilities who want children from a role that for many women validates their womanhood.

Men who are disabled are better able to validate their manhood. In the traditional heterosexual husband role, a man expects care from his wife and expects to support and protect her and their children. Therefore, as long as a man with disabilities can earn an income and be present for his children, he can fulfill his family role obligations. However, sexuality and its machismo qualities are particularly devastating minefields for men with disabilities, as it is for men who have had prostate surgery and older men. The immense popularity of Viagra and similar drugs indicates that actual or imagined sexual dysfunction is widespread, even among healthy men; their use by men with disabilities is therefore normalized. In short, despite the conventional wisdom that "'disabled man' is a self-contradiction, because men are stereotypically supposed to be 'able,' strong, and powerful" (Lakoff 1989, 368), a man with disabilities may be quite able to function well as a husband, father, and lover.

The conventional norms of masculinity push men with disabilities to find ways of feeling independent, even when they need to rely on white canes (Kudlick 2005). Looking at masculinity and physical disability in the lives of 10 men, Thomas Gerschick and Adam Stephen Miller (1994) found that those who ascribed to conventional ideals of masculinity felt they had to demonstrate physical strength, athleticism, sexual prowess, and independence. Their self-image was tied into heroics and risk-taking, but they often felt inadequate and incomplete because they couldn't do what they wanted or go where they wanted. The men who reformulated these norms defined their ways of coping with their physical limitations as demonstrations of strength and independence. For example, two quadriplegics who needed round-the-clock, personal care assistants did not feel they were dependent on others, but had hired helpers whom they directed and controlled. The men who rejected the standard version of masculinity put more emphasis on relationships than on individual accomplishments, were comfortable with varieties of sexuality, and felt they were non-conformists.

DISABILITY AND GENDERED SEXUALITY

Conceptions of masculine sexuality as assertive and penetrative in effect "unman" an adult male with physical impairments. Although he conceded that there were many ways to make love, Robert Murphy, a paraplegic, bleakly assessed his future sexuality:

> Most forms of paraplegia and quadriplegia cause male impotence and female inability to orgasm. But paralytic women need not be aroused or experience orgasmic pleasure to engage in genital sex, and many indulge regularly in intercourse and even bear children, although by Caesarean section. ... Paraplegic women claim to derive psychological gratification from the sex act itself, as well as from the stimulation of other parts of their bodies and the knowledge that they are still able to give pleasure to others. ... Males have far more circumscribed anatomical limits. Other than having a surgical implant that produces a simulated erection, the man can no longer engage in genital sex. He either becomes celibate or practices oral sex—or any of the many other variations in sexual expression devised by our innovative species. Whatever the alternative, his standing as a man has been compromised far more than has been the woman's status. He has been effectively emasculated. (1990, 96)

Irving Kenneth Zola's version of sexuality is much more diffuse and emotional than Murphy's, but hardly emasculated. In the following excerpt, he describes mutual love-making with a severely paralyzed woman, an activity that begins with his doing all her physical care, as well as the more conventional undressing, and ends with him feeling that she had made love to him as well.

Tell Me, Tell Me

◆◆◆

Irving Kenneth Zola

Now I was the one who was nervous. Here we were alone in her room thousands of miles from my home.

"Well, my personal care attendant is gone, so it will all be up to you," she said sort of puckishly. "Don't look so worried! I'll tell you what to do."

This was a real turn-about. It was usually me who reassured my partner. Me who, after putting aside my cane, and removing all the clothes that masked my brace, my corset, my scars, my thinness, my body. Me who'd say, "Well, now you see 'the real me.'" How often I'd said that, I thought to myself. Saying it in a way that hid my basic fear—that this real me might not be so nice to look at . . . might not be up to "the task" before me.

She must have seen something on my face, for she continued to reassure me, "Don't be afraid." And as she turned her wheelchair toward me she smiled at me that smile that first hooked me a few hours before. "Well," she continued, "first we have to empty my bag." And with that brief introduction we approached the bathroom.

Anger quickly replaced fear as I realized she could get her wheelchair into the doorway but not through it.

"Okay, take one of those cans," she said pointing to an empty Sprite, "and empty my bag into it."

Though I'd done that many times before it wasn't so easy this time. I quite simply couldn't reach her leg from a sitting position on the toilet and she couldn't raise her foot toward me. So down to the floor I lowered myself and sat at her feet. Rolling up her trouser leg I fumbled awkwardly with the clip sealing the tube. I looked up at her and she laughed, "It won't break and neither will I."

I got it open and her urine poured into the can. Suddenly I felt a quiver in my stomach. The smell was more overpowering than I'd expected. But I was too embarrassed to say anything. Emptying the contents into the toilet I turned to her again as she backed out. "What should I do with the can?" I asked.

"Wash it out," she answered as if it were a silly question. "We try to recycle everything around here."

Proud of our first accomplishment we headed back into the room. "Now comes the fun part…getting me into the bed." For a few minutes we looked for the essential piece of equipment—the transfer board. I laughed silently to myself. I seemed to always be misplacing my cane—that constant reminder of my own physical dependency. Maybe for her it was the transfer board.

When we found it leaning against the radiator I reached down to pick it up and almost toppled over from its weight. Hell of a way to start, I thought to myself. If I can't lift this, how am I going to deal with her? More carefully this time, I reached down and swung it onto the bed.

She parallel parked her wheelchair next to the bed, grinned, and pointed to the side arm. I'd been this route before, so I leaned over and dismantled it. Then with her patient instructions I began to shift her. The board had to be placed with the wider part on the bed and the narrower section slipped under her. This would eventually allow me to slip her across. But I could do little without losing my own balance. So I laid down on the mattress and shoved the transfer board under her. First one foot and then the other I lifted toward me till she was at about a 45 degree angle in her wheelchair. I was huffing but she sat in a sort of bemused silence. Then came the scary part. Planting myself as firmly as I could behind her, I leaned forward, slipped my arms under hers and around her chest and then with one heave hefted her onto the bed. She landed safely with her head on the pillow, and I joined her wearily for a moment's rest. For this I should have gone into training, I smiled silently. And again, she must have understood as she opened her eyes even wider to look at me. What beautiful eyes she has, I thought, a brightness heightened by her very dark thick eyebrows.

"You're blushing again," she said.

"How can you tell that it's not from exhaustion?" I countered.

"By your eyes … because they're twinkling."

I leaned over and kissed her again. But more mutual appreciation would have to wait, there was still work to be done.

The immediate task was to plug her wheelchair into the portable recharger. This would have been an easy task for anyone except the technical idiot that I am.

"Be careful," she said. "If you attach the wrong cables you might shock yourself."

I laughed. A shock from this battery would be small compared to what I've already been through.

But even this attaching was not so easy. I couldn't read the instructions clearly, so down to the floor I sank once more.

After several tentative explorations, I could see the gauge registering a positive charge. I let out a little cheer.

She turned her head toward me and looked down as I lay stretched out momentarily on the floor, "Now the real fun part," she teased. "You have to undress me."

"Ah, but for this," I said in my most rakish tones, "we'll have to get closer together." My graceful quip was, however, not matched by any graceful motion.

For I had to crawl on the floor until I could find a chair onto which I could hold and push myself to a standing position.

As I finally climbed onto the bed, I said, "Is this trip really necessary?" I don't know what I intended by that remark but we both laughed. And as we did and came closer, we kissed, first gently and then with increasing force until we said almost simultaneously, "We'd better get undressed."

"Where should I start?" I asked.

My own question struck me as funny. It was still another reversal. It was something I'd never asked a woman. But on those rare occasions on which I'd let someone undress me, it was often their first question.

"Wherever you like," she said in what seemed like a coquettish tone.

I thought it would be best to do the toughest first, so I began with her shoes and socks. These were easy enough but not so her slacks. Since she could not raise herself, I alternated between pulling, tugging, and occasionally lifting. Slowly over her hips, I was able to slip her slacks down from her waist. By now I was sweating as much from anxiety as exertion. I was concerned I'd be too rough and maybe hurt her but most of all I was afraid that I might inadvertently pull out her catheter. At least in this anxiety I was not alone. But with her encourage-ment we again persevered. Slacks, underpants, corset all came off in not so rapid succession.

At this point a different kind of awkwardness struck me. There was something about my being fully clothed and her not that bothered me. I was her lover, not her personal care attendant. And so I asked if she minded if I took off my clothes before continuing.

I explained in a half-truth that it would make it easier for me to get around now "without all my equipment." "Fine with me," she answered and again we touched, kissed and lay for a moment in each other's arms.

Pushing myself to a sitting position I removed my own shirt, trousers, shoes, brace, corset, bandages, undershorts until I was comfortably nude. The comfort lasted but a moment. Now I was embarrassed. I realized that she was in a position to look upon my not so beautiful body. My usual defensive sarcasm about "the real me" began somewhere back in my brain but this time it never reached my lips. "Now what?" was the best I could come up with.

"Now my top...and quickly. I'm roasting in all these clothes."

I didn't know if she was serious or just kidding but quickness was not in the cards. With little room at the head of the bed, I simply could not pull them off as I had the rest of her clothes.

"Can you sit up?" I asked.

"Not without help."

"What about once you're up?"

"Not then either ... not unless I lean on you."

This time I felt ingenious. I locked my legs around the corner of the bed and then grabbing both her arms I yanked her to a sitting position. She made it but I didn't. And I found her sort of on top of me, such a tangle of bodies we could only laugh. Finally, I managed to push her and myself upright. I placed her arms around my neck. And then, after the usual tangles of hair, earrings and protestations that I was trying to smother her, I managed to pull both her sweater and blouse over her head. By now I was no longer being neat, and with an apology threw her garments toward the nearest chair. Naturally I missed . . . but neither of us seemed to care. The bra was the final piece to go and with the last unhooking we both plopped once more to the mattress.

For a moment we just lay there but as I reached across to touch her, she pulled her head back mockingly, "We're not through yet."

"You must be kidding!" I said, hoping that my tone was not as harsh as it sounded.

"I still need my booties and my night bag."

"What are they for?" 1 asked out of genuine curiosity.

"Well my booties—those big rubber things on the table—keep my heels from rubbing and getting irritated and the night bag . . . well that's so we won't have to worry about my urinating during the night."

The booties I easily affixed, the night bag was another matter. Again it was more my awkwardness than the complexity of the task. First, I removed the day bag, now emptied, but still strapped around her leg and replaced it with the bigger night one. Careful not to dislodge the catheter I had to find a place lower than the bed to attach it so gravity would do the rest. Finally, the formal work was done. The words of my own thoughts bothered me for I realized that there was part of me that feared what "work" might still be ahead.

She was not the first disabled woman I'd ever slept with but she was, as she had said earlier, "more physically dependent than I look." And she was. As I prepared to settle down beside her, I recalled watching her earlier in the evening over dinner. Except for the fact that she needed her steak cut and her cigarette lit, I wasn't particularly conscious of any dependence. In fact quite the contrary, for I'd been attracted in the first place to her liveliness, her movements, her way of tilting her head and raising her eyebrows: But now it was different. This long process of undressing reinforced her physical dependency.

But before I lay down again, she interrupted my associations. "You'll have to move me. I don't feel centered." And as I reached over to move her legs, I let myself fully absorb her nakedness. Lying there she somehow seemed bigger. Maybe it was the lack of muscle-tone if that's the word—but her body seemed somehow flattened out. Her thighs and legs and her breasts, the latter no longer firmly held by her bra, flapped to her side. I felt guilty a moment for even letting myself feel anything. I was as anxious as hell but with no wish to flee. I'm sure my face told it all. For with her eyes she reached out to me and with her words gently reassured me once again, "Don't be afraid."

And so as I lay beside her we began our loving. I was awkward at first, I didn't know what to do with my hands. And so I asked. In a way it was no different than with any other woman. In recent years, I often find myself asking where and how they like to be touched. To my questions she replied, "My neck . . . my face . . .

especially my ears…." And as I drew close she swung her arms around my neck and clasped me in a surprisingly strong grip.

"Tighter, tighter, hold me tighter," she laughed again. "I'm not fragile … I won't break."

And so I did. And as we moved I found myself naturally touching other parts of her body. When I realized this I pulled back quickly, "I don't know what you can feel."

"Nothing really in the rest of my body."

"What about your breasts," I asked rather uncomfortably.

"Not much … though I can feel your hands there when you press."

And so I did. And all went well until she told me to bite and squeeze harder, then I began to shake. Feeling the quiver in my arm, she again reassured me. So slowly and haltingly where she led, I followed.

I don't know how long we continued kissing and fondling, but as I lay buried in her neck, I felt the heels of her hands digging into my back and her voice whispering, "tell me… tell me."

Suddenly I got scared again. Tell her what? Do I have to say that I love her? Oh my God. And I pretended for a moment not to hear.

"Tell me… tell me," she said again as she pulled me tighter. With a deep breath, I meekly answered, "Tell you what?"

"Tell me what you're doing," she said softly, "so I can visualize it." With her reply I breathed a sigh of relief. And a narrative voyage over her body began; I kissed, fondled, caressed every part I could reach. Once I looked up and I saw her with her head relaxed, eyes closed, smiling.

It was only when we stopped that I realized I was unerect. In a way my penis was echoing my own thoughts. I had no need to thrust, to fuck, to quite simply go where I couldn't be felt.

She again intercepted my own thoughts—"Move up, please put my hands on you," and as I did I felt a rush through my body. She drew me toward her again until her lips were on my chest and gently she began to suckle me as I had her a few minutes before. And so the hours passed, ears, mouths, eyes, tongues inside one another.

And every once in a while she would quiver in a way which seemed orgasmic. As I thrust my tongue as deep as I could in her ear, her head would begin to shake, her neck would stretch out and then her whole upper body would release with a sigh.

Finally, at some time well past one we looked exhaustedly at one another. "Time for sleep," she yawned, "but there is one more task—an easy one. I'm cold and dry so I need some hot water."

"Hot water!" I said rather incredulously.

"Yup, I drink it straight. It's my one vice."

And as she sipped the drink through a long straw, I closed my eyes and curled myself around the pillow. My drifting off was quickly stopped as she asked rather archly, "You mean you're going to wrap yourself around that rather than me?"

I was about to explain that I rarely slept curled around anyone and certainly not vice-versa but I thought better of it, saying only, "Well, I might not be able to last this way all night."

"Neither might I," she countered. "My arm might also get tired."

We pretended to look at each other angrily but it didn't work. So we came closer again, hugged and curled up as closely as we could, with my head cradled in her arm and my leg draped across her.

And much to my surprise I fell quickly asleep—unafraid, unsmothered, and more importantly rested, cared for, and loved.

Excerpted from Irving Kenneth Zola, *Ordinary Lives: Voices of Disability and Disease*, pp. 208–216. Copyright © 1982 by Apple-wood Books, Inc. Reprinted by permission.

Heterosexual women with disabilities do not find it easy to be sexual. One study comparing heterosexual women with and without disabilities found that women with a disability have less sexual knowledge and less experience with intercourse, and they are less satisfied with their sexual situation, since they have the same sexual desires and fantasies as women without a disability (Vansteenwegen, Jans, and Revell 2003). If they are in a relationship, though, they are equally sexually involved. There was no comparison with lesbian women.

Some writers have pointed out the parallels in the experiences of non-disabled lesbians and gays and heterosexuals with disabilities (Sherry 2004). Both are often isolated from families and subject to stereotyping and discrimination. Both have to make difficult choices about trying to pass as "normal" or being upfront about who they are. The feelings of isolation are compounded for lesbian women and gay men with disabilities (Clare 1999).

For women and men of any sexual orientation who have disabilities, social life is complicated by difficulties in dating, going to parties, and casual socializing. One lesbian who lost her eyesight long after she came out writes of missing terribly "regular validation of my status through visual interaction with other dykes"—the winks and smiles exchanged with strangers who recognize they are members of the same community (Peifer 1999, 33). She has the alienating sense of living two disparate worlds. A lesbian mother with no hearing feels that she and her non-hearing, school-age daughter live in communities that have little overlap and sometimes, little tolerance of diversity (D'aoust 1999). These communities are the world of the physically challenged (she uses a wheelchair for mobility), the Deaf, White mothers of adopted non-White children, and lesbians. She says of her daughter that she "is part of a community that welcomes Deaf people as members but does not have the same history of dealing with other differences" (117). She and her daughter are accepted as Deaf, but she is isolated as a lesbian mother.

TRANSCENDING THE BODY

With all the mainstreaming, bravery, skillful caretaking, and innovative technology, the body itself persists. Susan Wendell, a philosopher who has had myalgic encephalomyelitis or chronic fatigue immune dysfunction syndrome since 1985, experiences "constant muscle pain, muscle weakness...periods of profound fatigue…overlapping periods of dizziness and/or nausea and/or depression, head-aches lasting for several days, and intermittent problems with short-term memory, especially verbal recall" (1996, 3). She has creative work, a good income, a pres-tigious position, and a loving partner, but her need to accommodate her body, she says, gives her and others defined as disabled a point of view different from those whose bodies give them little trouble. This perspective is a standpoint, or what Nancy Mairs, a wheelchair user, calls "sitpoint." As with other standpoints, it comes from experiences in a social, cultural, and physical world, and it constitutes "a significant body of knowledge" (Wendell 1996, 73). In the following excerpt, Wendell challenges feminism's call for women to valorize and exert control over their bodies. For her, living through her body entails a form of transcendence.

The Suffering and Limited Body

◆◆◆

Susan Wendell
Simon Fraser University

Feminism's continuing efforts on behalf of increasing women's control of our bodies and preventing unnecessary suffering tend to make us think of bodily suffering as a socially curable phenomenon. Moreover, its focus on alienation from the body and women's bodily differences from men has created in feminist theory an unrealistic picture of our relationship to our bodies. On the one hand, there is the implicit belief that, if we can only create social justice and overcome our cultural alienation from the body, our experience of it will be mostly pleasant and rewarding. On the other hand, there is a concept of the body which is limited only by the imagination and ignores bodily experience altogether. In neither case does feminist thought confront the experience of bodily suffering. One important consequence is that feminist the-ory has not taken account of a very strong reason for wanting to transcend the body. Unless we do take account of it, I suspect that we may not only underestimate the subjective appeal of mind-body dualism but also fail to offer an adequate alternative conception of the relationship of consciousness to the body.…

Attempting to transcend or disengage oneself from the body by ignoring or discounting its needs and sensations is generally a luxury of the healthy and able-bodied. For people who are ill or disabled, a fairly high degree of attention to the body is necessary for survival, or at least for preventing significant (and sometimes irreversible) deterioration of their physical conditions. Yet illness and disability often render bodily experiences whose meanings we once took for granted dif-ficult to interpret, and even deceptive. Barbara Rosenblum described how a "crisis of meaning" was created by the radical unpredictability of her body with cancer:

> In our culture it is very common to rely on the body as the ultimate arbiter of
> truth.…By noticing the body's responses to situations, we have an idea of how

we "really feel about things." For example, if you get knots in your stomach every time a certain person walks into the room, you have an important body clue to investigate.... Interpretations of bodily signals are premised on the uninterrupted stability and continuity of the body.... When the body, like my body, is no longer consistent over time... when something that meant one thing in April may have an entirely different meaning in May, then it is hard to rely on the stability—and therefore the truth—of the body. (Butler and Rosenblum 1991, 136–37)

Chronic pain creates a similar (but more limited) crisis of meaning, since, to a healthy person, pain means that something is wrong that should be acted upon. With chronic pain, I must remind myself over and over again that the pain is meaningless, that there is nothing to fear or resist, that resistance only creates tension, which makes it worse. When I simply notice and accept the pain, my mind is often freed to pay attention to something else. This is not the same as ignoring my body, which would be dangerous, since not resting when I need to rest can cause extreme symptoms or a relapse into illness that would require several days' bed rest. I think of it as a reinterpretation of bodily sensations so as not to be overwhelmed or victimized by them. This process has affected profoundly my whole relationship to my body, since fatigue, nausea, dizziness, lack of appetite, and even depression are all caused by my disease from time to time, and thus all have changed their meanings. It is usually, though not always, inappropriate now to interpret them as indications of my relationship to the external world or of the need to take action. Unfortunately, it is often much easier to recognize that something is inappropriate than to refrain from doing it.

For this reason, I have found it important to cultivate an "observer's" attitude to many bodily sensations and even depressive moods caused by my illness. With this attitude, I observe what is happening as a phenomenon, attend to it, tolerate the cognitive dissonance that results from, for example, feeling depressed or nauseated when there is nothing obviously depressing or disgusting going on, accommodate to it as best I can, and wait for it to pass....

In general, being able to say (usually to myself): "My body is painful (or nauseated, exhausted, etc.), but I'm happy," can be very encouraging and lift my spirits, because it asserts that the way my body feels is not the totality of my experience, that my mind and feelings can wander beyond the painful messages of my body, and that my state of mind is not completely dependent on the state of my body. Even being able to say, "My brain is badly affected right now, so I'm depressed, but I'm fine and my life is going well," is a way of asserting that the quality of my life is not completely dependent on the state of my body, that projects can still be imagined and accomplished, and that the present is not all there is. In short, I am learning not to identify myself with my body, and this helps me to live a good life with a debilitating chronic illness.

I know that many people will suspect this attitude of being psychologically or spiritually naive. They will insist that the sufferings of the body have psychological and/or spiritual meanings, and that I should be searching for them in order to heal myself (Wilber and Wilber 1988). This is a widespread belief, not only in

North America but in many parts of the world, and... I do not reject it entirely. I too believe that, if my stomach tightens every time a particular person enters the room, it is an important sign of how I feel about her/him, and I may feel better physically if I avoid or change my relationship to that person. But, having experienced a crisis of meaning in my body, I can no longer assume that even powerful bodily experiences are psychologically or spiritually meaningful. To do so seems to me to give the body too little importance as a cause in psychological and spiritual life. It reduces the body to a mere reflector of other processes and implicitly rejects the idea that the body may have a complex life of its own, much of which we cannot interpret.

When I look back on the beginning of my illness, I still think of it, as I did then, as an involuntary violation of my body. But now I feel that such violations are sometimes the beginnings of a better life, in that they force the self to expand or be destroyed. Illness has forced me to change in ways that I am grateful for, and so, although I would joyfully accept a cure if it were offered me, I do not regret having become ill. Yet I do not believe that I became ill *because* I needed to learn what illness has taught me, nor that I will get well when I have learned everything I need to know from it. We learn from many things that do not happen to us because we need to learn from them (to regard the death of a loved one, for example, as primarily a lesson for oneself, is hideously narcissistic), and many people who could benefit from learning the same things never have the experiences that would teach them.

When I began to accept and give in to my symptoms, when I stopped searching for medical, psychological, or spiritual cures, when I began to develop the ability to observe my symptoms and reduced my identification with the transient miseries of my body, I was able to reconstruct my life. The state of my body limited the possibilities in new ways; but it also presented new kinds of understanding, new interests, new passions, and projects. In this sense, my experience of illness has been profoundly meaningful, but only because I accepted my body as a cause. If I had insisted on seeing it primarily as reflecting psychological or spiritual problems and devoted my energy to uncovering the "meanings" of my symptoms, I would still be completely absorbed in being ill. As it is, my body has led me to a changed identity, to a very different sense of myself even as I have come to identify myself less with what is occurring in my body.

References

Butler, Sandra, and Barbara Rosenblum. 1991. *Cancer in Two Voices.* San Francisco: Spinster Book Company.
Wilber, Ken, and Treya Wilber. 1988. "Do We Make Ourselves Sick?" *New Age Journal* September/October 50–54, 85–90.

CRITICAL SUMMARY

In addition to an ethics of care, feminists have contributed other concepts to disability studies: the intersection of body functioning with gender and sexual orientation in discrimination patterns; the standpoints of people of different body and social statuses, especially gender, racial ethnic group, class, and age; the gendered social construction of disabling processes; gendered discourse and language as shaping how we think about body functioning; a systemic view of "disability" as subordinating and silencing, especially for women (Garland 2005).

The stories of people with disability convey mixed messages. One is that body limitations can be overcome through one's own efforts and the help of other people. The other message is that body limitations become part of one's status because of the way other people see you. The gendering of physical disability makes men less masculine, reducing them to the status of women. Zola said,

> Whoever I was, whatever I had, there was always a sense that I should be grateful to someone for allowing it to happen, for like women, I, a handicapped person, was perceived as dependent on someone else's largesse for my happiness, or on someone else to *let* me achieve it for myself. (1982a, 213)

In order to restore their public persona of masculinity, men often go to great lengths to try to make their disability irrelevant to their identity. At a time when disability was much more stigmatizing than it is today, Franklin Delano Roosevelt, a polio victim who served as president of the United States from 1932 to 1944, masked his inability to walk or to stand without supports, and the press respected his privacy (Gallagher 1985). In contrast, John Hockenberry, a paraplegic due to an automobile accident, has gone around the world as a reporter in his wheelchair, flaunting his physical state (Hockenberry 1995).

While men with disabilities try to project masculine strength, women with disabilities cannot come across as conventionally feminine because it might exaggerate their dependence. So, paradoxically, they do what the men now do—project an image of strength in adversity. As Nancy Mairs says,

> People—crippled or not—wince at the word "cripple," as they do not at "handicapped" or "disabled." Perhaps I want them to wince. I want them to see me as a tough customer, one to whom the fates/gods/viruses have not been kind, but who can face the brutal truth of her existence squarely. As a cripple, I swagger. (1986, 9)

People with disabilities may be praised for the heroic ways in which they live "normal" lives, but there is always an undercurrent of "difference." It is this difference, a combination of the physical and the social, that gives those with permanent or long-term body problems a special standpoint (or sitpoint), a way of looking at the world that is different from those safely on the right side of "normal." It is an "outsider" viewpoint, just as women have an outsider viewpoint on the male-dominated world, and people of color have an outsider viewpoint on the White world. It necessitates fighting for a place in the hegemonic world and not taking any privileges for granted. A person who is at the intersection of several outsider statuses—a lesbian with cerebral palsy, a Black man in a wheelchair—has complex knowledge that could be very special to convey because it shows "normals" how much they take for granted that their environment will be physically accessible and socially welcoming.

REFERENCES AND RECOMMENDED READINGS

Adelson, Betty M. 2005. *The Lives of Dwarfs: Their Journey from Public Curiosity toward Social Liberation*. New Brunswick, NJ: Rutgers University Press.

Araton, Harvey. 2001. "A Champion Slips Away Unnoticed." *New York Times*, 30 August, D1.

Asch, Adrienne, and Michelle Fine. 1988. "Introduction: Beyond Pedestals," in *Women with Disabilities: Essays in Psychology, Culture, and Politics*, edited by Michelle Fine and Adrienne Asch. Philadelphia: Temple University Press.

Barnartt, Sharon N., and Richard Scotch (eds.). 2001. *Disability Protests: Contentious Politics, 1970–1999*. Washington, DC: Gallaudet University Press.

Bayley, John. 1998. *Elegy for Iris*. New York: St. Martin's Press.

Blumenfeld, Warren J. (ed.). 1999. Queer and Dis/Abled. Special issue of *International Journal of Sexuality and Gender Studies* 4: 1–123.

Brownworth, Victoria A., and Susan Raffo (eds.). 1999. *Restricted Access: Lesbians on Disability*. Seattle, WA: Seal Press.

Clare, Eli. 1999. *Exile and Pride: Disability, Queerness, and Liberation*. Cambridge, MA: South End Press.

D'aoust, Vicky. 1999. "Complications: The Deaf Community, Disability and Being a Lesbian Mom—A Conversation with Myself," in *Restricted Access: Lesbians on Disability*, edited by Victoria A. Brownworth and Susan Raffo. Seattle, WA: Seal Press.

Davis, Lennard (ed.). 2006. *The Disability Studies Reader*, 2nd edition. New York: Routledge.

Deutsch, Helen, and Felicity Nussbaum (eds.). 2000. *"Defects": Engendering the Modern Body*. Ann Arbor: University of Michigan Press.

Fine, Michelle, and Adrienne Asch. 1985. "Disabled Women: Sexism without the Pedestal," in *Women and Disability: The Double Handicap*, edited by Mary Jo Deegan and Nancy A. Brooks. New Brunswick, NJ: Transaction Books.

—— (eds.). 1988. *Women with Disabilities: Essays in Psychology, Culture, and Politics*. Philadelphia: Temple University Press.

Frank, Geyla. 2000. *Venus on Wheels: Two Decades of Dialogue on Disability, Biography, and Being Female in America*. Berkeley: University of California Press.

Gallagher, Hugh Gregory. 1985. *FDR's Splendid Deception*. New York: Dodd Mead.

Garland Thomson, Rosemarie (ed.). 1996. *Freakery: Cultural Spectacles of the Extraordinary Body*. New York: New York University Press.

——. 1997. *Extraordinary Bodies: Figuring Physical Disability in American Culture and Literature*. New York: Columbia University Press.

——. 2005. "Feminist Disability Studies." *Signs* 30: 1557–1587.

Gerschick, Thomas J., and Adam Stephen Miller. 1994. "Gender Identities at the Crossroads of Masculinity and Physical Disability." *Masculinities* 2: 34–55.

Grealy, Lucy. 1994. *Autobiography of a Face*. New York: Perennial Press.

Hall, Kim (ed.). 2002. Feminist Disability Studies. Special issue, *NWSA Journal* 14 (3).

Hawking, Stephen. "My Experience with ALS." http://www.hawking.org.uk/disable/dindex.html.

Hockenberry, John. 1995. *Moving Violations: War Zones, Wheelchairs, and Declarations of Independence*. New York: Hyperion.

Hillyer, Barbara. 1993. *Feminism and Disability*. Norman: University of Oklahoma Press.

Juette, Melvin, and Ronald J. Berger. 2008. *Wheelchair Warrior: Gangs, Disability, and Basketball*. Philadelphia: Temple University Press.

Kaye, Lenard W., and Jeffrey S. Applegate. 1990. *Men as Caregivers to the Elderly: Understanding and Aiding Unrecognized Family Support*. Lexington, MA: Lexington Books.

Kelley, Tina. 2009. "Fencing Their Way, and Loving it." *New York Times*, 12 October, A20.

Kittay, Eva, Alexa Schriempf, Anita Silvers, and Susan Wendell (eds.). 2001. Feminism and Disability: Part I. Special issue, *Hypatia* 16 (4).

———. 2002. Feminism and Disability: Part II. Special issue, *Hypatia* 17 (3).

Killoran, Carrie. 1994. "Women with Disabilities Having Children: It's Our Right, Too." *Sexuality and Disability* 12: 121–126.

Kudlick, Catherine. 2005. "The Blind Man's Harley: White Canes and Gender Identity in America." *Signs* 30: 1549–1606.

Linton, Simi. 1998. *Claiming Disability: Knowledge and Identity*. New York: New York University Press.

Lipton, Benjamin (ed.). 2004. *Gay Men Living with Chronic Illnesses and Disabilities: From Crisis to Crossroads*. New York: Routledge.

Litsky, Frank. 2001. "Diana Golden Brosnihan, Skier, Dies at 38." *New York Times*, 28 August, D7.

Lonsdale, Susan. 1990. *Women and Disability*. New York: St. Martin's Press.

Lorber, Judith. 2000. "Gender Contradictions and Status Dilemmas in Disability," in *Expanding the Scope of Social Science Research on Disability*, edited by Barbara M. Altman and Sharon N. Barnartt. Stamford, CT: JAI Press.

Mairs, Nancy. 1986. *Plaintext*. Tucson: University of Arizona Press.

———. 1996. *Waist-High in the World: A Life among the Nondisabled*. Boston: Beacon.

Mathers, Colin D., Ritu Sadana, Joshua A. Salomon, Christopher J.L. Murray, and Alan D. Lope. 2001. "Healthy Life Expectancy in 191 Countries, 1999." *Lancet* 357: 1685–1691.

McGrath, Charles. 2005. "Hell on Wheels." *New York Times*, 26 March, B7, 13.

McRuer, Robert, and Abby L. Wilkerson (eds.). 2003. Desiring Disability: Queer Studies Meets Disability Studies. Special issue, *GLQ: A Journal of Lesbian and Gay Studies* 9: (1–2).

Murphy, Robert F. 1990. *The Body Silent*. New York: Norton.

Noddings, Nel. 2002. *Starting at Home: Caring and Social Policy*. Berkeley: University of California Press.

Nosek, Margaret A., Mary Ellen Young, Diana H. Rintala et al. 1995. "Barriers to Reproductive Health Maintenance Among Women with Physical Disabilities." *Journal of Women's Health* 4: 505–518.

O'Brien, Ruth. 2005. *Bodies in Revolt: Gender, Disability, and an Alternative Ethic of Care*. New York: Routledge.

Peifer, D. 1999. "Seeing is Be(liev)ing," in *Restricted Access: Lesbians on Disability,* edited by Victoria A. Brownworth and Susan Raffo. Seattle, WA: Seal Press.

Rohrer, Judy. 2005. "Toward a Full-Inclusion Feminism: A Feminist Deployment of Disability Analysis." *Feminist Studies* 31: 34–63.

Rousso, Harilyn, and Michael L. Wehmeyer (eds.). 2001. *Double Jeopardy: Addressing Gender Equity in Special Education.* Albany: State University of New York Press.

Saxton, Marsha. 1994. Women with Disabilities: Reproduction and Motherhood. Special issue, *Sexuality and Disability* 12 (Summer).

Saxton, Marsha, and Florence Howe (eds.). 1987. *With Wings: An Anthology of Literature by and about Women with Disabilities.* New York: Feminist Press.

Schillinger, Liesl. 2005. "Arms and the Man: The Star of 'The Flid Show.'" *New York Times* Arts & Leisure, 30 January, 8.

Serlin, David. 2003. "Crippling Masculinity: Queerness and Disability in U.S. Military Culture, 1800–1945." *GLQ: A Journal of Lesbian and Gay Studies* 9: 149–179.

Shakespeare, Tom, Kath Gillespie-Sells, and Dominic Davies (eds.). 1996. *The Sexual Politics of Disability: Untold Desires.* New York: Cassell.

Sherry, Mark. 2004. "Overlaps and Contradictions Between Queer Theory and Disability Studies." *Disability & Society* 19: 769–783.

Smith, Bonnie G., and Beth Hutchison (eds.). 2004. *Gendering Disability.* New Brunswick, NJ: Rutgers University Press.

Taylor, Chris. 2001. "Who Goes There and How?: Lesbians and Disability." *Women Writers: A Zine,* edited by Kim Wells. Online Journal. Published 11 May. http://www.womenwriters.net/may2001/taylor.htm.

Thomas, Carol. 1999. *Female Forms: Experiencing and Understanding Disability.* Philadelphia: Open University Press.

Tommasini, Anthony. 2004. "It's the Vocal Cords That Matter Most." *New York Times,* 28 January, E1, 6.

Tremain, Shelley (ed.). 1996. *Pushing the Limits: Disabled Dykes Produce Culture.* Toronto: Women's Press.

Tronto, Joan C. 1993. *Moral Boundaries: A Political Argument for an Ethic of Care.* New York, Routledge.

———. 2006. "Moral Perspectives: Gender, Ethics, and Political Theory," in *Handbook of Gender and Women's Studies,* edited by Kathy Davis, Mary Evans, and Judith Lorber. London: Sage.

Vansteenwegen, Alfons, I. Jans, and Arlynn T. Revell. 2003. "Sexual Experience of Women with a Physical Disability: A Comparative Study." *Sexuality and Disability* 21: 283–290.

Weiss, Meira. 1994. *Conditional Love: Parental Relations Toward Handicapped Children.* Westport, CT: Greenwood Press.

Wendell, Susan. 1996. *The Rejected Body: Feminist Philosophical Reflections on Disability.* New York: Routledge.

Willmuth, Mary, and Lillian Holcomb (eds.). 1993. *Women with Disabilities: Found Voices.* New York: Haworth.

Zola, Irving Kenneth. 1982a. *Missing Pieces: A Chronicle of Living with a Disability.* Philadelphia: Temple University Press.

——— (ed.). 1982b. *Ordinary Lives: Voices of Disability and Disease.* Cambridge, MA: Apple-wood Books.

CHAPTER 8

Violent Bodies
Violence and Violations

Key concepts
femicide, gender-based violence, government-sponsored violence, honor crimes, imprisoned bodies, military bodies, sex slaves, sexual torture, suicide bombers

The theme we have been developing throughout this book is how bodies are constructed to be masculine or feminine, how they are shaped to conform to gendered expectations, and how these expectations are modified or resisted. At the same time as individual bodies are gendered, bodies are gendered in the mass. Particularly in times of conflict, bodies in the mass are subject to violent, injurious actions. They suffer bombings, war injuries, imprisonment, torture, rape, and sexual slavery. As with so much of social embodiment, violence to bodies is not "equal opportunity." Men and women suffer differently, and the poor and disadvantaged are the most likely victims.

Governments in Western societies maintain social order through masculine values—coercion, domination, and military and police strength. Men swell the ranks of military institutions and the corporations that benefit from the military—the "military industrial complex." In the prison industrial complex, men are overwhelmingly the wardens, prison guards, and the prisoners. Even in peacetime, nations often behave as if they are under attack by some enemy or violent criminals, which stirs up fear and anxiety among their citizens and justifies spending a large part of the national budget on the criminal justice system and the military and its weapons. Nations also encourage citizens to join the military voluntarily or to submit to required military service. These are all instances of government-sponsored, legitimated violence.

The gendered issues in body violence are not straightforward. The military and prison systems are major sources of violence to bodies through injuries, physical abuse, and torture. Women as well as men are soldiers and prisoners, but the bodies that suffer are predominantly those of men. When women are the perpetrators of violence, as prison guards or suicide bombers, their rarity makes them major news. Their actions call into question the conventional and feminist views of women as nurturing, empathic caretakers. We are more familiar with women's vulnerability in times of conflict—as rape victims and sexual slaves. This familiarity often makes the violence done to their bodies invisible.

MILITARY BODIES

In many societies, the government reserves the right to require military service of its citizens—called conscription or the draft. Except for Chile and Israel, which also draft women, other countries with required military service only draft men. In the United States, women may volunteer for the military, but if there were a national emergency requiring a draft, there would be a political issue over gender equality, because historically only men have been drafted.

In the volunteer military in the United States, Black people are overrepresented, and people of Hispanic origin are underrepresented. In 2002, 13.1 percent of the U.S. population aged 18–24 was categorized as Black, and 13.3 percent was categorized as Hispanic; Black people were 21.8 percent of enlisted military personnel on active duty, and 10 percent were Hispanic (Adamshick 2005, Table 1). In contrast, commissioned officers are overwhelmingly White. In 2002, 38.8 percent of the enlisted military personnel were classified as "minority," but only 19.7 percent of the officers (Adamshick 2005, Table 2). In 2004 and 2005, the number of Black recruits declined considerably, presumably because of lack of support for the war in Iraq (White 2005). Among all groups, volunteering for the military rose again in 2008 and burgeoned in 2009, a surge attributed to high unemployment (Alvarez 2009a, Lake 2009).

In 2008, women comprised about 14 percent of the 1.4 million people on active duty in the U.S. military (Swarns 2008). Of active duty women serving in the U.S. Armed Forces in 2008, the Air Force had the highest percentage of women (19.6 percent) and the Marine Corps the lowest (6.1 percent) (The Women's Memorial Fund 2009). Women in the U.S. military are not supposed to serve in combat, but there isn't a clear front line nor are there safe areas in modern wars (Alvarez 2009b, Myers 2009). In Iraq, women are drivers in supply convoys, military police, and checkpoint patrollers, where they are needed to search and question Iraqi women. In all these jobs, they are vulnerable to roadside bombs, suicide bombers, and mortar fire. They are not supposed to be part of combat units, but according to newspaper accounts, when more soldiers are needed for bomb disposal and intelligence, women are "attached" rather than "assigned" to the front line (Alvarez 2009b). The presence of women as embodied beings in the U.S. military is clearly troublesome to the masculine status quo, and women fighting and dying alongside men soldiers hasn't eradicated sexual harassment and rape. As sociologists Monica Casper and Lisa Jean Moore argue,

> Through practices of rape and sexual harassment exemplified by the 1991 Tailhook and the 1996 Aberdeen scandals, the military as an institution continues to have hostility to fully integrating women into its ranks. Aberdeen Proving Ground, the U.S. Army base in Maryland, was the site of sexual assault and rape of female trainees by their male superiors, twelve of whom were indicted. The very materiality of women's bodies and their routine sexualization is clearly troublesome to the military. The pain and suffering of women's bodies at the hands of the enemy is deployed symbolically as a means to bolster the military's masculinity and nationalism—"we can and will protect our women." But the actual bodies and experiences of women are missing in action when their pain and suffering is caused by the military itself....(2009, 141, 143)

In her memoir, *Love My Rifle More Than You,* Kayla Williams (2005), a translator and former U.S. Army sergeant, reports being offered money in exchange for showing her breasts to her male comrades.

Women's participation in military occupations and peacekeeping forces has also changed the techniques of maintaining peace. For example, in 2010, in the African country of Liberia, a special all-woman United Nations police unit from India has been used to "employ distinctive social skills in a rugged macho domain" (Carvajal 2010). These women comprise about 14 percent of the police peacekeepers in Liberia. Liberian officials report that women of this unit act as mediators rather than invaders and invoke a type of "mother culture," getting people to change their behavior in line with gendered expectations. Similarly, in Afghanistan "female engagement teams," four to five member units that accompany patrols are beginning to be used as a means to engage with Afghan women. These women Marines have greater access to "rural Afghan women, rarely seen by outsiders, [who] have more influence in their villages than male commanders might think, and that the Afghan women's good will could make Afghans, both men and women, less suspicious of American troops" (Bumiller 2010, 1, 4).

In the United States, many women and men of color volunteer for the military as a way to attain an education and a good job or to escape violent and deteriorated inner cities. White women and men who enlist in the armed services tend to come from impoverished small towns or rural areas. The recruiters often entice poor and vulnerable young people to enlist by claiming that they can make something of themselves and see the world by joining the military. Rarely is there a discussion of battles, having to kill or be killed, losing limbs and eyes, being paralyzed, scarred, or suffering post-traumatic stress disorder. The strategies of recruitment and staffing the ranks of the military indicate that in a society stratified by class, race, and ethnicity, the bodies of poor people, especially those of color, are not as valuable as middle and upper-class White bodies. Poor bodies of color may be considered more "disposable." Who better to fight and put their bodies on the line than those who uphold the society's values of achievement but don't have access to resources to achieve? Offered a legitimate way up the social ladder, many are willing to risk their bodies and lives.

The survival rate among the U.S. military in Iraq is higher than in previous wars, but wounds are multiple and severe:

> Survivors are coming home with grave injuries, often from roadside bombs, that will transform their lives: combinations of damaged brains and spinal cords, vision and hearing loss, disfigured faces, burns, amputations, mangled limbs, and psychological ills like depression and post-traumatic stress. (Grady 2006, 1)

Many of these multiple wounds are from explosions—improvised explosive devices, or I.E.D.'s, mortars, bombs, and grenades. As of March 2009, the Defense Department reported that 31,131 members of the U.S. military had been wounded in action since the beginning of the war in Iraq (Fischer 2009, Table 1). Women who have been in combat suffer all these traumas, too, and like men with post-traumatic stress disorders, they tend to suffer in silence (Cave 2009).

IMPRISONED BODIES

In times of high anxiety about personal and national security, there is an increase in the scope and amplitude of mechanisms of social control. These systems of social control do not treat people equally. The prison industrial complex has thrived by incarcerating particular types of bodies—primarily poor, male, and non-White (Davis 1998). Once in prison, incarcerated men are vulnerable to the violence per-petrated by other inmates and guards.

The United States population has about 5 percent of the global population, but the U.S. prison population accounts for almost a quarter of the world's pris-oners (roughly 2.3 million in 2008) (Liptak 2008). One explanation is that the United States criminal justice system has stricter federal and state legal codes and sentencing mandates, so particular individuals are criminalized at a greater rate than in other countries. For example, the United States' war on drugs cre-ated very strict sentencing mandates that led drug offenders (sometimes drug addicts and sellers, but also casual users) to swell the ranks of prisoners (Austin et al. 2007).

There is a great racial and ethnic disparity among prisoners, which appears to be increasing. Between 1990 and 2008, Hispanic jail inmates increased at a faster average annual growth than White or Black inmates and Blacks were three times more likely than Hispanics and five times more likely than Whites to be in jail (U.S. Department of Justice 2009). Statistics from 1995 reveal that one in three Black men between the ages of 20 and 29 years old were under correctional supervision or control (Mauer and Huling 1995). Although incarceration rates for women are lower than those of men at every age, they show the same racial ethnic breakdown (Harrison et al. 2005).

The racial ethnic disparities are due in part to differences in sentencing for non-White men and boys compared to their White counterparts. A review of 40 studies investigating the link between race and sentence severity found evidence of direct racial discrimination that resulted in significantly longer and more severe sentences for Black and Hispanic young, unemployed men (Spohn 2000). Racial group is a determinant in who receives the death penalty, particularly when it comes to the racial group of the victim. A study conducted by the Associated Press reviewed 1,936 indictments in Ohio from October 1981 through 2002. One of the most significant findings was that offenders facing a death penalty charge for kill-ing a White person were twice as likely to go to death row than if they had killed a Black victim (Welsh-Huggins 2005). These different rates of incarceration and sentencing are evidence that in the United States, the least valued bodies are those of Black men.

SEXUAL TORTURE

Torture is a violation of body and mind. Tortured bodies are maimed and often killed, but those who survive often suffer the psychological effects for the rest of their lives. Sexual torture specifically targets minds—the sense of oneself as a man or a woman. Torture involving the genitalia may maim or kill, but its purpose is to cause humiliation as well as excruciating pain. Based on her study of 27 civil-war-torn countries, Kathryn Farr (2009) coined the term "extreme war rape" to describe regularized, war-normative acts of sexual violence accompanied by intentional serious harm, including physical injury, physical and psychological torture, and sometimes murder. These pervasive intentional and violent assaults terrorize communities and are overwhelmingly perpetrated against women, often with genocidal intentions. That is, female bodies are raped in order to impregnate and through forced procreation, contaminate not only her body, but her family, tribe, and nation.

Men as well as women have been subject to sexual torture, although men are extremely reluctant to talk about it. The following excerpt is from a report of the Medical Centre for Human Rights. It documents the prevalence of sexual torture of men, and the ways that masculinity is attacked through defiling the male body.

Sexual Torture of Men

◆◆◆

Pauline Oosterhoff
Medical Committee, Netherlands

Prisca Zwanikken
Royal Tropical Institute, Amsterdam

Evert Ketting
Sexual and Reproductive Health Center, Amsterdam

Rape and other forms of sexual torture are a means of terrorising and controlling a population, e.g. to terrorise an ethnic minority. Governments have probably always used it in both war and peacetime. Sexual torture of women in detention during peacetime has been documented in recent years in dozens of countries, including China, Egypt, Spain and France,[4,5] and is also common during war.[1] In every armed conflict investigated by Amnesty International in 1999 and 2000, sexual torture of women was reported, including rape.[5] Rape of male prisoners and sexual torture of homosexual men are also well documented.[6]

When sexual torture occurs, it often follows arrests and round-ups of the local population, particularly where repressive governments are faced with armed rebellion. Torture might take place in a field, a school, the victim's own house or a torture chamber or prison.[7,8] Like other forms of torture, sexual torture usually takes place during the first week of captivity, most often at night and often when guards are drunk.[8] . . .

Before World War II, rape and sexual violence were considered inevitable by-products of war or ascribed to renegade soldiers. Even at the Nuremberg trials, not a single case of rape was punished.[7]

The 1949 Geneva Conventions on the Protection of Civilians in Time of War were the first in which international law addressed wartime sexual violence. Protocol II to the Geneva Conventions explicitly outlaws "outrages upon personal dignity, in particular humiliating and degrading treatment, rape, enforced prostitution, and any form of indecent assault."[9] The 1984 Convention against Torture and Other Cruel, Inhuman or Degrading Treatment or Punishment, which in Article 1 gives the definition of torture still accepted today,[2] does not specifically mention sexual violence as a form of torture, however.

Legal recognition that sexual violence could constitute torture came as a result of the war in the former Yugoslavia, with its abundant testimony by female rape survivors. The International Criminal Tribunal for the Former Yugoslavia (ICTY) was mandated to try the perpetrators of heinous crimes (genocide, crimes against humanity, violations of the laws of war and serious breaches of the 1949 Geneva Conventions) committed during the conflict.

In its Celebici judgment, the ICTY established that sexual violence constitutes torture when it is intentionally inflicted by an official, or with official instigation, consent or tolerance, for purposes such as intimidation, coercion, punishment, or eliciting information or confessions, or for any reason based on discrimination.[3] ...

Incidence of Sexual Torture of Men

It was not possible to calculate or even estimate the incidence of sexual torture in wartime Croatia. Only a small proportion of survivors are likely to have admitted to having been sexually tortured. Many victims may have been killed. Their remains, even if discovered, may not show evidence of sexual torture. Thus, the study was not designed to measure incidence. However, it is possible to try to develop a broad sense of whether sexual torture of men occurred often enough to be considered a regular feature of wartime violence or limited to a few exceptions.

Among the 22 male torture survivors in the International Rehabilitation Council for Torture (ICRT) Victims Programme, 14 reported having suffered some type of sexual torture, ten suffered genital beatings or electroshock, and four had been raped.

Of the 1,648 testimonies screened by Medical Centre for Human Rights (MCHR) staff, 78 self-reported sexual torture. Among the 55 survivors of sexual torture who sought help from MCHR, 24 were subjected to genital beatings or electroshock, 11 were raped, seven were forced to engage in sexual acts and 13 were fully or partially castrated. In addition, MCHR staff had found six post-mortem cases of total castration.

Comparatively few self-reported cases of sexual torture were found by the Centre for Psychotrauma. Of the 5,751 Croatian war veteran patients, nine reported having suffered genital beatings and/or electroshock, and five reported rape. Among the unknown number of male civilians, one reported having been raped and three reported genital beatings.

The data from the ICRT and the MCHR support the conclusion that sexual torture of men was a regular, unexceptional component of violence in wartime Croatia, not a rare occurrence. The data from the Centre for Psychotrauma were probably at variance because of the nature of the sample and the attitudes of at least one therapist....

An Open Secret

One of the striking points to emerge from the study is how silent male survivors of sexual torture have remained about their experiences. In the MCHR therapy group, specifically advertised as a group for male survivors of sexual torture, none of the men who showed up would initially admit to having suffered sexual torture themselves; they claimed they had come on behalf of friends. It was only after some time that group members acknowledged they had been tortured. In the ICRT group, none of the survivors mentioned sexual torture during intake interviews. Other types of torture were discussed relatively openly, but sexual torture was not broached until later in therapy, according to the therapists.

Torture is often carried out in public to demonstrate the power of the perpetrators. Narratives by male survivors show that torture was frequently perpetrated by groups and in full and deliberate view of bystanders. The example below illustrates the public nature of the sexual torture:

> First they grabbed X and pushed him down by the road. He was the weakest.... Four men pushed him down and were holding his head, legs and arms. Y approached him, she had a scalpel in her hand. The men who pushed him down took his trousers off. She castrated him. We had to watch. I was watching, but I was so scared that I did not see much. ... One of the Chetniks had a wooden stick and he hit X a few times across his neck. X showed no signs of life anymore. Then three Chetniks shot at X. The fourth took a pistol and shot him in the head. (Unpublished testimony, a soldier at MCHR)

The silence that envelopes the sexual torture of men in the aftermath of the war in Croatia stands in strange contrast to the public nature of the crimes themselves.

As shown in the literature and confirmed by our study, sexual torture of men in wartime occurs regularly. While there are certain specific differences in the sexual torture of men and women and its effects, the psychological symptoms experienced by male and female survivors seem to be substantially similar.

In fact, perpetrators seem to torture both men and women sexually. Although more women than men have reported sexual torture in some studies, lack of recognition may discourage male survivors from reporting sexual torture even more than women, and professionals may fail to recognise cases. Few men admit being sexually tortured or seek help. Health professionals, the legal system and human rights advocates have proven to be somewhat gender-biased about sexual torture and have only recently begun to acknowledge that men as well as women are potential victims. It is difficult enough for survivors of sexual torture to come forward; men should not have to face the additional problem of disbelief that it could even happen to them at all.

The occurrence of sexual torture of men during wartime and in conflict situations remains something of an open secret, although it happens regularly and often takes place in public. These shortcomings are a critical barrier for those needing treatment and legal assistance, and limit the possibility of action against the perpetrators. The challenge is to turn this open secret into a recognised fact, so that it can be deterred and prosecuted alongside the sexual torture of women.

References

1. Shanks, L, Ford N, Schull M, et al. *Responding to rape.* Lancet 2001; 357 (9252): 304.
2. Convention against Torture and Other Cruel, Inhuman or Degrading Treatment or Punishment, G.A. Res. 39/46. [Annex, 39 U.N. GAOR Supp. (No. 51) at 197, U.N. Doc. A/39/51 (1984)], entered into force June 26, 1987. Geneva: United Nations, 1984.
3. Celebici Judgement, *Prosecutor v. Delalic, Mucic, Delic, and Landzo*, Case No. IT-96–21-T, Para. 770, November 1998.
4. Amnesty International, International Centre for Human Rights and Democratic Development. Documenting Human Rights Violations by State Agents: Sexual Violence. Montreal: ICHRDD, 1999.
5. Amnesty International. "Broken bodies, shattered minds, torture and ill-treatment of women." Amnesty International Index: ACT 40/001/2001: 2001. London: Amnesty International Publications, 2001.
6. Amnesty International, "Crimes of hate, conspiracy of silence: torture and ill-treatment based on sexual identity." Amnesty International Index: ACT 40/016/2001. London: Amnesty International Publications, 2001.
7. Asian Legal Resource Centre. Specific contexts of sexual torture and cruel, inhuman and degrading treatment. Armed conflict, Police/Penal. At: http://www.alrc.net. Accessed 11 November 2002.
8. Amnesty International. *A Glimpse of Hell: Reports on Torture Worldwide.* Forrest, D (editor). New York: New York University Press, June 2002.
9. Geneva Conventions, Protocol II, Article 4(2)(e). Protocol Additional to the Geneva Conventions of 12 August 1949, and relating to the Protection of Victims of Non-International Armed Conflicts (Protocol II), 8 June 1977. At: http://www.icrc.org. IHL.nsfl0lf9cbd575d47ca6c8c12563cd0051e783?OpenDocument. Accessed 2 February 2004.

Less physically damaging but culturally and psychologically traumatic has been the prevalent sexual humiliation of Muslim men prisoners in Iraq, Afghanistan, and Guantánamo Bay. Deplored publically, American women soldiers' collaboration raises serious questions about their use as sexual subjects. According to an official Pentagon report:

> There were several instances when female soldiers rubbed up against prisoners and touched them inappropriately. In April 2003, a soldier did that in a T-shirt after removing her uniform blouse. Following up on an F.B.I. officer's allegation that a female soldier had done a "lap dance" on a prisoner, the report described this scene from the interrogation of the so-called 20th hijacker from the 9/11 attacks: A female soldier straddled his lap, massaged his neck and shoulders, "began to enter the personal space of the subject," touched him and whispered in his ear. ... These practices are as degrading to the women as they are to the prisoners. (Editorial 2005, A18)

Why do women soldiers agree to be "pseudo lap dancers," to smear fake menstrual blood on prisoners, to be photographed holding a naked hooded man on a leash? One feminist response to the highly publicized abuses at Abu Ghraib prison in Baghdad was that the young women soldiers "succumbed to a culture of power that they did not create and could not change, though they likely didn't try" (Enda 2004). Another rationale was that the ones who were complicit were too far down the military hierarchy, and the woman general who was in charge of the prison had no other women at her level. The "critical mass" needed to change organizational culture was missing: "On the one hand, we think that women can change things. But on the other hand, if you just have a handful of women in a very militarized system, they aren't going to be any different, unfortunately," said Sanam Naraghi Anderlini, director of the Women Waging Peace policy commission (Enda 2004). These rationales don't excuse the complicity with torture; feminists have argued that women have agency, and that means taking responsibility for one's actions. We also don't hear much about the women (and men) who did protest the torture and sexual humiliation.

SUICIDE BOMBERS

So far, we have concentrated on the victims of violence and the violations done to them. A suicide bomber—a person carrying explosives with awareness and consent to detonate them strategically to kill or damage other people or property—is a human weapon. The term suicide bomber is value laden; in different circumstances, these individuals have been called homicide bombers or martyrs. Historically, rebels and revolutionaries have planted bombs in civilian areas. Also in the past, there have been occasional suicide bombers, but since September 11, 2001, "suicide bombings have rapidly evolved into perhaps the most common method of terrorism in the world, moving west from the civil war in Sri Lanka in the 1980s to the

Palestinian intifada of recent years to Iraq today" and the bombings in London in July 2005 (Eggen and Wilson 2005, A01). Suicide bombings in crowded civilian areas like marketplaces have been a daily occurrence in Afghanistan and Pakistan in 2009.

Most of the contemporary suicide bombers are men, but in 1991, a woman Tamil Tiger assassinated Prime Minister Rajiv Gandhi of India by detonating explosives strapped to her body. Since women are not often thought of as suicide bombers, the news of the first woman Palestinian suicide bomber, 27-year-old college-educated Wafa Idris, made global headlines in January 2002. In interviews after Wafa Idris's death, many attributed her suicide bombing to her frustration and loss of hope after working as a Red Crescent Society emergency paramedic and witnessing so much pain and suffering from the Palestinian-Israeli conflict (Bennet 2000a). The second woman suicide bomber blew herself up at an Israeli checkpoint just a month later. She was a 22-year-old college student, Darin Abu Eisheh, who said she was following in the footsteps of Wafa Idris, who had been praised in some of the Arab-language press as an Islamic Joan of Arc (Bennet 2002b). Al Aqsa reportedly set up a women's unit named for Wafa Idris, and the third and fourth women suicide bombers struck a few weeks later.

The use of feminist metaphors to celebrate Idris made her a hero, but body imagery kept her very much a woman: "'She bore in her belly the fetus of a rare heroism, and gave birth by blowing herself up,' the columnist Mufid Fawzie wrote in the Egyptian Daily Al Aalam al Youm" (Bennet 2002b, A8). The videotape Darin Abu Eisheh left also used birth imagery. She stated, "Let Sharon the coward know that every Palestinian woman will give birth to an army of suicide attackers, even if he tries to kill them while still in their mother's wombs, shooting them at the checkpoints of death" (Greenberg 2002, A10).

The imagery may have been feminine, but these women also projected their commitment to the Palestinian cause. Frances Hasso, who analyzed the gendered discourse around the first four Palestinian women "suicide bombers/martyrs," notes that the three women who left videos, pictures, and messages depicted themselves in militant poses and "represented their acts as explosive and embodied action, recognizing that it was more dramatic and dangerous because they are women" (2005, 29). Two of them were long-time activists, and all were politically aware. The response by Arab men was mixed, with some of the religious leaders uncomfortable with these women's public role, but activists welcomed their joining the battle. Many young Arab women "interpreted and responded to the attacks as calls for *women's* political action in defense of community" (Hasso 2005, 30). The public memorial for Wafa Idris was attended by about 3,000 people, mostly women; the funeral procession was led by the head of the Fatah women's committees. Hasso says,

> ... [T]he daring of the women's acts also generated feminist pride and increased public display of militance among Arab, including Palestinian, women and girls throughout the region.... It is as if when they inserted themselves—by dying and killing—into a sphere of politics dominated by men, the Palestinian women

militants allowed other Arab girls and women to contest their own marginality in national and regional politics. (2005, 35)

Israel is not the only place where women are using their bodies as conduits for bombs. In at least 15 separate attacks, women have been deemed responsible for the suicide bombing of public markets, train stations, and aircraft in the Russian-Chechnyan conflict (Myers 2004). Their motives are attributed to grief over the deaths of fathers, sons, and husbands. These attributions of womanly motives of grief and empathy are in marked contrast to the nationalistic and religious motives attributed to men suicide bombers, whose masculinity is interwoven into their heroic martyrdom:

> The martyr is a young, unmarried (virgin, innocent) man, fearless and strong. He is depicted with eyes cast forward to *jihad* and the blessed state of martyr-dom. His hair is dark and held back with a bandana with Qur'anic inscriptions. If depicted in full figure, he wears white, the color of a coffin, while holding a gun. Sometimes he is depicted in the foreground, leading a group of women and older male martyrs; or he is depicted in the foreground of fully veiled women and young girls, protecting them and the country's honor. (Gerami 2003, 267)

Other rationales for women suicide bombers have implied that they were forced to choose between martyrdom and an honor killing for adultery or an out-of-wedlock pregnancy. Three Chechnyan women who are suspected of bombing a plane were said to have been divorced because they couldn't have children, a severe stigma in Muslim society (Myers 2004).

Amal Amirah (2005) argues that these Western denigrations of Muslim women suicide bombers are a form of "death by culture," an erasure of their choice to be martyrs for national liberation. Much media attention is given to female suicide bombers and struggles for asserting nationalism. In the following excerpt, Dorit Naaman, a cinema studies scholar, examines how the use of the female body as a weapon conflicts with the stereotypical cross-cultural constructions of femininity.

Brides of Palestine/Angels of Death: The Case of the Palestinian Female Suicide Bombers

◆◆◆

Dorit Naaman
Queen's University

In January 2002, Wafa Idris, a 27-year-old Palestinian woman, strapped ten kilo-grams of explosives to her body and killed herself and two Israelis on a crowded Jerusalem street. Idris was the first Palestinian female suicide bomber, to be followed by nine others and several dozen failed attempts. The female suicide bomber is a social phenomenon that has left Israel and the West shocked, signaling (in both Arab and Western views) an escalation in the conflict. Idris was not the first Palestinian woman to be recruited for the fight for national liberation, as women have taken part in the Palestinian struggle from its onset, with some, including Leila Khaled and Dalal el Moughrabi, having partaken in highly publicized hijacking operations. Idris was not the first female suicide bomber either, with Hezbollah and the Tamil Tigers utilizing female suicide bombers since the 1980s. The reactions to Idris's actions vary widely, as labels such as *martyr*, *hero*, *monster*, and *terrorist* indicate. But reactions in the Arab world, in Israel, and in the West cannot be reduced to simple labels. Instead, the reactions all highlight junctures of ideological crises in the perceived roles of women in armed struggles, religion, and traditional gendered settings. Particularly in the Arab world these actions were not simply hailed but actually debated—pragmatically, morally, and, most notably, religiously. For instance, Sheikh Ahmed Yassin, spiritual leader of Hamas until his assassination by Israel in March 2004, objected to the inclusion of women initially, then altered his principled position, and in 2004 Hamas sent its first female suicide bomber, Reem el Riyashi.[1] The debates in the Arab world around Western-style feminism, religion, and the roles women should take in armed struggles are complex and, I would argue, push the already highly charged gender debate to its logical limits....

Gender and War

War generally brings with it images that fall into normative gender categories: men are fighters, women the victims. Images of women and children as widows and orphans fleeing war zones to become refugees, or media focus on rape as a war tactic in Rwanda and the former Yugoslavia, figure women as fragile, vulnerable, and in need of defense by men. Rape and forced pregnancies in particular bring forth issues of ethnic purity and position women as vehicles for the production of the next generation of ethnically pure fighters but as defenseless in and of themselves.[2] Furthermore, one aspect of any occupation (and colonization) is the perceived feminization of the occupied men. Men who were used to being sovereign agents are now subject to the rules, regulations, and whims of the occupier. As the economic situation in the occupied Palestinian territories deteriorated and as the limitations on freedom of movement increased, men were stripped of their stereotypically masculine qualities—independence, courage, ability to provide economically, and protection of the weak (women and children in particular)....

When women opt to fight alongside men, they challenge the dichotomy of woman as victim/man as defender. Women fighters are physically strong, are active (therefore agents), and, most important, are willing to kill (hence, they are violent). They challenge not only the images of women as victims of war but also the traditional patriarchal binary opposition that postulates women as physically and emotionally weak and incapable of determining and defending the course of their own lives. As a result, women fighters have often been represented—especially in mass media—as deviant from prescribed forms of femininity, forms that emphasize a woman's delicacy and fragility but also her generosity, caring nature, motherliness, and sensitivity to others' needs.[3]

Suicide operations complicate these stereotypical dynamics further—not only does the woman willingly sacrifice herself, but her actions also carry a performative aspect typical of terrorist actions by substate groups. Since these groups do not have large and well-equipped armies, they organize their political violence as spectacles that attract media and public attention. When women partake in such operations, their performance of violence and political agency—so drastically different from that of typical female roles in both news and entertainment media—enhances the sense of perplexity, fear, and aversion to the perpetrators of the acts....

Relying on the stereotypical gap between traditional feminine qualities (i.e., engaged to be married, good student) and political, violent, and supposedly masculine actions, journalists and analysts alike could not explain the phenomenon. The solution was to search for a personal explanation. For instance, after Idris's suicide attack, Western media focused on the fact that Idris was infertile and had allowed her husband to marry another woman, watching him live nearby as he became a father. It was claimed that she was unhappy and, as she could not bear children, that her life was unworthy to her. This explanation is typical, but in many of the cases that followed, the logic of such explanations is unfounded. Some of the women were happy, engaged to be married (Ayat Akhras), good students (Dareen Abu Aisheh), professionals (Hanadi Jaridat), and mothers (Reem el Riyashi). What this attempt at explanation exposes is how gendered the discussion around the female suicide bombers is. While the dozens of male suicide bombers' identities and life stories are hardly ever delved into, their reasons are assumed to be clear and grounded in both political and religious ideology. In contrast, a woman as a suicide bomber seems so oxymoronic that an individualized psychological explanation for the deviation must be found.

However, this sort of psychological explanation fails time and again. The image of woman as the symbolic nurturer, healer, and spiritual mother of the nation is challenged beyond repair, a rupture that is dealt with in the Arab world quite differently than it is in the West. Idris in particular highlights this symbolic contradiction; in her spare time Idris volunteered as a medic on an ambulance, caring for the wounded of the intifada. How did the "angel of mercy" become an "angel of death," asked one headline (Beaumont 2002). Indeed, the idea that a woman who heals people could turn around and kill others seemed so improbable that it could indicate to Western media and society only that something was wrong with this particular individual or else that there is something monstrous about the society that produces such a person.[4] In the Arab press the discourse generally focuses on the harshness of the occupation, which drives women to defend the land and the people. Although suicide bombing is met with ambivalence in the Arab world, it is nevertheless understood as an extreme means derived from an extreme situation.[5]...

Suicide Operations in the Context of Gender and Media

The phenomenon of Palestinian female suicide bombers ignited the cultural imagination in Western societies, which have produced a *Suicide Bomber Barbie*, a recent American independent film about a would-be female suicide bomber, and artworks, to name just a few responses.[6] This response highlights the gender discrepancies in reporting, editing, and exposure in mass media coverage. It is a common practice for Palestinian suicide bombers to leave videotapes of themselves, filmed against the Palestinian flag or the Dome of the Rock, holding a rifle.[7] The text is somewhat scripted and incorporates a medley of religious and nationalistic language. In Arab media the tapes are aired repeatedly, and the suicide bomber is culturally classified as a *shaheed*.[8] But in the West we rarely see the videos of the men, and even their names are often not disclosed. The case with the women is quite different, as their names are publicly emphasized and the videos aired; furthermore, they are contrasted with photos of the women from their previous lives, photos that emphasize the fact that they were young women engaged in traditional teenage habits and activities. In particular, pictures of Idris and Akhras in ordinary and secular settings were publicized and compared to pictures taken just before they headed out on their missions. The result is a demonization not only of these particular women but also of the society that could produce such monsters. In the context of mass media (especially but not only television outlets), the need for shows to sell advertisements (and ultimately products) make women a major target audience....

Furthermore, Western media tend to focus on the mothers of both men and women suicide bombers, showing them ululating and celebrating their children's actions. These images are used as supporting evidence for the ills of Palestinian society at large. But Maha Abu-Dayyeh Shamas claims that "compounding their private pain, women are subjected to extreme social pressure to behave in a certain way in public. Their private pain has to be denied for the sake of the public. Some women who have not been able to meet such societal demands (i.e. suppressing their grief in public) have actually been tranquilized by local doctors" (2003, 9). Mothers, then, are expected to perform the loss of their children in certain cultural codes that deny them their own expression of grief and that are used in Western media to mark them as uncaring mothers. This performance masks their personal pain and robs them of a genuine expression of political position, both gender-wise and via the conflict....

That is, while female suicide bombers are hailed as heroes and martyrs, they are also elevated to mythic realms that solve the problem of dealing with nontraditional gender behavior in their own society. Since women have always been accepted in national liberation struggles as the symbol of the mother nation, the designation of the title *bride* suggests a comfortable place in the patriarchal nationalist project (Abdo 2002, 592).[9] Interestingly, Frances Hasso shows that the application of the title *bride* (implying also "feminine beauty, female weakness and womanly sacrifice" [Hasso 2005, 42]) is selective and does not apply to all female suicide bombers. Particularly telling is the lack of attention in the Arab media to the second female suicide bomber, Dareen Abu Aisheh. Abu Aisheh was a brilliant student of English at Al Najah University in Nablus, an outspoken feminist, and a devout Muslim. She was also a militant and was the first to leave a videotape recording indicating her intentions and implicating Arab leaders as weak in their response to the Palestinian situation. Hasso argues that Arab media ignored Abu Aisheh "because she can be constructed in no other way but as a militant *woman* and a devout Muslim. The words, images, and known history of Abu Aisheh were not conducive to deployments of heterosexual romance, desire, frailty, and feminized beauty" (2005, 42).[10] Regardless of the narratives the women tried to communicate in their actions and videos, the dominant narrative in the Arab public sphere (political, media, and local) tied these women into heteronormative narratives as mothers and brides, narratives that affirmed the gender status quo. Whether discussing mythic brides or monsters, the discourse in both the Arab world and the West generally avoids uncomfortable questions of subjectivity, agency, and aggression, all qualities that are not befitting women according to patriarchal norms....

Narratives of Martyrdom

...Female suicide bombers use their bodies as weapons, thus circumventing the patriarchal system and entering the symbolic order as (dead) symbols or as myths. Most feminist critics agree that national movements, particularly in the postcolonial context, have for the most part betrayed women's struggle for gender equality and blocked their participation in the newly established nation-state (see, e.g., Abdo and Lentin 2002; Giles et al. 2003). The phenomenon of female suicide bombers highlights some of the problematic relations of gender to the nationalist project of liberation, but at the same time, female suicide bombers get more attention than women combatants because of their ahistorical (either mythic or terrorist) classification. I believe the reason for this discrepancy is that women fighters challenge the patriarchal army order in more profound ways than suicide bombers, ways that are harder to dismiss or subvert. Khaled, perhaps the best-known Palestinian woman fighter, has commented about the reception of the Palestinian female suicide bombers by religious leaders: "When the religious leaders say that women who make those actions are finally equal to men, I have a problem. Everyone is equal in death—rich, poor, Arab, Jew, Christian, we are all equal. I would rather see women equal to men in life" (quoted in Victor 2003, 63–64). Like Khaled and Kamila Shamise, other feminists call for nuanced attention to the way that gender plays into the already complex medley of politics, nationalism, religion, patriarchy, economy, tradition, honor, and social norms in the Palestinian Israeli conflict.

Conclusion

...Now let us return to Idris, the medic and first Palestinian female suicide bomber. Is she a monster? A terrorist? A freedom fighter? A martyr? A victim? The answer clearly lies not in her action or even in her choice of how to represent herself but in the diverse and often competing narratives of politicians and media alike. The politicians' narratives tend to frame the actions of women suicide bombers in ways that minimize and subvert the overt confrontation of gender politics present in the women's own narratives and actions. Ultimately, this co-optation renders the affront on gender politics ineffective, or effective only insofar as it serves the nationalist and patriarchal project.

Notes

1. For Yassin's and others' positions on the matter, see MEMRI (2002).
2. For an extended discussion, see Coomaraswamy (2003). There are also reports of women joining the Liberation Tamil Tiger Eelam in Sri Lanka as a way to defend themselves against the danger of rape by Indian soldiers of the Indian Peacekeeping Force units. I thank Neloufer De Mel for pointing this out.
3. A good feminist analysis of those stereotypes can be found in Heinecken (2003).
4. For instance, Olivia Ward of the *Toronto Star* writes: "The participation of women and, sometimes, teenage girls in an increasing number of deadly acts has horrified the international public, and a wave of revulsion has rolled through the media at female violence in its most ruthless form. Yet, the extent and causes of women's violence are uncertain and remain unpredictable in a world in which aggression has been the province of men, and violent women considered mentally unbalanced or possessed by unimaginable evil" (2004, A6).
5. For a good overview of the discourse in Arab media surrounding suicide operations and martyrdom, see Hasso (2005). In the conclusion to the article, Frances S. Hasso writes: "My analysis and understanding of suicide/martyrdom attacks takes for granted that Palestinians in the West Bank and Gaza Strip undertake them to resist settler-colonial domination at a historical point of Zionism's almost complete (ideological, economic, diplomatic and military) 'triumph' over the native population" (2005, 43).
6. For *Suicide Bomber Barbie*, see http://www.theculture.net/barbie/index.html. *Day Night Day Night* (2006) describes the last forty-eight hours in the life of a would-be female suicide bomber in New York City. The film never explains her personal motivation, her social background, or even the goals of those who sent her on the mission, and as such is vacuous at best. Dror Felier, an Israeli-born Swedish citizen, created an art installation in which Hanadi Jaradat's picture floats in a pool of blood. The work inspired a diplomatic incident whereby the Israeli ambassador to Sweden tried to destroy it during a gala opening. Tamil Tiger female suicide operations in Sri Lanka have already inspired an Indian film, *The Terrorist* (1999).
7. There are also posters produced in the local towns and villages that are collages of an image of the person with the Dome of the Rock, the flag, and other nationalist symbols as well as accompanying text. These posters produce a narrative of the act of martyrdom that conforms to a script. For a good discussion of the role of the posters, see Abu Hashhash (2006).
8. It is important to note that anyone who dies from Israeli fire is considered a *shaheed*, regardless of whether she or he has been violent or involved in fighting.
9. For a fuller discussion of the mother nation, see Naaman (2000).
10. I would also like to point out that while testimonies from Abu Aisheh's friends and family account for diverse reasons for her action, Victor's own selective narrative concludes that "Darine Abu Aisheh is...a woman who killed herself because she couldn't face the prospect of an arranged marriage when her goal in life was to continue her education

and work in academia" (Victor 2003, 196). Nowhere in the friends' interviews is it suggested that if Abu Aisheh did marry she would be barred from an academic career. Such a reading is not only reductive, but it also conforms to and reaffirms stereotypes about the gender backwardness of Muslim society. Hasso's own (2005) reading—while critical of the manipulation of women in the patriarchal structure of Palestinian society—accounts for the complexity of the situation.

References

Abdo, Nahla. 2002. "Women, War and Peace: Reflection from the Intifada." *Women's Studies International Forum* 25(5): 585–93.

Abdo, Nahla, and Ronit Lentin, eds. 2002. *Women and the Politics of Military Confrontation: Palestinian and Israeli Gendered Narratives of Dislocation*. New York: Berghahn.

Abu-Dayyeh Shamas, Maha. 2003. "Women in Situations of Organized Violence: A Case of Double Jeopardy." Report, Women's Centre for Legal Aid and Counseling. http://www.wclac.org/reports/violence.pdf.

Abu Hashhash, Mahmoud. 2006. "On the Visual Representation of Martyrdom in Palestine." *Third Text* 20(3/4): 391–404.

Beaumont, Peter. 2002a. "From an Angel of Mercy to Angel of Death." *Guardian*, January 31. http://www.guardian.co.uk/Archive/Article/0,4273,4346503,00.html.

Coomaraswamy, Radhika. 2003. "A Question of Honour: Women, Ethnicity, and Armed Conflict." In Giles et al. 2003, 91–102.

Giles, Wenona, Malathi de Alwis, Edith Klein, and Nekula Silva, eds. 2003. *Feminists under Fire: Exchanges across War Zones*. Toronto: Between the Lines.

Hasso, Frances S. 2005. "Discursive and Political Deployments by/of the 2002 Palestinian Women Suicide Bombers/Martyrs." *Feminist Review* 81: 23–51.

Heinecken, Dawn. 2003. *The Warrior Women of Television: A Feminist Cultural Analysis of the New Female Body in Popular Media*. New York: Peter Lang.

MEMRI (Middle East Media Research Institute). 2002. "The Celebration of the First Palestinian Female Suicide Bomber, Part 1." *Al-Sharq Al-Awsat*, February 12. http://www.imra.org.il/story.php3?id=10155.

Naaman, Dorit. 2000. "Woman/Nation: A Postcolonial Look at Female Subjectivity." *Quarterly Review of Film and Video* 17(4): 333–42.

The Terrorist. 1999. Directed by Santosh Sivan. Port Washington, NY: Fox Lorber.

Victor, Barbara. 2003. *Army of Roses: Inside the World of Palestinian Women Suicide Bombers*. Emmaus, PA: Rodale.

Ward, Olivia. 2004. "The Changing Face of Violence." *Toronto Star*, October 10, A6.

WOMEN'S VULNERABILITY

Women suicide bombers and sexual humiliators show that women's experiences of violent conflict are not all the same. During World War II, women were concentration camp victims and members of the resistance in Nazi-occupied countries. German women were concentration-camp guards and victims of rape by the Russian and American post-war occupation armies. Korean women were abducted into military sexual slavery for Japanese soldiers, and Japanese women who survived the atom bombing of Hiroshima and Nagasaki were sterile and badly scarred. In the twentieth century, nine out of ten people killed in wars were civilians, and these were overwhelmingly women and children (Hynes 2004).

Women may be combatants, prison guards, and resistance fighters, but they are more commonly ordinary citizens vulnerable to rape, forced pregnancy, and sexual slavery. As the United Nations Security Council on Women and Peace and Security reported in 2004:

> Gender-based violence is a form of discrimination that seriously inhibits the ability of women to enjoy their rights and freedoms on a basis of equality with men. The unacceptable violence against women and girls in peacetime is further exacerbated during armed conflict and in its aftermath. Both State and non-State actors are responsible for severe violations of women's human rights, including killings, abductions, rape, sexual torture and slavery, as well as denial of access to food and health care, with dramatic consequences. (p. 16)

In many destabilized and devastated countries, women often end up becoming prostitutes through coercion or economic necessity to help their families survive. Much of the global trafficking in sex workers since the fall of communism has been from countries in the former Soviet Union to Western Europe, Israel, and the United States. There is a concentration of child and teenage sex workers in Asia and South America; some are boys but most are girls.

Another persistent source of violence against women are "honor crimes"— family killings of wives, sisters, and daughters who have been raped, had sexual relations outside of marriage, or committed adultery. These crimes take place in the context of patriarchal cultures. Nadera Shalhoub-Kevorkian, a social worker and criminologist who has done first-hand research with women living with the threat of honor crimes, says that they are part of a culture of oppression of women and should be called *femicide*.

Reexamining Femicide

◆◆◆

Nadera Shalhoub-Kevorkian
Hebrew University, Jerusalem

Femicide is cloaked in silence and has rarely been investigated. This article aims to break the silence by reexamining the definition of the crime. The current definition, which deals only with the actual killing of the victim, is quite narrow, indicating that the phenomenon is still misunderstood. I will suggest how this definition can be expanded, contextually grounded, and improved.

The current definition adequately describes the crime of killing a woman, but it fails to cover the arduous process leading up to her death. In this context, death needs redefining. Death in femicide is currently defined medicolegally as the inability to breathe. In the new definition that I propose, death has already occurred by the time a female is put on "death row"—that is, when she is effectively sentenced to death by murder and lives under the continual threat of being killed. Even at this point, I consider her a victim of femicide, and I thus redefine death as the inability to live. Although victims of femicide are technically alive, they are in a mode of life that they never wanted and completely reject, a mode that is perhaps best described as death-in-life.

Living on death row, always in fear of execution, results in an inability to live and is a major part of the death process. This view of femicide derives from the central argument (which I believe should be at the heart of human rights and feminist debates) that *sexism* and *gender oppression* do not just refer to the binary relations between men and women, or the causal relations between patriarchy and female abuse, but constitute the central social dynamic of the world that recreates, maintains, and justifies a pervasive, inhumane social abuse.[1] The political, social, and economic contexts within which femicide crimes take place affect the social reaction to them. Therefore, studying femicide as a cultural or traditional practice will reveal that it is not about culture but, rather, is part of a sociopolitical and economic legacy that reflects a hidden machinery of oppression....

The Center for Women's Policy Studies (1991) regards femicide as fitting accepted definitions of hate crimes since it is based on gender and on the intimidation and terrorization of women by men. Femicide is a universal crime found in India, Pakistan, Afghanistan, Brazil, Canada, the United States, the United Kingdom, and other countries around the world (Radford and Russel 1992). Indeed, the number of men who kill women is much larger than the number of women who kill men (Stout 1992). For example, on the Island of Montreal, women were the main homicide victims (1954–62 and 1985–89), and the offenses usually occurred within the residence the victim shared with the perpetrator. While demographic and situational factors affect the killing of females by their male relatives (Stout 1992), gender and the possessiveness of males toward their female partners emerge as major features of male violence in situations of sexual intimacy. This has caused researchers to call for a reexamination of cases of intimate violence leading to homicide, especially in light of their epidemic and escalating increase (Radford and Russel 1992)....

Most writers who have dealt with this issue state that this is the tradition and the culture (Ginat 1982). Edward Said criticizes such orientalists, stating that they portray oriental women as part of harem life—exotic and erotic—without looking at the political, colonial, and social contexts in which Middle Eastern women live (1979, 15). Looking at femicide as a cultural traditional practice that occurs only in the "Orient" empowers the existing patriarchal mechanisms and strategies and helps maintain such criminal behavior as "normal."

Femicide also occurs in the West, but, while Westerners attribute the etiology of femicide to individual violent behavior, orientalists attribute femicide to primitive cultural practices and beliefs. Such orientalist notions thus construct the system of analysis in a discriminatory, stereotypical manner. Naming femicide as "crimes of passion" in the West and "crimes of honor" in the East is one reflection of the discriminatory constructions of frames of analyses, which build a simplistic system that hides the intersectionality among political, economic, cultural, and gender factors....

One of the methods for defining and imprisoning women within the bars of honor is the use of metaphors to explain the significance of honor in their society. One famous metaphor is that women's honor is like glass; any scratch may ruin it. The continuous use of this metaphor by both men and women further oppresses, controls, and objectifies women. Objectifying a woman prevents relating to her feelings, suffering, and pain. This denies a woman the right to redefine femicide based on her voice, forcing her to stay with the classical, politically acceptable definition. The use of metaphors provides an interpretive framework that guides and affects social meanings and serves as a mental map for understanding the world. The metaphor mentioned above, reflecting the larger system of structural power, has provided suggestive maps for years of gender oppression....

Voices of the Silent—Words of Pain and Resistance

My work with abused women, who believed that they were or who actually were under the threat of murder, has revealed that they all shared similar experiences of fearing death and living in continual danger. Fear of death was so great that they clearly perceived the act of killing as easier to bear. The expansion of the definition of femicide is, therefore, based on the factors given below.

Voices leading to death

THE VICTIM: FEAR OF DEATH CREATES A LIVING DEATH

The women living on death row expressed their continuous fear of being killed and hoped to die, knowing that one day a family member would kill them. They kept repeating expressions such as "I wish I would die," "I die millions of times every day," and "death is easier for me than this agony, suffering, misery." And many of these women have indeed attempted suicide or succeeded in committing suicide.

One sixteen-year-old girl was raped by a taxi driver on her way home from school. The fact that she was late reaching home and that her face and body were injured signaled to the family that something serious had taken place. She explained:

> I spent many hours circling around the house, wondering what can I do, what should I say, how am I going to survive the disaster, who will kill me?...I cried and cried, but then realized that my tears were not going to help me explain my rape. Everybody would blame me. And then I started walking toward my

home…my legs were walking home, but my mind stayed in the field…that same place were he [the rapist] dropped me…I imagined myself walking into the house and telling my father that I had been beaten by strangers…but I know he is no stranger…he is my neighbor…and he might tell them that I gave up my honor *"farratet bi-sharifi"*…he is a man…why should he worry. I imagined myself telling my parents that I had been raped, but then what would happen? They would kill me immediately…or no…maybe they would ask him to marry me…he always wanted to marry me. I don't want to marry him…he is an animal…a beast. But then, after it became too dark…I couldn't stay in the field…and started walking. I was walking like a dead body…walked toward the real death. No the real death is not stabbing or strangulation…real death was to look them in the eyes…and I reached the house…went in and started screaming: "Kill me, go ahead and kill me! I can't bear it anymore!" I remember hitting myself, taking a knife from the kitchen and cutting myself.…They all thought I had lost my mind…but I knew I had lost everything. Never mind that I look alive to you now.…I was killed when I was raped, when I met my family…and I am killed everyday by all the gossip and rumors in the village that question my rape, my behavior, my sanity…that question my purity and honor.

THE FAMILY: "SHE SHOULD DIE"

The second factor is that the women's words reflect not only their belief that they are living dead or that they are dying every day but also that their families and members of society use the same expressions and share similar beliefs. In discussing a woman's situation as a potential murder victim, relatives would say, "I hope she dies," "I should slaughter and get rid of her," "I could make believe that she has never been born," or "killing her would be as easy as drinking water." Others asked, "Do you think that she will be the first woman to die from burns or who fell into a well?" or said "She should die." Many expressions, words, and threats were used to state that killing a woman is easy and that her death is a good solution that should be kept in mind. One father said that it is hard to fight a whole society when they all think that killing is the best method of dealing with such cases. He stated, "If your people/your collective lose their sanity, your wisdom and reason won't do you any good."…

Although no empirical evidence exists, my clinical experience in working with mothers of victims threatened with femicide suggests that they hold contradictory perspectives and beliefs. Some mothers wished the victim would die in order to cleanse the tarnished honor of the family. Some mothers, however, wished to help the victim but feared their help would be construed as supporting a "dishonorable" person—a move that could jeopardize not only the life of the daughter but also those of the mother and other female members of the family. Other mothers were torn between their need to observe the patriarchal codes and their inner need to help their daughters; as one stated:

No one knows what happens to mothers when their daughters are raped. No punishment is harder on a mother than raping her daughter because everybody is accusing me of not teaching her to protect herself from being raped. Now I need to deal with her fears and pains. I need to deal with the family's threat to kill her. I need to deal with the worry about my other daughters. You know, my son-in-law sent my daughter back with her baby, stating that he does not want to have any connection with our family—forgetting that his uncle was the one who raped my daughter. My husband might do the same to me. You know...we all feel like we are dying...and it seems to me that this feeling will never go for even if they will kill her and kill the rapist...the harm is done...and the family is destroyed.

THE HIDDEN VOICE: HELPING CONSTRUCT "DEATH ROW."

Not only words and social perceptions but also actions (explicit and implicit) may contribute to the slow process of femicide. Overt and covert social reactions (i.e., socialization) support the construction of a social readiness to propose death and killing as a solution in cases of sexual abuse related to "family honor." Women and men in the family and society in general have used various methods to cause the victim's death. In one case, the father of a three-year-old girl, raped by a relative, ordered the mother to kill the girl in order to conceal the social shame and avoid the ridicule that might confront him (Shalhoub-Kevorkian 1998). In another case, a victim of incest poured gasoline on her body in order to burn herself. When her father realized what she was doing he brought her heating oil, suggesting that it is more effective than gasoline. One father wrapped his daughter's sandwiches in a newspaper article titled "A Father Killed His Daughter as a Crime of Honor." One man bought new knives and hung them in the middle of the house without a word, repeatedly sharpening them while staring at his sister. An aunt convinced an incest victim that she had no reason to live after losing her virginity. All these acts strengthen the argument that the processes leading up to death are as criminal as the actual death....

Social pressure on both the victim and her family or collective

Social pressure, including moral panic (Cohen 1973), plays a great role in the process of femicide. In the case below, a social worker shared her observations and discussed the family's reaction to her client's killing:

> One of our clients at the Women's Center for Legal Aid and Counseling was killed. The first information we received was that she had committed suicide. We knew her well as a very strong woman, who faced much abuse but kept fighting it, searching in her own way for love and safety. We felt it impossible that she would commit suicide unless she had been forced to, i.e. murdered. When we visited her family after her death, the father showed us how she had "killed" herself, showing us the well in which she threw herself. We all looked at the well while thinking to ourselves: "But you killed her, why are you lying? We know that one of you killed her." Our conjecture was reinforced by the unspoken words in her sister's eyes. She must have thought that if she were to disclose to us that her sister had been killed, she could be next. But she collapsed soon thereafter, and the whole family panicked. They tried to mute even that silent voice that spoke through her fainting and all the voices that resisted death and claimed a right to live. Afterwards

it transpired that the mother had supported the brother in killing his sister. She cried in anguish when we went to visit her.

The mother's crying was brimming with dissonance. She had lost her daughter and she would need to look in her granddaughter's eyes everyday hiding the fact that she supported the killing of the girl's mother. As she told me later, her brother was left with no choice other than to kill. The villagers kept insinuating to him that he should "control" his sister and her "unacceptable behavior." They accused him of not being able to protect his own honor. He was ostracized by his relatives, friends, and the community. Furthermore, she stated, "I am in pain for I have lost my daughter. I am in pain, for my son is now in jail because he killed his sister, he wanted to save the family honor, and ended up in jail. I am in pain, because my granddaughter will learn one day that her mother was killed on the so-called basis of 'honor.' I am in pain because our society has no mercy...they will definitely punish the little girl for what her mother did." The killing in this case did not help anybody but rather exacerbated the anguish and pain.

As we see in the above case, the process of femicide ended in the killing of the victim. This case, like so many others, shows that the family chose to kill their daughter not out of conviction but rather as a reaction to social pressure....

Femicide: The Expanded Definition

The expanded definition of femicide that I propose is that *femicide* is the process leading to death and the creation of a situation in which it is impossible for the victim to "live." That is, femicide is all of the hegemonic masculine social methods used to destroy females' rights, ability, potential, and power to live safely. It is a form of abuse, threat, invasion, and assault that degrades and subordinates women. It leads to continuous fear, frustration, isolation, exclusion, and harm to females' ability to control their personal intimate lives. This definition challenges the exclusion of women, writing women into the theoretical agenda. However, changes in the theoretical agenda alone are not sufficient to move toward any sort of social change.

By offering this new definition, I am not only enlarging the conceptual framework of the crime of femicide, but I am also showing how unjust power relations create crimes that have not been defined as such in criminological, victimological, or gender studies. Moreover, the new definition calls for building new policies that address femicide in a more serious manner, calling for harsher punishments for offenders. This analysis of the women's victim's (group) experience of the whole process of femicide shows how historical legacy, ethnicity, class, politics, and gender mutually construct one another to create the crime of femicide as acknowledged by its victims but not yet by society. The new definition is best understood through analyses of the victims' voices, social institutions (extended and nuclear family and society), organizational structures (tribal laws and codes, cultural practices, and formal legal practices), and patterns of social interactions (mainly social reactions to "crimes of family honor," "purity," "virginity," and "shame"). The intersection of the different power relations (such as ones related to ethnicity, economic context, sexuality, gender, and politics) places women in a distinctive social location that, in some cases, not only specifies their exact self-definition but also their actions and future destinies....

Accepting the expanded definition of femicide is only one step in explaining and fighting the sexism of femicide and the long, draining process of death. The more we study femicide, the more we discover how puzzling a phenomenon it is, for we do not cross borders, voice the previously unvoiced, or lift veils of denial in a static atmosphere. The machinery of oppression and the processes of building denial remain in continuous action. Thus, only by taking actions such as constructing public campaigns, conducting research to build a body of knowledge, explaining to the public the effect that killing women and girls has on the socialization and acculturation of both males and females, and changing the current laws that justify the killing of women would we be able to effect change. Only by taking responsibility and believing that femicide is not a gender issue that should be solved by women but rather a political issue that should be dealt with in a public manner are we able to break down the door of oppression and injustice.

Note

1. For more details, see Ilkkaracan 2000.

References

Center for Women's Policy Studies. 1991. "Violence against Women as Bias Motivated Hate Crime: Defining the Issue." Report. Center for Women's Policy Studies, Washington, D.C.

Cohen, Stan. 1973. *Folk Devils and Moral Panic*. London: Paladin.

Ginat, Joseph. 1987. *Blood Disputes among Bedouin and Rural Arabs in Israel*. London: Feffer & Simons.

Ilkkaracan, Pinar, ed. 2000. *Women and Sexuality in Muslim Societies*. Istanbul: Women for Women's Human Rights.

Radford, Jill, and Diana Russel. 1992. *Femicide: The Politics of Woman Killing*. Buckingham: Open University Press.

Said, Edward. 1979. *Orientalism*. New York: Vintage.

Shalhoub-Kevorkian, Nadera. 1998. "Reactions to a Case of Female Child Sexual Abuse in the Palestinian Society: Protection, Silencing, Deterrence, or Punishment." *Plilim* 7:161–95.

Stout, Karen. 1992. "'Intimate Femicide': Effect of Legislation and Social Services." In Radford and Russel 1992, 133–40.

CRITICAL SUMMARY

The history and current practices of body violation and violence during and after armed conflict are well documented—we have barely touched on it. We have seen that the violence is government-sponsored and also perpetrated by insurgents against governments. We may not think of imprisonment as a form of body violence, but beyond deprivation of liberty, people in prison are subject to physical abuse by guards and beatings and killing by other prisoners. Most of those imprisoned in the United States are Black and Hispanic men. They are more likely to be arrested even if they have not committed a crime, and if convicted, they receive longer sentences than White men. They are also more likely to get the death penalty, especially if the murder victim is White.

Women and girls are the victims of different body violations than men. They are often referred to as the spoils of war. In wartime, they are not only subject to killing, maiming, and sexual torture, as men are, but also to rape, sexual slavery, and forced pregnancies. In many countries, men are drafted into the military and trained to be violent. In other countries, men volunteer, as do women, and in two countries, Chile and Israel, women are drafted. Women can be the violators—sexual humiliation is a mild form of what women are asked to do as members of the military and what they did as Nazi concentration camp guards.

Governments, the military, and insurgencies are dominated by men and men's valorization of violence, but women do have agency and also believe in nationalist and religious causes. Suicide bombers would seem to be the ultimate in violence by choice, but is it? Our feminist response is that it is violence to women and men and boys and girls when they are induced by a resistance movement to use their bodies to kill themselves and others. The non-violence movements of Gandhi in the liberation of India and Martin Luther King, Jr. in the U.S. civil rights fight were, in our view, a better form of resistance. The bodies of their followers were vulnerable to beatings, imprisonment, and murder, but the violence came from the oppressors, not the oppressed.

One form of violence against women is embedded in patriarchal cultures and is part of the codes of family honor. These are killings of wives, sisters, and daughters by male relatives because they have been raped, had sexual relations before marriage, or committed adultery. They are seen as having violated family purity and the family's good name; the price is death.

Violence to bodies and minds may not be spread evenly in the population, but its disastrous and ugly manifestations affect everyone and its prevalence must not be rendered invisible.

REFERENCES AND RECOMMENDED READINGS

Armed Conflict

Adamshick, Mark. 2005. "Social Representation in the U.S. Military Services." Circle Working Paper 32, May. http://www.civicyouth.org/PopUps/WorkingPapers/WP32Adamshik.pdf.

Alvarez, Lizette. 2009a. "More Americans Joining Military as Jobs Dwindle." *New York Times,* 18 January. http://www.nytimes.com/2009/01/19/us/19recruits.html.

———. 2009b. "Women at Arms: G.I. Jane Stealthily Breaks the Combat Barrier." *New York Times,* 6 August, 1, 20–21.

Baum, Dan. 2004a. "The Casualty: An American Soldier Comes Home from Iraq." *New Yorker,* 9 March, 64–73.

———. 2004b. "Two Soldiers: How the Dead Come Home." *New Yorker,* 9 & 16 August, 76–95.

Bumiller, Elisabeth. 2010. "Letting Women Reach Women in Afghan War." *New York Times,* 6 March, 1, 4.

Carvajal, Doreen. 2010. "A Female Approach to Peacekeeping." *New York Times,* 6 March. http://www.nytimes.com/2010/03/06/world/africa/06iht-ffpeace.html.

Casper, Monica J., and Lisa Jean Moore. 2009. *Missing Bodies: The Politics of Visibility.* New York: New York Uuniversity Press.

Cave, Damien. 2009. "Women at Arms: A Combat Role and Anguish, Too." *New York Times,* 1 November, A1, 34–35.

Enloe, Cynthia. 2000. *Maneuvers: The International Politics of Militarizing Women's Lives.* Berkeley: University of California Press.

———. 2007a. *Globalization and Militarism: Feminists Make the Link.* New York: Rowman and Littlefield.

———. 2007b. "Feminist Readings on Abu Ghraib." *International Journal of Feminist Politics* 9: 35–37.

Fischer, Hannah. 2009. "United States Military Casualty Statistics: Operation Iraqi Freedom and Operation Enduring Freedom." Congressional Research Service. RS 22452. U.S. Congress.

Grady, Denise. 2006. "Struggling Back from War's Once-Deadly Wounds." *New York Times,* 22 January 1, 24.

Hawkesworth, Mary, and Karen Alexander. 2007. Special Issue: War and Terror I: Race-Gendered Logics and Effects in Conflict Zones. *Signs* 32: 833–1075.

Hynes, H. Patricia. 2004. "On the Battlefield of Women's Bodies: An Overview of the Harm of War to Women." *Women's Studies International Forum.* 27: 431–445.

Lake, Eli. 2009. "Droves of Recruits to Ease Burden on Troops." *Washington Times,* 14 October. http://washingtontimes.com/news/2009/oct/14/droves-of-recruits-likely-to-ease-burden-on-troops/.

Moser, Carolyn, and Fiona Clark (eds.). 2001. *Victims, Perpetrators, or Actors? Gender, Armed Conflict, and Political Violence.* London: Zed Books.

Myers, Steven Lee. 2009. "Women at Arms: Living and Fighting Alongside Men, and Fitting In." *New York Times,* 17 August, A1, 6.

Scheper-Hughes, Nancy, and Philippe I. Bourgois (eds.). 2003. *Violence in War and Peace: An Anthology.* Oxford, UK: Blackwell.

Sutton, Barbara, Sandra Morgen, and Julie Novkov. (eds.). 2008. *Security Disarmed: Critical Perspectives on Gender, Race, and Militarization.* New Brunswick, NJ: Rutgers University Press.

Swarns, Rachel. 2008. "A Step Up for Women in the U.S. Military." *New York Times,* 30 June. http://www.nytimes.com/2008/06/30/world/americas/30iht-army.1.14093138.html.

White, Josh. 2005. "Steady Drop in Black Army Recruits." *Washington Post,* 9 March, A01.

Williams, Kayla with Michael E. Staub. 2005. *Love My Rifle More Than You: Young and Female in the U.S. Army.* New York: W. W. Norton.

Women's Memorial Fund. 2009. Statistics on Women in the Military. www.womensme-morial.org/PDFs/StatsonWIM.pdf.

Zarkov, Dubravka. 2007. *The Body of War: Media, Ethnicity, and Gender in the Break-up of Yugoslavia.* Durham, NC: Duke University Press.

Gender and Genocide

Baer, Elizabeth, and Myrna Goldenberg (eds.). 2003. *Experience and Expression: Women, the Nazis, and the Holocaust.* Detroit: Wayne State University Press.

Bergoffen, Debra B. 2006. "From Genocide to Justice: Women's Bodies as a Legal Writing Pad." *Feminist Studies* 32: 11–37.

Delbo, Charlotte. 1997. *Convoy to Auschwitz: Women of the French Resistance.* Boston: Northeastern University Press.

Fuchs, Esther. 1999. *Women and the Holocaust.* Lanham, MD: University Press of America.

Morrison, Jack G. 2000. *Ravensbrück: Everyday Life in a Women's Concentration Camp 1935–45.* New York: Marcus Wiener.

Ofer, Dalia, and Lenore J. Weitzman (eds.). 1998. *Women in the Holocaust.* New Haven, CT: Yale University Press.

Saidel, Rochelle G. 2004. *The Jewish Women of the Ravensbrück Concentration Camp.* Madison: University of Wisconsin Press.

Tec, Nechama. 2003. *Resilience and Courage: Women, Men, and the Holocaust.* New Haven, CT: Yale University Press.

Totten, Samuel (ed.). 2009. *Plight and Fate of Women During and Following Genocide.* New Brunswick, NJ: Transaction.

Tydor Baumel, Judith. 1998. *Gender and the Holocaust: Double Jeopardy.* London: Valentine Mitchell.

Honor Killings

Hossain, Sara, and Lynn Welchman. (eds.). 2005. *"Honour": Crimes, Paradigms, and Violence Against Women.* London: Zed Books.

Husseini, Rana. 2009. *Murder in the Name of Honor: The True Story of One Woman's Heroic Fight Against an Unbelievable Crime.* Oxford, UK: Oneworld Publications.

Mai, Mukhtar. 2007. *In the Name of Honor: A Memoir,* translated by Linda Coverdale. New York: Washington Square Press.

Mayell, Hillary. 2002. "Thousands of Women Killed for Family 'Honor.'" *National Geographic News,* 12 February. http://news.nationalgeographic.com/news/2002/02/0212_020212_honorkilling.html.

Mojab, Shahrzad. 2002. "'Honor Killing': Culture, Politics and Theory." *The Middle East Women's Studies Review.* 22 March.

Onal, Ayse. 2008. *Honour Killing: Stories of Men Who Killed.* London: Saqi Books.

Imprisonment

Alexander, Randolph. 2005. *Racism, African Americans and Social Justice.* New York: Roman and Littlefield.

Austin, James, Todd Clear, Troy Duster, David F. Greenberg, John Irwin, Candace McCoy, Alan Mobley, Barbara Owen and Joshua Page. 2007. *Unlocking*

America: Why and How To Reduce America's Prison Population. NCJ 222403.
Washington, DC: JFA Institute.

Davis, Angela Y. 1998. "Masked Racism: Reflections on the Prison Industrial Complex."
ColorLines Fall. http://www.thirdworldtraveler.com/Prison_System/Masked_
Racism_ADavis.html.

Harrison, Paige M., and Allen J. Beck. 2005. "Prison and Jail Inmates at Midyear 2004."
Bureau of Justice Statistics. Washington, DC: U.S. Department of Justice, April.

Liptak, Adam. 2008. "US Prison Population Dwarfs that of Other Nations." *New York
Times,* 23 April. http://www.nytimes.com/2008/04/23/world/americas/23iht-23-
prison.12253738.html.

Mauer, M., and T. Huling. 1995. *Young Black Americans and the Criminal Justice System:
Five Years Later.* Washington, DC: The Sentencing Project.

Spohn, Cassia C. 2000. "Thirty Years of Sentencing Reform: The Quest for a Racially
Neutral Sentencing Process." *Criminal Justice 2000,* Vol. 3. National Institute of
Justice.

U.S. Department of Justice. 2009. Bureau of Justice Statistics. Demographic Trends in
Correctional Populations. http://www.ojp.usdoj.gov/bjs/gcorpop.htm.

Welsh-Huggins, Andrew. 2005. "Death Penalty Unequal." *Cincinnati Enquirer,* 7 May.
news.enquirer.com/apps/pbcs.dll/article?AID=/20050507/NEWS01/505070402.

Rape and Prostitution

Anonymous. 2000. *A Woman in Berlin: Eight Weeks in the Conquered City.* New York:
Picador.

Barstow, Anne Llewellyn (ed.). 2000. *War's Dirty Secret: Rape, Prostitution and Other
Crimes Against Women.* Cleveland, OH: Pilgrim Press.

Barry, Kathleen. 1995. *Prostitution of Sexuality: Global Exploitation of Women.* New York:
New York University Press.

Bos, Pascale R. 2006. "Feminists Interpreting the Politics of Wartime Rape: Berlin, 1945;
Yugoslavia, 1992–1993." *Signs* 31: 995–1025.

Brownmiller, Susan. 1975. *Against Our Will: Men, Women, and Rape.* New York: Simon
and Schuster.

Cho, Grace M. 2008. *Haunting the Korean Diaspora: Shame, Secrecy, and the Forgotten
War.* Minneapolis: University of Minnesota Press.

Engle Merry, Sally. 2003. "Rights Talk and the Experience of Law: Implementing Women's
Human Rights to Protection from Violence." *Human Rights Quarterly* 25: 343–381.

Farr, Kathryn. 2009. "Extreme War Rape in Today's Civil-War-Torn States: A Contextual
and Comparative Analysis." *Gender Issues* 26: 1–41.

Frederick, Sharon. 2000. *Rape: Weapon of Terror.* Hackensack, NJ: World Scientific
Publishing Company.

Hicks, George. 1995. *The Comfort Women: Japan's Brutal Regime of Enforced Prostitution
in the Second World War.* New York: W.W. Norton.

Moon, Katharine H.S. 1997. *Sex Among Allies: Military Prostitution in U.S.-Korea
Relations.* New York: Columbia University Press.

Oh, Bonnie B.C., and Margaret D. Stetz (eds.). 2001. *Legacies of the Comfort Women of
WWII.* Armonk, NY: M. E. Sharpe.

Schmidt, David Andrew. 2000. *Ianfu—The Comfort Women of the Japanese Imperial
Army of the Pacific War: Broken Silence.* Lewiston, NY: Mellen.

Scoular, Jane. 2004. "The 'Subject' of Prostitution: Interpreting the Discursive, Symbolic and Material Position of Sex/Work in Feminist Theory." *Feminist Theory* 5: 343–355.

Sturdevant, Saundra Pollack, and Brenda Stoltzfus. 1992. *Let the Good Times Roll: Prostitution and the U.S. Military in Asia*. New York: The New Press.

U.N. Security Council. 2004. "Women and Peace and Security." Report of the Secretary-General S/2004/814: 1–26, 13 October.

Suicide Bombers

Amireh, Amal. 2005. "Palestinian Women's Disappearing Act: The Suicide Bomber Through Western Feminist Eyes." *MIT Electronic Journal of Middle East Studies*, 5 (Spring): 228–242. http://web.mit.edu/cis/www/mitejmes/.

Atran, Scott. 2004. "Mishandling Suicide Terrorism." *Washington Quarterly* 27: 67–90.

Bennet, James. 2002a. "Arab Woman's Path to Unlikely 'Martyrdom.'" *New York Times*, 31 January, A1, 10.

———. 2002b. "Arab Press Glorifies Bomber as Heroine." *New York Times*, 11 February, A8.

Brunner, Claudia. 2007. "Occidentalism Meets the Female Suicide Bomber: A Critical Reflection on Recent Terrorism Debates: A Review Essay. *Signs* 32: 957–971.

Editorial. 2005. "The Women of Gitmo." *New York Times*. 15 July, A18.

Eggen, Dan, and Scott Wilson. 2005. "Suicide Bombs Potent Tools of Terrorists: Deadly Attacks Have Been Increasing and Spreading Since Sept. 11, 2001." *Washington Post*, 17 July, A01.

Faludi, Susan. 2007. *The Terror Dream: Fear and Fantasy in Post 9-11 America*. New York: Metropolitan Books.

Gerami, Shahin. 2003. "Mullahs, Martyrs, and *Men*: Conceptualizing Masculinity in the Islamic Republic of Iran," *Men & Masculinities*, 5: 257–275.

Greenberg, Joel. 2002. "Portrait of an Angry Young Arab Woman." *New York Times*, 1 March, A10.

Hasso, Frances S. 2005. "Discursive and Political Deployments by/of the 2002 Palestinian Women Suicide Bombers/Martyrs." *Feminist Review* 81: 23–51.

Kimmel, Michael S. 2003. "Globalization and its Mal(e)contents: The Gendered Moral and Political Economy of Terrorism." *International Sociology* 18: 603–620.

Myers, Steven Lee. 2004. "From Dismal Chechnya, Women Turn to Bombs," *New York Times*, 10 September, A1, 6.

Torture

Burr, Viv, and Jeff Hearn (eds.). 2008. *Sex, Violence and the Body: The Erotics of Wounding*. New York: Palgrave Macmillan.

Enda, Jodi. 2004. "Female Face of Abuse Provokes Shock." *Women's Enews*, 14 May. http://www.womensenews.org/article.cfm?aid=1828.

McKelvey, Tara (ed.). 2007. *One of the Guys: Women as Aggressors and Torturers*. Berkeley, CA: Seal Press.

Philipose, Liz. 2007. "The Politics of Pain and the Uses of Torture." *Signs* 32: 1047–1071.

Zarkov, Dubravka. 2001. "The Body of the Other Man: Sexual Violence and the Construction of Masculinity, Sexuality and Ethnicity in Croatian Media," in *Victims, Perpetrators or Actors? Gender, Armed Conflict and Political Violence*, edited by C. Moser and F. Clark. London: Zed Books.

Conclusion
Social Bodies in an Interconnected World

Key concepts
biopolitics, body economics, embodied citizenship, social bodies

In this book, we have seen the extent to which bodies are shaped according to gendered norms and ideals of masculinity and femininity. We have explored the resistances and revolution in meanings of bodies with impairments, the battles by and about intersexed and transgender people, and the horrors of body violations in war, disasters, and imprisonment. We argue that bodies become social entities through membership in a community and conformity to its informal rules. They are also mediated by political structures that control the body with formal laws. Carol Bacchi and Chris Beasley coined the term "social flesh"

> ...to capture a vision of interacting, material, embodied subjects. When we use the term "social" we mean to draw attention to how fleshly materiality highlights intersubjectivity and interdependence. This use of "social" captures a full range of intersubjective bodily experiences—based on movement and communication, the bodily requirements of sustenance and attention, the social relations around touch and non-touch.... Our use of "flesh" is meant to highlight our embodied existence. There is no suggestion of unchanging bodily essences; all bodies are necessarily social. Indeed, how we experience our bodies reflects the social messages we receive about them. (2002, 330)

Our bodies are valued according to their gender, social class, religion, racial ethnic, and national status. Our bodies survive and thrive depending upon economic resources and social power. Men's bodies are at risk of military, athletic, and industrial exploitation, and, for disadvantaged men, imprisonment. Women's bodies are controlled by institutions dominated by men, namely, medicine and religion, but body knowledge gives women increased autonomy. Finally, it is possible for the marginalized—disadvantaged people, the elderly, those with disabilities, intersexed and transgender people—to forge communities that give their bodies value.

SOCIAL BODIES

Instead of exclusively understanding our bodies as containers of unique individuals, throughout this book we have demonstrated that individual bodies are not the asocial, physical expression of individuality. Rather, individual bodies are constrained and conditioned by social circumstances and are produced through the ongoing negotiation of social power, historical trends, and cultural expectations. Individual bodies are thus part of the social and political, just as the social and the political are made up of individual bodies (Scheper-Hughes and Lock 1987).

Social bodies are understood in two distinct ways. First, a social body is the entity formed of a community of individual bodies. Second, our physical bodies become social bodies through recognition by a community and application of the community's body norms and practices. For example, New York City is a social body, a metropolis populated by heterogeneous individual bodies. These individual bodies become social bodies in interaction with other individual bodies. As social bodies, New Yorkers walk on streets crowded with other bodies, careful not to bump into them; they ride on subway cars watched by police; those in wheelchairs expect bus drivers to operate the stair lifts for them and other passengers to give them their seats. They may even survive a heart attack, thanks to the timely intervention of medical personnel on the same subway train (Winerip 2009). They are strangers to each other, but recognize each other's presence, and that makes them social bodies. In contrast, when a homeless person sleeps in someone's doorway, and people walk by as if that body were invisible, the person has been excluded from the community. Community inclusion makes us social bodies, which is why excommunication and exile are such harsh punishments.

Social bodies also create and interact with political bodies. A political body is made up of the local, regional, and federal entities that structure daily life through rules and regulations. These laws and policies organize our mundane and profound bodily activities—giving birth, consuming food, taking medication, disposing of dead bodies. Gendered bodies particularly are socially constructed through the constant negotiation and interaction with and between individual, social, and political bodies.

Environmental, economic, and geopolitical disasters bring to the fore the ways in which physical bodies are made into social bodies. Who dies and who survives, who is mourned and who is reviled, who eats and who starves, who is helped and who is ignored, who is in control and who is vulnerable—these are all ways in which communities create social bodies out of physical bodies. Through the multiplicity of media coverage—24/7 news broadcasts, podcasts, traditional and alternate newspapers, and the Internet—we can see bodies interacting in real time physically and socially. Through our viewing, these bodies enter our own social lives, and become part of a global social community. We form opinions about how survivors are being aided—or not—and we may deplore and protest the conditions that led to the disaster or its magnitude. We are moved to help, through donations of money, clothing, and other material items and through volunteering to lend our bodies to rescue and recovery efforts.

In the first year of the twenty-first century, bodies rammed into New York City's World Trade Center twin towers on September 11, 2001, and bodies jumped out of them before the 110-story buildings collapsed. Fragments of bodies were carefully collected from the tons of rubble and painstakingly identified as people. The names of the almost 3,000 dead are read by their kin at Ground Zero in downtown New York City on every anniversary, symbolic bodies that recall physical bodies.

On December 26, 2004, a tsunami in the Indian Ocean drowned hundreds of thousands in Indonesia, Sri Lanka, India, and Thailand. The bodies of foreign tourists became people to us in the tears of the local survivors on television and photos left in cameras. In contrast, the hundreds of thousands of bodies of people who had lived in wiped-out villages and towns and who died or were displaced by the massive devastation to the terrain and economy of Southeastern Asia, were rendered nearly invisible in the West, identified only by where they had once lived (Dewan 2005). The most visible survivors of the people who had lived there were the orphaned children featured in many television accounts. On the first anniversary, the stories in the media about how the survivors fared turned them into the symbolic bodies of that disaster (Berak 2005).

On August 28, 2005, we saw the effects of Hurricane Katrina on the U.S. Gulf Coast and the flooding of New Orleans and sections of Mississippi when levees broke. The disintegration of a once vibrant community, ineptitude and apathy of government officials, and years of neglect of the physical infrastructure caused the uprooting of thousands of mostly poor and African-American mothers and children, and the deaths of sick and old men and women, many with disabilities (Fink 2009). They were very visible as people, thanks to constant television coverage and interviews where they told what was happening to them. They became part of the national and global community, a visual indictment of America's neglect of poor African-Americans.

In 2010, the news of the devastation from the 7.0 earthquake in Haiti on January 12 and the 8.8 earthquake in Chile on February 27 was immediately broadcast to the world through pictures sent by social media and used in 24-hour reporting on cable news. In Haiti, reporters and rescue and aid teams from many countries arrived the next day. Shots of the dead and wounded, and the crowds just walking, dazed, in the streets—bodies, all—dominated what we saw. The mass paralyzes our reaction, but one body makes the disaster hit home:

> All the massiveness contained in the troubled injury
> Of her tiny dark glance at the camera: an eye torn away, the other
> Under a limp pink ribbon, scathing like the sun. (Gosetti-Ferencei 2010)

More bodies have been disabled and killed in earthquakes in Kashmir; mud slides in Managua; and from continuing drought, civil war, and starvation in Darfur; but the further we get from our own social worlds, the less attention we pay to these disasters. Yet we are all connected in networks of social communities.

In "Violence, Mourning, Politics," feminist philosopher Judith Butler asks, "Who counts as human? Whose lives count as lives? And, finally, What *makes for a grievable life?* ... Loss has made a tenuous 'we' of us all" (Butler 2004, 20).

BODY ECONOMICS

When communities neglect people, the social and individual bodies suffer. Disasters may push people past their breaking point, but for those who live in poor economic conditions, their bodies have already been under constant assault. In nations that experience economic crisis, research has found that bodies, particularly of mothers who must care for children and scrounge for food, are increasingly fatigued, stressed, overworked, malnourished, and sick (Sutton 2005). The effects of disasters, like those of wars, fall most heavily on women and children, especially if they have few economic resources. Disasters take everyday vulnerability to a higher degree because social networks break down. According to the U.N. Population Fund:

> When conflict or natural disaster strikes, women survivors usually bear the heaviest burden of relief and reconstruction. They become primary caretakers for other survivors—including children, the injured or sick, and the elderly. The vulnerability and responsibilities of women are further increased by the loss of husbands and livelihoods and the need to procure essentials for family survival.
>
> Gender-specific needs have often been overlooked when it comes to relief and recovery planning. The vulnerability of girls and women to exploitation, trafficking and abuse has largely been ignored, as have their needs for pregnancy-related care, sanitary supplies, and locally appropriate clothing. The distribution of emergency assistance has often been managed by, and delivered to, men, without attention to whether women and their dependents will benefit. (2005, ch. 8)

In another form of body exploitation that only government intervention can change, the owners of factories, mines, and plantations push workers to exhaustion. Given the global dominance of free-market capitalism and agribusinesses, bodies are drained of their physical, emotional, and procreative resources in sweat shops manufacturing cheap clothing and electronics, gold and diamond mines, slaughter houses, food processing factories, and fruit and vegetable farms and orchards. We benefit by low prices for clothing and food and for those who can afford them, a supply of jewelry and other luxuries.

Male bodies often take on the greatest occupational risks because men are encouraged to work at dangerous jobs and to hide injuries and illnesses (Courtenay 2000). A study of black lung disease demonstrated how the men who worked in coal mines were expected to normalize the symptoms of disease—since everybody coughed and spat black sputum, it was just part of life in coal mines. When a miner could not breathe well enough to work, he was denied compensation by physicians working for the mining industry. Instead of identifying the toxins of the work environment, the owners and the medical profession blamed the workers' lifestyles—smoking and drinking—for their ill health (Smith 1987).

Years of potential life lost (YPLL) is a statistic that estimates the number of years of life lost owing to premature death in a population. Premature death is usually defined as death at the age of less than 65 or 75 years, or less than the average life expectancy for a region. YPPL is used as a measure of the economic burden of premature death to society, since it represents the loss of productive workers, consumers, and taxpayers. International comparative research has demonstrated that suicide and premature death due to coronary heart disease, violence, homicides, accidents, drug or alcohol abuse are a strikingly male phenomena, particularly in the young and middle-aged (Möller-Leimkühler 2003). Much of this research suggests that the social expectations of traditional masculinity make men and boys vulnerable to an early death (Courtenay 2000, Riska 2004, Rosenfeld and Faircloth 2006).

The scourge of untreated AIDS, particularly in sub-Saharan Africa, has wiped out a whole generation of young women and men, leaving orphaned children to the care of impoverished grandparents and other relatives. Nearly two-thirds of the world's HIV-positive people live in sub-Saharan Africa, which has a little over 10 percent of the world's population. Not only are innumerable years of potential productive life lost, but family networks fall apart, and there are fewer health workers and teachers, farmers, and urban workers (Avert 2005).

HIV is mostly transmitted heterosexually in Africa, and women and girls, especially those aged 15–24, have higher rates of infection than men and boys (U.N. AIDS 2008). Three-quarters of the women with HIV/AIDS live in Africa. Their vulnerability comes from economic dependence, high rates of rape, migrant labor patterns that send husband to cities to work and to find other sex partners, and "transactional sex" with older men for money or gifts. In the United States, poor and marginalized communities are also highly vulnerable. African-American women and Latinas are less than one-quarter of the population, but they accounted for 80 percent of the reported cases of HIV/AIDS in the United States in 2000. In 2006, African-American men and women were estimated to have an incidence rate seven times higher than the incidence rate of White Americans (Hall, Ruiguang, and Rhodes 2008).

In sum, the economics of the body—occupational exploitation, the toll of poverty, vulnerability in disasters and epidemics—are both gendered and classed, with much of the effects of racial ethnic social differences reflective of economic differences. Women and men suffer from poor economic conditions in different ways, men from exhaustive physical labor, and women from trying to care for children with little food or adequate shelter. They scrounge for food, and if they cannot earn some money in home-based work, they prostitute their bodies. The poorest women, men, and children become the least valued social bodies.

POLITICAL BODIES AND EMBODIED CITIZENSHIP

The concept of political body goes beyond the informal norms and expectations that socially construct our bodies. Bodies become political when they are governed by formal laws and bureaucratic regulations. Michel Foucault, the French social scientist whose work has documented the myriad ways bodies are socially controlled, coined the term *biopolitics* to refer to the social policies and institutions established to regulate a population's quality (and quantity) of life (2008).

In order to have a say in one's ruling regime, you need to be a legitimate member of that jurisdiction—a *citizen*. The process of becoming a citizen can be as simple as being born within certain borders, or proving your familial lineage in a particular region or country, or as complicated as convincing a governmental agency that you are worthy of permanent legitimate residence. Citizenship comes with certain rights and responsibilities —paying taxes, voting—and certain benefits, such as receiving welfare.

Even with legitimate citizenship, certain groups do not have an equal say in producing the laws and regulations that govern their bodies. Across the globe, governments are not representative of the gender distribution of the general population, and thus, not unsurprisingly, their practices are not gender neutral. Rather, the ruling regime is often overwhelmingly made up of men and imbued with dominant men's values. These values translate into laws and regulations that affect men and women and boys and girls quite differently.

Historically, in the United States, many of the rights of citizenship were exclusively bestowed upon White male bodies. African-American men got the right to vote and run for office in 1870, but it took the Civil Rights Act of 1965 to ensure that they could fully use those political rights. Women in the United States did not get the right to vote until 1920. Because of this legacy of racial and gendered citizenship, all women and African-American men are still not treated equally (Brown 1992). African-American men are much more likely to be arrested on suspicion, and more likely to be convicted of crimes and serve long sentences. Much of the government's control over women's bodies considers them potential mothers and men's sexual partners. In these contexts, women and girls are highly regulated through policies governing age of consent to sexual relations, encouragement or discouragement of child-bearing, abortion, breast-feeding, maternity leave, child care provisions, and so on. White Women become "government-approved" citizens by not violating these policies; Black women and men may find it much harder, if not impossible, to always be treated as first-class citizens.

Since ruling regimes produce a gendered social order, bodies that challenge conventional gendering make problems for gendered laws and regulations. In most Western countries, the primary legal ruling concerning gender is that there are only two—male and female—and that everyone must be put into one of those categories, preferably permanently and at birth. Just as women are controlled through their procreative and sexual bodies, intersexed people are medically manipulated through their sexed bodies:

> ... [T]he child who cannot be identified at birth as "either" male or female becomes their body through a process of objectifying hyperembodiment, rendering them a physical site that is open for an unusual level of intervention by

medical practitioners and family. That is to say, from the time of birth, and the attendant "medical emergency," the enormous amount of external medical and familial pressure and surveillance to which intersexual people are subjected indicates that their "abnormal" corporeality renders them somehow more "mappable" and, crucially, less autonomous than people who appear to be more clearly sexed. (Grabham 2007, 43)

Since "intersex" is not a legally recognized bureaucratic category, their very existence as a legal person is questioned. Those who construct a gender and a body to match, as most do, can achieve full-fledged citizenship.

For transgender people, who have full citizenship rights in their original gender, the bureaucratic rules and laws affect their status when they change genders. At issue is often the primary document of identity—the birth certificate—and whether a primary identification status, sex, can be changed retroactively. Since one's gender is such a major part of one's legal identity, and the birth certificate the testament to citizenship, inability to change the birth certificate to reflect a gender change virtually erases the person as a legitimate citizen (Currah and Moore 2009, Monro and Warren 2004).

The formal laws and regulations governing gender for anybody establish a set of criteria for what a government will recognize as a legitimate gendered citizen with a male or female body, masculine or feminine outward appearance (for ease of social placement), and appropriate men's and women's behavior. Nonconformity not only incurs penalties and punishments, but can result in loss of citizenship status through incarceration in a mental hospital, imprisonment, or deportation.

CONCLUSION

Our bodies are material; they are flesh and blood. Our bodies are invested with social meaning when we are part of a community; then we become people with biographies, stories of our personal social bodies. Community norms and expectations determine the meanings of bodies and their relative value. Whether a body is handled with reverence or contempt, whether it is nourished or starved, whether its owner has control over it or must succumb to others' control—these are all determined by the intertwining of communities, families, and individuals. As political bodies, we are even more under social control.

Even though our bodies are regulated every day through laws and regulations that guide our social interaction, we are not wholly determined by this control. Bodies are shaped by conforming to norms, expectations, and laws, but bodies can also be used to rebel, to flaunt differences and celebrate them, such as in gay pride parades. Bodies have been used as weapons, and as a means of resistance and protest—in civil rights and anti-war demonstrations, hunger strikes, picket lines, sit-ins, take-back-the-night and other feminist marches.

What this adds up to is that our bodies are material, physical, and biological, but it is communities that give us humanity. From birth to death, we are social bodies in social worlds.

REFERENCES AND RECOMMENDED READINGS

Albertson Fineman, Martha, Jack E. Jackson, and Adam P. Romero (eds.). 2009. *Feminist and Queer Legal Theory: Intimate Encounters, Uncomfortable Conversations*. Surrey, UK: Ashgate Press.

Avert. 2005. "The Impact of HIV and AIDS on Africa." http://www.avert.org/aidsimpact.htm.

Bacchi, Carol Lee, and Chris Beasley. 2002. "Citizen Bodies: Is Embodied Citizenship a Contradiction in Terms?" *Critical Social Policy* 22: 324–352.

Bearak, Barry. 2005. "The Day the Sea Came." *New York Times Magazine*, 27 November, 46–66, 70, 97, 101.

Beasley, Chris, and Carol Bacchi. 2000. "Citizen Bodies: Embodying Citizens—A Feminist Analysis." *International Feminist Journal of Politics* 2: 337–358.

Bridges, Tristan S. 2010. "Men Just Weren't Made To Do This: Performances of Drag at 'Walk a Mile in Her Shoes' Marches." *Gender & Society* 24: 5–30.

Brown, Wendy. 1992. "Finding the Man in the State." *Feminist Studies* 18: 7–34.

Butler, Judith 1993. *Bodies that Matter: On the Discursive Limits of 'Sex'*. New York: Routledge.

———. 2004. *Precarious Life: The Powers of Mourning and Violence*. New York: Verso.

Casper, Monica J., and Lisa Jean Moore. 2008. *Missing Bodies: The Politics of Visibility*. New York: New York University Press.

Chase, Cheryl. 1998. "Hermaphrodites with Attitude: Mapping the Emergence of Intersex Political Activism." *GLQ: A Journal of Gay and Lesbian Studies* 4: 189–211.

Courtenay, W.H. 2000. "Constructions of Masculinity and Their Influence on Men's Well-Being: A Theory of Gender and Health." *Social Science and Medicine* 50: 1385–1401.

Currah, Paisley, Richard M. Juang, and Shannon Price Minter (eds.). 2006. *Transgender Rights*. Minneapolis: University of Minnesota Press.

Currah, Paisley, and Lisa Jean Moore. 2009. "'We Won't Know Who You Are': Contesting Sex Designations on New York City Birth Certificates." *Hypatia: Journal of Feminist Philosophy* 24: 113–135.

Dewan, Shaila. 2005. "Disasters and Their Dead." *New York Times*, Week in Review, 16 October, 4.

Editorial Collective. 2009. The Politics of Embodiment. *Feminist Studies* 35 (Fall): 447–665.

Enarson, Elaine, and Betty Hearn Morrow (eds.). 1998. *The Gendered Terrain of Disaster: Through Women's Eyes*. Miami: Florida International University Press.

Fink, Sheri. 2009. "Strained by Katrina, a Hospital Faced Deadly Choices." *New York Times Magazine*, 30 August. http://www.nytimes.com/2009/08/30/magazine/30doctors.html.

Foucault, Michel. 2008. *The Birth of Biopolitics: Lectures at the College de France, 1978–1979*, edited by Michel Senellart, Arnold I. Davidson, Alessandro Fontana, and Francois Ewald; translated by Graham Burchell. New York: Palgrave Macmillan.

Gallagher, Catherine, and Thomas Laqueur (eds.). 1987. *The Making of the Modern Body*. Berkeley: University of California Press.

Gatens, Moira. 1997. *Imaginary Bodies: Ethics, Power, and Corporeality*. New York: Routledge.

Gosetti-Ferencei, Jennifer. 2010. "Earthquake in Haiti," used by permission of the author.

Grabham, Emily. 2007. "Citizen Bodies, Intersex Citizenship." *Sexualities* 10: 29–48.

Grosz, Elizabeth. 1994. *Volatile Bodies: Toward a Corporeal Feminism.* Bloomington: Indiana University Press.

Grosz, Elizabeth. 1996. *Space, Time and Perversion: Essays on the Politics of the Body.* New York: Routledge.

Hall, H.I., S. Ruiguang, P. Rhodes et al. 2009. "Estimation of HIV Incidence in the United States." *Journal of the American Medical Association* 300: 520–529.

Hawthorne, Susan, and Bronwyn Winter. 2002. (eds.). *September 11, 2001: Feminist Perspectives.* North Melbourne, Australia: Spinifex.

King, L. 2002. "Demographic Trends, Pronatalism, and Nationalist Ideologies in the Late Twentieth Century." *Ethnic and Racial Studies* 25: 367–389.

Möller-Leimkühler, Anne Maria. 2003. "The Gender Gap in Suicide and Premature Death or: Why Are Men So Vulnerable?" *European Archives of Psychiatry & Clinical Neuroscience* 253: 1–9.

Monro, Surya. 2005. *Gender Politics: Citizenship, Activism, and Sexual Diversity.* London, UK: Pluto Press.

Monro, Surya, and Lorna Warren. 2004. "Transgendering Citizenship." *Sexualities* 7: 345–362.

Price, Janet, and Margrit Shildrick (eds.). 1999. *Feminist Theory and the Body.* New York: Routledge.

Rahman, Momin, and Anne Witz. 2003. "What Really Matters? The Elusive Quality of the Material in Feminist Thought." *Feminist Theory* 4: 243–261.

Riska, Elianne. 2004. *Masculinity and Men's Health: Coronary Heart Disease in Medical and Public Discourse.* Lanham, MD: Rowman & Littlefield.

Rosenfeld, Dana, and Christopher Faircloth (eds.). 2006. *Medicalized Masculinities.* Philadelphia: Temple University Press.

Salzinger, Leslie. 2003. *Genders in Production: Making Workers in Mexico's Global Factories.* Berkeley: University of California Press.

Scheper-Hughes, Nancy, and Margaret Lock. 1987. "The Mindful Body: A Prolegomenon to Future Work in Medical Anthropology." *Medical Anthropology Quarterly* 1: 6–41.

Scheper-Hughes, Nancy, and Loïs Wacquant (eds.). 2004. *Commodifying Bodies.* Thousand Oaks, CA: Sage.

Shilling, Chris. 2005. *The Body in Culture, Technology and Society.* Thousand Oaks, CA: Sage.

Smith, Barbara Ellen. 1987. *Digging Our Own Graves: Coal Miners and the Struggle over Black Lung Disease.* Philadelphia: Temple University Press.

Sutton, Barbara. 2005. "The Bodily Scars of Neoliberal Economics: A Feminist Analysis." Paper presented at American Sociological Association Annual Meeting, Philadelphia.

Take Back the Night Foundation. http://www.takebackthenight.org/index.html.

Turner, Bryan S. 1996. *The Body and Society: Explorations in Social Theory,* 2nd ed. Thousand Oaks, CA: Sage.

U.N. AIDS. 2008. "Report on the Global AIDS Epidemic." http://www.unaids.org/en/KnowledgeCentre/HIVData/GlobalReport/2008/2008_Global_report.asp.

U.N. Population Fund. 2005. "State of World Population 2005." http://www.unfpa.org/swp/2005/english/ch8/index.htm.

Weiss, Meira. 2002. *The Chosen Body: The Politics of the Body in Israeli Society.* Stanford, CA: Stanford University Press.

Winerip, Michael. 2009. "As Luck Would Have It…" *New York Times,* Sunday Styles, 8 November, 2.

Class Exercises
Lisa Jean Moore

EXERCISE I

Body Variables

Procedure: Hand out chart to all students and ask them to fill it in to the best of their abilities in about 10 minutes. Then go over in class together using board or projector. After students have filled in the chart, ask them if there are people who do not have the assumed correspondence of categories. For example, they can begin with themselves. Do they fit the logic of an entire column? Do they know anyone else who doesn't?

Aim: This exercise is intended to demonstrate to students the ways in which binary thinking about human bodies forces us to think in pre-existing dichotomous categories. By placing terms in each box, students are likely to fill out the chart as if there is a logical coherence down each column. There are assumptions we make about individuals from their gendered performances—these assumptions are often about some "natural" or biological facts. Although we do not see penises or vaginas, we assume they are lurking beneath clothing and that is what drives certain gendered performances. But when students confront real-life experiences of individuals who do not neatly fit into the categories, the class can begin discussions of how social structures work to re-insert or force people into categories or to shun them. Students can then discuss how the naturalness of the body is really a fiction or an imaginary that we construct as real and use for our perceptions of others.

Instructions for Students
Please fill in the chart to the best of your ability. You have 10 minutes to complete the chart.

BODY VARIABLES: SEX AND GENDER CHART

CATEGORY	NORMATIVE SEX/GENDER ASSUMPTIONS	NORMATIVE SEX/ GENDER ASSUMPTIONS
Descriptor	Feminine	Masculine
Hormones		
Chromosomes		
Genitalia		
Symbols		
Childhood Term		
Sphere		
Labels/Slang		
Social Behavior		
Gender Performance		
Sexual Attraction to—		
Adjectives to Describe		

EXERCISE II

What are Normal Bodies?

Procedure: Hand out chart to all students and ask them to fill it in to the best of their abilities in about 10 minutes. Then go over in class together using board or projector. In a discussion, ask them to focus on the social construction and purpose of "normal bodies." It is also useful for students to use this chart as a form of an interview. They can collect data from their friends and family and return to class with a data set that can be aggregated in small groups. These small groups can then discuss these findings and present their findings to the larger class. A larger class discussion can present findings on the board and also begin to explore any outliers as well as rationales for outliers.

Aim: This exercise is designed to demonstrate how becoming normal is a social process of managing one's performance through the consumption of discourses, products, and practices. Although people often say that "being normal is natural," this exercise aims to deconstruct that notion and get students to begin to look at the ways the "range of normal" is quite limited and used to control individuals' body practices and appearances.

Questions for Discussion
How are normal bodies made?
What is normal for women and men?
Why is it important for women/men to have these normal body characteristics?
How do normal and natural become interchangeable terms?
What happens when they are used interchangeably?
What are the consequences of non-normality?

Instructions for Students
For this exercise, go through column one and describe the social and individual expectations for the normal body for men and for women. Second column: give one example of how people attempt to attain it. Third column: think of what is considered abnormal. Fourth column: list some consequences of abnormality. Please fill in the chart to the best of your ability. You have 10 minutes to complete the chart.

WHAT IS THE NORMAL BODY?

TOPIC	DESCRIPTION OF THE APPROPRIATE RANGE OF NORMAL		HOW DO PEOPLE ATTEMPT TO ATTAIN THE NORMAL		WHAT IS ABNORMAL	WHAT ARE THE CONSEQUENCES OF ABNORMALITY
	MEN	WOMEN	MEN	WOMEN		
Normal Weight						
Normal Height						
Normal Physical Appearance						
Normal Health						
Normal Gender						
Normal Sex						
Normal Sexuality						

EXERCISE III

Body Projects

Procedure: Students conduct informal interviews with one to five individuals outside of class over two weeks. (The number interviewed depends on the class size.) The first week, students interview girls/women, and the second week students interview boys/men. If students are interviewing more than one person, it is important that they try to vary the sexual orientation, religion, ability, age and/or racial or ethnic group of those they are interviewing. They ask six questions and bring the data back to class the next session. This data is then aggregated on the board for students to make some general sociological observations about gendered body projects. Generally, despite sampling from a diverse group, certain trends emerge in the aggregated data, which leads to interesting discussions about what types of body projects exist and how they are gendered.

Aim: This exercise is designed to demonstrate similarities and differences in contemporary body projects of women and men. During an in-class discussion, students are asked to consider these questions:

- What patterns do they see?
- What is the range of variation for women's/men's ideal bodies and body projects?
- In what ways are they similar? In what ways are they different?
  Additionally, the professor can ask students to discuss:
  - difficulties of informants discussing their bodies
  - interviewing across gender lines
  - truth-telling regarding potentially stigmatizing body analysis

Instructions for Students
Please interview X individual women/men about their bodies. After establishing the demographic variables, ask each person the following six questions. Please bring this data into class for a group exercise.

BODY PROJECTS INTERVIEW SCHEDULE

Demographics
Age
Race/Ethnicity
Religion
Sexual Orientation

Questions
1. In your opinion, what is the ideal female/male body?
2. How do you feel about your own body?
3. What is one thing you would like to change about your body?
4. How would you change this?
5. What is one thing you love about your body?
6. Is there anything you are currently doing to fit into the ideal female/male body?

EXERCISE IV

Taking Care of Bodies

Procedure: For this exercise, students are provided with a sheet to tally their labor performed in the service of the body. Be clear that this labor is unpaid and often invisible until noted. In a week-long journal, students are asked to keep track of tasks that they themselves do in the service of their own bodies, those of their children, their parents, and other loved ones. After creating a log of unpaid or (in)visible labor for the body, students are asked to determine a salary for their time for the tasks and to calculate the amount of money that is saved by doing these tasks themselves.

This Web site provides various wages that can be modified to help students to determine their hourly wage had they been compensated for their labor: U.S. Bureau of Labor Statistics at http://www.bls.gov/bls/blswage.htm.

Aim: The purpose of this assignment is threefold. First, it is an accounting of unpaid, informal labor routinely done in service of the body. Second, it is a mathematical calculation of cost savings because the labor is done in the private and unpaid sector. Finally, it leads to a gender analysis of childcare and eldercare that women are often expected to perform in the service of bodies. It provides students with an opportunity to see the effects of deskilling; the gendered division of caregiving and informal, unpaid care work; and the state/corporate benefit from informal, unpaid caregivers. In particular, older women seem to be very affected by the consciousness-raising of their work and its worth.

Instructions for Students

Please create a log of your informal, unpaid labor that you perform in the service of bodies: your own, children, parents, lovers: this includes cleaning, grooming, dressing, applying cosmetics, giving/taking injections or medications, changing diapers, bandages, and so on. Do this log for a week and bring it to class. This chart can be used as a model. Feel free to modify to fit your needs. We will fill in the columns with the wages in class together. Three examples have been provided for you.

TAKING CARE OF BODIES: CHART

TASK	TIME IN WEEK	PROFESSIONAL CAREER IF PAID	HOURLY WAGE	WEEKLY WAGE	YEARLY WAGES
Diaper Changing/ Diaper Rash Treatment	5 hours	Childcare Provider			
Purchasing/ Preparing/ Cooking for Family	22 hours	Chef			
Administer Meds/ Vitamins to Children and Mother	1 hour	Pediatrican/ Pharmacist/ Case Worker			
TOTAL					

◆◆◆

Films with Somatic Themes

Apocalypse Now (1979)—Vietnam War captain is sent to assassinate a renegade Green Beret in Cambodia

Becoming Ayden (2008)—Documentary profile of a young trans man in Toronto who must deal with the objections of his father, a conservative rabbi

Big Enough (2004)—Explorations of "otherness" in twenty-year documentary follow-up to *Little People*. Available from Fanlight Productions, www.fan-light.com

Black Women On: The Light, Dark Thang (1999)—Explores the politics of color, skin hues, in the Black community

The Beauty Myth: The Culture of Beauty, Psychology, & the Self (2008)—Hosted by Naomi Wolf, exposes the beauty myth as a distinct cultural narrative—a fiction that "beauty" exists objectively and universally. DVD available from Into the Classroom Media, www.classroommedia.com

The Body Beautiful (1991)—White mother has radical mastectomy while Black daughter begins modeling career

Bombay Eunuch (2001)—Documentary profiling the lives of hijras, gender-variant persons often called "eunuchs" in India

Boy I Am (2006)—Documentary that engages with feminist and lesbian critiques of trans identities through exploring the lives of three FTMs

Boys Don't Cry (1999)—Teena Brandon story of transgender identity and violent reactions

Casa De Los Babies (2003)—Western women waiting to adopt babies in South America

Chutney Popcorn (2000)—Interracial lesbian couple and pregnancy

Cruel and Unusual (2006)—The plight of transgender women in men's prisons

The Crying Game (1992)—Transgendered person in IRA psychological thriller

Dare to Dream: The Story of the U.S. Women's Soccer Team (2005)—From their beginning in the 1980s as "the red-headed stepchild" of sports through four World Cups and three Olympic games (HBO documentary)

The Day I Will Never Forget (2002)—Ritual genital cutting in Kenya

The Deer Hunter (1978)—Expendable working-class male bodies and minds in Vietnam

Defiance (2008)—Four Jewish brothers escape from Poland to lead resisters to form a safe haven for Jewish refugees during WWII

Dirty Pretty Things (2002)—Organ donation for travel documents

Dying to be Thin (2000)—Eating disorders and the American obsession with thin women

The Elephant Man (1980)—Carnivalesque use of body for freak show

Gattaca (1997)—Two men exchange genetic identity in a DNA future

Georgie Girl (2001)—Documentary about Georgina Beyers, a Maori transsexual elected to Parliament in New Zealand

G.I. Jane (1997)—Feature-length film on a woman going through grueling Navy SEALS training as a litmus test for women in combat

Girl Inside (2007)—Portrait of a young MTF and her close relationship with her grandmother

Girlfight (2000)—Young Brooklyn woman trains as a boxer

Good Hair (2009)—Documentary in which Chris Rock investigates the multibillion dollar hair industry that promotes chemicals and painful processes to transform "nappy" hair into "good hair"

Hollywood Harems (1999)—Documentary about Hollywood's portrayal of Arab, Persian, Chinese, and Indian people

Hotel Rwanda (2005)—Genocide in Rwanda

The Hurt Locker (2009)—Feature-length film of an all-male squad of bomb defusers in Iraq

Is It a Boy or a Girl? (2000)—Controversy surrounding intersex medical treatment. Video available at www.isna.org

Juggling Gender (1992)—Documentary about a bearded woman performance artist who discusses the life of a "side show"

Junior (1994)—Male scientist (Arnold Schwarzenegger) experimentally carries a fetus in his own body

The Killing Fields (1984)—Cambodian genocide under Pol Pot

Killing Us Softly 3 (2000)—Women's bodies portrayed in advertising

The Laramie Project (2002)—Feature-length film about the murder of a young gay man, Matthew Shepard, in Laramie, Wyoming

The Life and Times of Sara Baartman: "The Hottentot Venus" (1998)—The life of a Khoikhoi woman who was taken from South Africa in 1810 and exhibited in Britain as a freak

Little Man (2005)—Lesbian couple adopt a seriously ill premature baby (documentary)

Ma Vie en Rose (1997)—Transgender child in Western Europe

Maria Full of Grace (2004)—Women who act as Colombian drug "mules"

Million Dollar Baby (2004)—Women's empowerment in athletics, ending with question of euthanasia

Mind If I Call You Sir? (2004)—Documentary about the lives of Latino FTMs in California

Miss Evers' Boys (1997)—U.S. government's 1932 Tuskeegee syphilis experiments, in which a group of Black men who were test subjects were left untreated, despite the development of a cure

Moolaade (2004)—Female genital cutting in Burkina Faso

Murderball (2002)—Wheelchair Rugby World Championships

My Left Foot (1989)—Christy Brown, born with cerebral palsy, learned to paint and write with his only controllable limb, his left foot

Naked Acts (1996)—Feature-length film about Black women and body image

Paper Dolls (2005)—Documentary of five Filipino MTF transgender immigrants to Israel who care for Orthodox Jewish men during the day and perform in a drag troupe at night

Paradise Now (2005)—Two Palestinian best friends on a suicide mission

Paternal Instinct (2003)—Gay couple establish a relationship with a surrogate to start a family

Playing Unfair (2002)—Media images of women athletes

Period: The End of Menstruation? (2007)—Documentary presenting pro-menses and menstrual suppression arguments in the context of the medicalization of PMS and menopause

Pumping Iron (1977)—Arnold Schwarzenegger's first film

Pumping Iron II: The Women (1985)—Women body-builders and the sexism in body building world

Real Women Have Curves (2002)—Mexican American woman and sweatshops in the United States

The Sea Inside (2004)—Completely paralyzed man in 30-year fight to end his own life

Shinjuku Boys (1995)—Documentary about lives of Onnabes, gender-variant natal women in Japan who work as men to entertain heterosexual women

Silence Broken: Korean Comfort Women (1999)—Historical footage, interviews, and dramatic reenacts tell the true story of Korean women forced to work as prostitutes for the Japanese Army during World War II

Silkwood (1983)—Occupational toxic exposure and woman whistle blower

Slaying the Dragon (1988)—Documentary about media stereotypes of Asian and Asian American women in films

Southern Comfort (2001)—Struggle of an FTM who is dying from ovarian cancer and can't get medical treatment (documentary)

Super Size Me (2004)—Fast food industry and nutritional consequences

Switch (1991)—As punishment for his misogyny, a man is transferred into a sexy woman's body

Thirteen (2003)—Adolescent girls and self-injury

Toilet Training (2003)—Persistent discrimination, harassment, and violence that transgender people face in gender-segregated bathrooms. Video available at www.srlp.org

Tootsie (1982)—Feature-length comedy about an out-of-work actor living as a woman to get work

Transamerica (2005)—Pre-op MTF transgender must care for the son she never knew she had fathered

The Twilight of the Golds (1997)—Fictional family confronted with gay gene in fetus

Vera Drake (2004)—Abortionist in 1950s England

Warm Springs (2005)—President Franklin D. Roosevelt learning to live with paralysis from polio in the late 1920s. Cable film available at www.hbo.com

A Woman in Berlin (2008)—Feature-length depiction of the violent post-war rapes of German women by soldiers of the conquering Soviet Army and their survival strategies. Based on an autobiographical account.

The Women Outside: Korean Women and the U.S. Military (1996)–Documentary on the lives of women who work in the brothels, bars, and nightclubs around U.S. military bases in South Korea. Available from Third World News Reel.

Index